THOUSAND OAKS LIBRARY

THOUSAND OAKS LIBRARY

3 2052 00995 7989 ✓

JUN 2008

DISCARD

D0016295

COLLECTION MANAGEMENT

4/09	1 — 1	1/09
5/2012	1 — 1	7/2009

THOUSAND OAKS LIBRARY
1401 E. Janss Road
Thousand Oaks, California

ALSO BY JAMES SALTER

—FICTION—

Last Night
Dusk and Other Stories
Solo Faces
Light Years
A Sport and a Pastime
Cassada (previously published as *The Arm of Flesh*)
The Hunters

—NONFICTION—

There and Then
Gods of Tin
Burning the Days

LIFE IS MEALS

LIFE IS
MEALS

A Food Lover's Book of Days

JAMES AND KAY SALTER

WITH ILLUSTRATIONS BY FABRICE MOIREAU

ALFRED A. KNOPF
IN ASSOCIATION WITH CALLAWAY

NEW YORK
2006

THIS IS A BORZOI BOOK PUBLISHED BY ALFRED A. KNOPF

Copyright © 2006 by James and Kay Salter
Illustrations copyright © 2006 by Fabrice Moireau

All rights reserved. Published in the United States by Alfred A. Knopf,
a division of Random House, Inc., New York, in association
with Callaway Arts & Entertainment, and in Canada by
Random House of Canada Limited, Toronto.
WWW.AAKNOPF.COM   WWW.CALLAWAY.COM

Knopf, Borzoi Books, and the colophon are
registered trademarks of Random House, Inc.

Grateful acknowledgment is made to the following for permission
to reprint previously published material:

Excerpt from The Wind in the Willows by Kenneth Grahame (NY 1999).
Reprinted by permission of Atheneum Books for Young Readers, an imprint
of Simon & Schuster Children's Publishing Division.

"Soupe de Nevers"—Recipe adapted from Cuisine of the Rose by Mireille Johnston.
Copyright © 1982 by Mireille Johnston. Reprinted by permission of the author.

"Polpettone alla Toscana"—Recipe adapted from The Classic Italian Cook Book:
The Art of Italian Cooking and the Italian Art of Eating by Marcella Hazan.
Copyright © 1973 by Marcella Hazan. First Alfred A. Knopf Edition, February 1976.
Reprinted by permission of the author. All rights reserved.

Excerpt from A Child's Christmas in Wales by Dylan Thomas. Copyright © 1954 by New Directions
Publishing Corp. Reprinted by permission of New Directions Publishing Corp.

"Gratin Dauphinois Madame Cartet"—Recipe from Bistro Cooking by Patricia Wells.
Copyright © 1989 by Patricia Wells. Reprinted by permission of
Workman Publishing Co., Inc., New York. All rights reserved.

Library of Congress Cataloging-in-Publication Data

Salter, James
Life Is Meals: a food lover's book of days / James and Kay Salter ;
with illustrations by Fabrice Moireau. – 1st ed.
p.   cm.
ISBN 0-307-26496-3 (alk. paper)
1. Gastronomy. 2. Food. 3. Dinners and dining.
I. Salter, Kay. II. Title.
TX631.S225 2006   641′013—dc22

641.013

Manufactured in the United States of America

First Edition

I intend that my last work shall be a cookbook composed of memories and desires . . .

ALEXANDRE DUMAS, 1869

OUR HOUSE IN ASPEN, COLORADO, DATED BACK TO THE MINING days, and the kitchen was small—about ten feet by twelve—with not much counter space and a worn floor, but it was honest and comfortable to be in. The dishes were kept in a wooden display case, and the pantry was a shallow closet with no door.

It was in this kitchen that we began cooking together when we moved into the house in about 1976. Neither of us had had much cooking experience, and there was no real decision to do it, it just happened naturally. We cooked side by side or back to back if necessary, following recipes, James Beard's or Mireille Johnston's, which were among our early favorites.

The dining room was equally small and almost a part of the kitchen. It had a fireplace and a large framed mirror on one wall. Another wall was three shaky windows looking out onto the street and often on snow pouring down or, in the summer, light that lasted until ten in the evening. The early dinner parties were for friends or people who had come to town. Aspen was easygoing in those days. The streets had only been paved a few years before. Dogs were full-fledged citizens of the town.

When something we cooked turned out particularly well, we cooked it over and over, of course, and partly as a consequence began, in an old brown notebook, to keep a record of what we had served people so as not to give them the same thing, at least not too often. At the same time we began a handwritten book of recipes or versions of them that were worth keeping, often with when they'd first been served, and to whom.

Gradually, over the years, the descriptions in the brown notebook—the dinner book, we called it—became longer and more detailed: who sat where, what was drunk, some memorable things said. The notebook ran out of pages. There was another and then a third. They became a kind of archive, stories otherwise forgotten, couples that had parted, familiar names, others hard to place. The framed mirror had a long scorched section on one side. In the middle of a dinner and impassioned conversation one night, someone happened to remark, "I think your house is on fire." A candle had collapsed and was leaning against the wall, which was burning. We put it out and went on with the meal.

That had been noted in the dinner book. Dinner when someone, in need of a little fresh air, went out and was discovered an hour later, sleeping on the woodpile. The night a wild woman threw the roast beef onto the floor, pronouncing it inedible. There were also great successes, but in any case, we were always writing things down, not just things that happened but also from books we were reading, things of interest, bits of history, opinions, occurrences, odd facts. At breakfast—tea and oranges for a period, as in Leonard Cohen's beautiful song—we read aloud to one another and often leafed through cookbooks, deciding what to make for a party or simply at the end of the day. Life never felt richer.

Could any of this be put down in words and, if so, in what form? We began to imagine something for the kitchen, or even the bedside table, a book that could be opened at random or read day by day, like a diary or collection of letters, intimate, perhaps ending up with coffee stains or underlinings on certain pages.

In 1999 we mentioned the idea of a book to Nicholas Callaway, a young publisher and friend with whom we had sometimes dined. He liked the description and, coincidentally, had even been gathering guidebooks and travel books, most of them rare, that for him had a similar appeal.

For us, over the years, cooking had evolved, and though it was still done together, it was more on the lines of, you do the salad, I'll do the tart. We wrote this book the same way, not side by side but with an agreed idea of what it would be, and then both editing what we each had done. Nicholas Callaway was not quite as young by the time it was finished. There was research, travel, much more to writing it than we had anticipated.

We put the book together not to be definitive but rather to appeal to those for whom eating is something more than a mere necessity. It's not meant to replace favorite cookbooks but instead, in a way, to complement them, to give them further context and, in the course of doing it, to give a year, perhaps more, of pleasure. If there are any inaccuracies, feel free to amend them in your own hand on the page. If there should be improvements or changes in recipes, do the same. We hope the book will be used as well as read. Life is many things, and among the best of them, it is meals.

JANUARY

MEALS ARE EVERYTHING

The meal is the essential act of life. It is the habitual ceremony, the long record of marriage, the school for behavior, the prelude to love. Among all peoples and in all times, every significant event in life—be it wedding, triumph, or birth—is marked by a meal or the sharing of food or drink. The meal is the emblem of civilization. What would one know of life as it should be lived or nights as they should be spent apart from meals?

EIFFEL TOWER

The Eiffel Tower was intended to stand for only twenty years when it was built for the 1889 World's Fair. Though it always had its admirers, others scornfully referred to it as the tallest flagpole in existence. Guy de Maupassant called it a "giant and disgraceful skeleton" and ate his lunch underneath it every day, because that was the only place in the city where he didn't have to look at it.

When it came time to pull it down in 1910, it was saved by the development of the telegraph, which required a tower. Ten years later, it barely survived a request from the construction industry to melt it down for its iron. Only in 1964 did the French decide to keep it for good, designating it an historic structure. Maupassant, if his royalties were sufficient, could avoid looking at it today by dining at one of the most famous restaurants in Paris, the Jules Verne, stylish and animated, often booked months in advance for its food as well as its exceptional view from the second tier of the tower, more than four hundred feet above where he used to have his lunch.

3

JANUARY

DINNER WITH LORD BYRON

Samuel Rogers (1763–1855) was a wealthy minor poet whose elegant home on St. James Street in London became a gathering place for his literary friends, including William Wordsworth and Charles Lamb. In his book *Table Talk*, Rogers recalls first meeting Lord Byron when it was arranged he should come to dinner:

"When we sat down to dinner I asked Byron if he would take soup? No, he never took soup. Would he take fish? No, he never took fish. Presently I asked if he would take some mutton? No, he never ate mutton. I then asked if he would take a glass of wine? No, he never tasted wine.

"It was now necessary to inquire what he *did* eat and drink; and the answer was, nothing but hard biscuits and sodawater. Unfortunately, neither hard biscuits nor sodawater were at hand; and he dined upon potatoes bruised down on his plate and drenched with vinegar. My guests stayed till very late discussing the merits of Walter Scott and Joanna Baillie.

"Some days after, meeting Hobhouse, I said to him, 'How long will Lord Byron persevere in his present diet?' He replied, 'Just about as long as you continue to notice it.'

"I did not then know, what I now know to be a fact—that Byron, after leaving my house, had gone to a club in St. James's Street, and eaten a hearty meat-supper."

4

JANUARY

COFFEE

They have in Turkey a drink called Coffee . . . as Black as Soot,
and of a Strong Scent . . . which they take, beaten into Powder, in Water,
as Hot as they can Drink it; and they take it, and sit at it in their
Coffee Houses, which are like our Taverns.

— FRANCIS BACON

Some forty years after Bacon's death, coffee made its way from Turkey to France with the sultan's ambassador to the court of Louis XIV, where Mme de Sévigné predicted, with something less than her usual acuity, "There are two things the French will never swallow— Racine's poetry, and coffee." She lived long enough to find that she was wrong about both.

The coffee tree, a small evergreen with fragrant white flowers and dark red pods, each containing two beans, is thought to be native to

Ethiopia, and East Africa remains a producer, behind South America, where Brazil is the leader. The beverage was made of the roasted, crushed beans and probably developed in Arabia. It then moved northward to Egypt and Turkey, where it became so essential to daily life that in Constantinople, denying a wife her coffee gave her grounds for divorce. When it arrived in Europe and the Americas in the 1600s, it was the thick, unfiltered liquid still served in Turkey, Greece, and the Middle East. Gradually, as it traveled, its preparation was adapted to the taste of its public by filtering or adding milk, sugar, or flavorings.

Always valued for its stimulating effect, coffee contains more caffeine than any other drink. There are about 110 to 150 milligrams of caffeine in a cup of coffee made by the drip method and about 65 to 125 in a percolated cup, nearly twice the amount found in tea. Espresso, though stronger in taste because it is more concentrated, actually has less caffeine than regular coffee. Decaffeinated, which has been around for one hundred years, accounts for about twenty percent of coffee sales in the United States.

Balzac was in the habit of drinking up to thirty cups a day while writing for twelve-hour stretches, producing his vast body of fiction as he tried to scramble out of debt. Dead at fifty, the cause wasn't coffee, though medical authorities today more or less agree that four cups a day is about as many as most people can consume before experiencing the side effects of excessive caffeine.

TWELFTH NIGHT

Twelfth Night, the twelfth night after Christmas, is the eve of Epiphany, marking the arrival of the Three Wise Men who had seen the star on the night Jesus was born and followed it to Bethlehem.

The church didn't officially designate December 25 as the birthday of Jesus until 336 A.D., and chose the time of year to coincide with already immensely popular pagan celebrations. Twelfth Night, for example, grew out of much older rituals that marked the winter solstice, when the days started getting longer again, and the ancients, for twelve days, celebrated the return of the sun.

Some of the customs practiced by the pagans during this season are still part of post-Christmas celebrations all over the world, including a Twelfth Night cake. A bean was baked into the cake, and whoever got that slice became king for the night. Today in France and Spain, the *galette des rois,* "cake of kings," and the *gastel à fève orroriz,* "cake with the king's bean," are still served, during the holidays, as is the *Dreikönigskuchen,* "the three kings' cake," in Switzerland and Germany, conferring good luck on the one who gets the special token.

6

SALT

Salt appears in the Bible as well as in the works of Homer, who described nations as poor when they did not use salt in their food, and the word itself is found in almost identical form in many languages: *sel, sal, salz, sale, sol', salt*, etc. The word "salary" comes from the salt that was part of Roman soldiers' pay or that they bought with a special allowance.

Mined or drawn from seawater by evaporation, salt has been essential to life, as well as to the taste of food, which it enhances, bringing out the deep-lying flavors. It dehydrates certain vegetables—tomatoes, cucumbers, and especially eggplant—and brightens the color of others—spinach and green beans if it is in the cooking water. Through thousands of years it has been crucial to the preservation of food.

When roasting or sautéing meat, it has long been held that salt should be used only after browning so that the juices will not be drawn out, though not all cooks agree. It should always be used in pasta water, and a pinch of it, oddly enough, brings out the sweetness of pineapple and grapefruit.

About ¼ ounce is the daily human requirement, although the modern diet may provide several times this amount, and medical advice has been to keep salt intake low, particularly for older people and those with certain health problems such as high blood pressure or diseases of the heart, liver, or kidneys.

Rock salt comes from mining, and sea salt—which chefs often prefer for its taste—from evaporation. Kosher salt has no additives, but table salt often does, to provide iodine and to prevent sticking due to dampness.

"The best smell is bread, the best taste is salt," Graham Greene wrote, adding, "and the best love is that of children."

7
JANUARY

RUTH CLEVELAND

1904. Ruth Cleveland, daughter of President Grover Cleveland, dies on this day at age thirteen of diphtheria, four years before her father. They lie near one another in Princeton Cemetery in New Jersey. Born between her father's two terms, she had been adored by the public, and a candy bar was even named for her: Baby Ruth.

8
JANUARY

IMPORTANCE OF MEALS

The edicts of a Chinese emperor are said to have begun, "The world is based on agriculture," and food has shaped human society since the very beginning. Eating is a process more vital than sex and the need more recurrent. The rhythm of working and eating defines the life of every individual, and the dizzying edifice made up of all the civilizations and savage tribes of history is based on food.

Primitive man did not eat at certain hours but simply when hungry. Gradually a regularity developed. Families and clans ate together, and in fact, for ages most eating was communal.

Food is closely interwoven with religion—the sacrifice of animals, the blessing of fields, the Eucharist, the traditional feasts—and it has been crucial to medicine, which, for centuries, was based on dietary principles. In its wake, food has sown cities, formed politics, and been at the root of prosperity or war.

The most important human relationships are all celebrated with or nourished by the sharing of food. Even death is marked by the serving of food and drink.

9

JANUARY

CREAMED CHIPPED BEEF

Lorenzo Semple, a close friend and neighbor, often stopped by in the morning to have tea. He'd abandoned his self-constructed diet that included rules for foods he said had no calories: anything eaten from someone else's plate, anything eaten in the movies, anything brown. Recently, he'd been carrying a pack loaded with rocks to increase the number of calories he could burn on his walk to work. One day when he arrived at our house, there was a large bowl of rice pudding on the table, just out of the oven. It was intended for later in the day, but we knew he loved it.

"Help yourself," we said.

"No, no, please, I'm trying to lose weight," he insisted, "and anyway, I've already had breakfast."

We poured him some tea.

"Well, maybe just a bite, just one taste, to see if it's any good," he said.

Twenty minutes later, he'd eaten the entire bowl. He stormed out of the house, furious at us for tempting him beyond his strength. The recipe, from Jennie Grossinger's *The Art of Jewish Cooking*, was plainly worth putting into our own cookbook. "Serves eight or Lorenzo," we noted.

The next day, to show he'd forgiven us, he returned and made us one of his favorite breakfasts: creamed chipped beef on toast. In the 1910 *Manual for Army Cooks*, this is recipe no. 251, and servicemen through the decades have called it—none too affectionately—SOS (shit on a shingle). But Lorenzo's recipe might have turned them around:

CREAMED CHIPPED BEEF

1 4.5-ounce jar dried beef
2 tablespoons butter
Wondra flour, about 2 table-
spoons, but it's not necessary
to measure it out

1 cup 2 percent or fat-free
milk (more or less, depending
on desired thickness)

Soak the dried beef in water to eliminate most of the salt, pat dry, and tear into pieces. Melt the butter in a skillet over medium/medium-high heat, and add beef.

Shake in Wondra flour and lightly sautée. Add milk gradually, stirring, and heat until mixture thickens. Add more milk to achieve desired consistency. Serve over toast. Serves two.

He could even join us, since dried beef has very little fat and is low in calories (and is brown).

10

JANUARY

TALLEYRAND

Talleyrand, who was bishop of Autun before he became a great statesman, was nearly as famous for his table as for his diplomacy. His knowledge of food was impressive, and he spent time in his kitchens daily deciding on the dinner for the evening and questioning the staff on what they may have overheard from guests the night before.

Breakfast and lunch for him were not consequential, and at night, as one source said, he liked heavy dishes and light women.

In the winter of 1803, during a time when there was virtually no fish to be had in Paris, Talleyrand gave a state dinner. At the appropriate time, to sounds of appreciation, a servant entered with an enormous salmon on a great silver platter. To the horror of all, he tripped while carrying it, and fish and platter fell to the floor.

Seeing this, Talleyrand said calmly, "Have them bring in another salmon."

Almost immediately another appeared. The whole incident had been planned.

11

JANUARY

PINEAPPLE

On this day in 1813, the first pineapples were planted in Hawaii. They may have originally come from Brazil, though other sources say that Columbus encountered them first in Guadeloupe, their true home. As if in tribute, it was also on this day in 1935 that Amelia Earhart took off from Honolulu to make the first solo flight from Hawaii to California.

Fragrant and impressive to look at, most pineapples now come from Hawaii. Fifty years ago, the Royal Hawaiian Hotel had a fountain in the lobby that provided fresh pineapple juice.

Pineapples do not continue to ripen after picking. They will keep for some weeks but should not be refrigerated—temperatures below 45 degrees F are not beneficial. A distinctive aroma is one indication of a good pineapple, as well as being heavy for its size. The fruit is sweeter at the bottom, so if it is to be served plain, it should be cut lengthwise.

Pineapple sorbet is hard to rival. In France, you can occasionally find *ananas givré,* a pineapple hollowed out and filled with the sorbet made from its fruit. Sometimes this is frozen. At any time, it is nearly irresistible. Balzac, who was very fond of pineapple fritters, once planned to get rich by growing pineapples on his property near Paris, but couldn't afford a greenhouse.

There are a number of recipes for making pineapple sorbet, most of them similar. One is:

PINEAPPLE SORBET

1 fresh pineapple

2 cups sugar

4 cups water

  Rum to taste

Dissolve the sugar in the water. Cut the fruit of the pineapple into pieces and add to the sugar and water. Let stand for several hours, then purée in a blender and flavor with rum near the end. Freeze in an ice cream maker according to the manufacturer's instructions. Serves four.

12

JANUARY

WOMEN AT TABLE

It was a mere five hundred years or so ago that women, who since antiquity had been largely segregated during meals, began to be widely included at the table. In the early days, advice was available on how they should conduct themselves and be a civilizing influence, as in the *Ingenious Gentlewoman's Delightful Companion,* published by an unknown writer in 1653:

"Talk not when you have meat in your mouth, and do not smack like a pig, nor venture to eat spoon-meat so hot that the tears stand in your eyes; which is as unseemly as the gentlewoman who pretended to have as little a stomach as she had a mouth, and therefore would not swallow her peas by spoonsful, but took them one by one, and cut them into two before she could eat them. It is very uncomely to drink so large a draught that your breath is almost gone, and are forced to blow strongly to recover yourself; throwing down your liquor as into a funnel, is an action fitter for a juggler than a gentlewoman. . . . It will appear very comely and decent to use a fork; so touch no meat without it."

13

JANUARY

FORKS

Compared to spoons and knives, used since prehistoric times, forks were latecomers. By the year 100 A.D., they appeared on the tables of royalty in the Middle East, and one hundred years or so later, a Byzantine princess brought a case of them to Venice as part of her trousseau when she married the heir to the doge. Italians of the day were outraged that she should prefer a metallic instrument to the ten fingers God had given her, and when she died soon after her arrival, it was considered divine retribution.

Forks were gradually adopted by the upper classes across Europe over the next five hundred years and were mainly for sticky sweets or food that would stain the fingers. The English considered them effeminate, and it was a long time before they crossed the Channel. An Englishman, Thomas Coryat, claimed to be the first to use one, and he had to go to Europe to do it. In his book *Coryat's Crudities,* published in 1611, he writes that "the Italian cannot by any means endure to have his dish touched with fingers, seeing all men's fingers are not alike cleane." A fork in the left hand held the food to the plate while the right hand cut it with a knife, and then the fork delivered the food directly to the mouth.

Twenty years later, the fork had immigrated to America, but just barely. Governor Winthrop, of the Massachusetts Bay Colony, was said to have had the only one on the continent. Ordinary folk were still spearing food with their sharp-tipped knives to carry it to their mouths. When pointed-tipped knives gave way to blunt-ended at the table, people had to use their spoons to steady food while cutting it. They then switched the spoon to the right hand to scoop up the pieces of food. Once the use of forks became widespread, Americans used them in the right hand to bring food to the mouth.

14

CORDON BLEU

The term *cordon bleu* originally referred to the wide blue ribbon from which hung a cross designating the most prestigious Order of the Holy Spirit, the L'Ordre des Chevaliers du Saint Esprit, created by Henry III in 1578. The investiture banquets were as famous as the medal.

A century later, Mme de Maintenon broadened the meaning of the *cordon bleu*. She had been the governess of Louis XIV's illegitimate children and later became his second wife, married in secret because of her low social standing. Always interested in education, she spent much time at Saint-Cyr, the school founded to educate the daughters of impoverished nobility and orphans of French soldiers. There, she established the Cordon Bleu of Cookery, and the blue ribbon of honor eventually came to mean excellence in any field, but especially in the kitchen.

On this day in 1896, Le Cordon Bleu held its first classes in the culinary arts at the Palais Royale in Paris. It has become the most famous culinary institute in the world. Taught by some of the great chefs of the day, the school has produced its own luminaries. One was Julia Child, who qualified for professional training after World War II, when Le Cordon Bleu was accepted as an accredited school under the G.I. Bill.

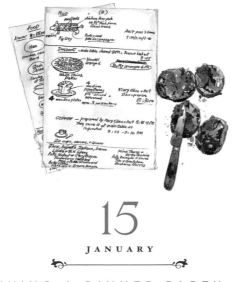

15

JANUARY

***

GIVING A DINNER PARTY (I)

You decide to give a dinner party. Someone is coming to town, or it seems a good idea to introduce someone to someone else, or you're just in the mood to have an evening with friends. You may choose the next night or one a few days or weeks off.

As W. S. Gilbert said, "When planning a dinner party, what's more important than what's on the table is what's on the chairs." The first thing is to invite the main guests. The others are chosen as complements—a mix, if possible, of couples and singles, men and women, though we don't try for a perfect balance. No more than seven, usually, including ourselves, since that's the most our table will comfortably seat. In general, two at a table makes for the most intimate talk, though that's not really a dinner party. Nor is three, though then the conversation is likely to be the most revealing. Four is congenial, and five the most interesting with its slight imbalance. Six is pleasant, but tends toward the conventional if it is three couples, especially if they're already acquainted.

There can be larger parties, of course, with two tables or else a buffet with people eating from plates in their laps or on low coffee tables. But then it is impossible for everyone to join in one conversation, and—if the guests are interesting—people end up feeling that wherever they sat, they've missed something.

If you've invited people far in advance, you might call the day of the dinner to remind them of the time.

16

JANUARY

GIVING A DINNER PARTY (II)

MENU

To approach this on a fundamental level, a dinner is more of an occasion if you have two courses before dessert. The first course might obviously be a soup (hot or cold), salad, smoked salmon with toast, bruschetta, a sautéed vegetable (leeks, sweet red peppers) with a dressing, or for a major feed, a risotto or pasta.

The main course needs something at its side—a potato or rice dish if it is meat, fish, or chicken, and possibly another vegetable. When pasta is the main course, you might serve it solo and add something afterward—a green salad or a cheese platter if the pasta hasn't included a lot of cheese.

Unless the meal is particularly heavy, chocolate or something rich can come as dessert, although a fruit tart or fruit in a liqueur is often our choice.

PREPARATIONS

Besides basic spirits—gin, vodka, beer, Scotch, bourbon—check the bar to make sure you have soda or seltzer, tonic, and olives/cocktail onions/lemon peel. Make or buy plenty of ice. Decide on the wine and chill the white before the evening begins. If you're going to serve drinks after dinner, have those and the glasses at hand.

Sometimes for a special occasion, you can write a single copy of the menu by hand and display it on the table.

After shopping for the ingredients, prepare anything possible ahead of time: dessert, salad and its dressing, assembling the main course if it will be baked, and the accompanying dishes up to the point of cooking.

When an important guest was expected in ancient Egypt, the entire household went into a frenzy of cleaning, brewing, and baking weeks in advance. That was then. Don't exhaust yourself by cleaning the house to inspection readiness. Tidy the bathroom guests will use, clear clutter, and let it go at that. Devote yourself instead to the elements that will actually be memorable: the food and the conversation.

GIVING A DINNER PARTY (III)

The Air Force taught Jim the value of knowing exactly what should happen and when—something crucial to a dinner party. He draws up a flow chart, working backward from the time we expect to sit down at the table. Especially important are the times certain dishes go into the oven or come off the stove. If the baked potatoes aren't ready when the meat is rare, you're going to be eating undercooked potatoes or overdone meat. Gavril Lourie, the son of friends, apprenticed at two-star restaurants in France, and he goes as far as making a diagram of each dish and how it will be arranged on the plates, then tacks it on the wall as he cooks.

We also have a basic master list: set table, set up bar, hors d'oeuvres out, open wine, light fire in fireplace, prepare cups and plates for later coffee and dessert. And just before sitting down, fill water glasses, cut bread, light candles.

As a child, you learn that promptness is a virtue, and we do have a few friends who arrive for dinner at exactly the designated hour. We know who they are, so on those evenings, we're ready. But usually, people show up about fifteen or twenty minutes later. As hosts, we can always use the extra time. If everything is actually done, we can sit down for a few minutes and congratulate ourselves.

We allow forty-five minutes to an hour for drinks, hors d'oeuvres, conversation, and unwinding, and to allow for guests who are late. Usually we serve something quite light with drinks—olives, nuts, sometimes a tapenade with crackers—depending on how rich the meal will be.

The end of the dinner is as important as any other part. It is like the "finish" of a wine, the aftertaste. We often bring a plate of chocolates or another sweet—butter-crunch candy or chocolate-coated candied oranges—to the table. Then, perhaps, liqueurs and small glasses or even cognac, occasionally in another room. The energy of the evening has died by this point, but one doesn't want a collapse. It is good to sign off with a flourish, sometimes even a game of poker.

18

JANUARY

GIVING A DINNER PARTY (IV)

It's more fun to cook with someone, even given differing opinions on exactly how it should be done. There are many men who are great in the kitchen and have a good time being there. It's worth remembering that the one who shops, chops, and is otherwise in a supporting role gets no credit and may be less inclined to be part of the team next time. Each cook likes to have a glory dish—the salad with the wonderful dressing, the memorable tart—that reliably gets compliments.

Serving should be decided on ahead of time. One system is to have the first course on the table when the guests sit down. Then you can present the main course and accompanying dishes around the table. They can be passed by the guests, or they can be served already on the plates. Flexibility is crucial: just because you've made a plan doesn't mean it can't be changed. If whoever is in charge of dessert is deep into a discussion of death and how to think about it, the other can take over those duties.

If you ask who wants coffee, there's usually an awkward moment when the guests wonder if they're putting you out by saying yes. A better way is to go ahead and make it, bring it to the table, and then ask.

19

JANUARY

GIVING A DINNER PARTY (V)

The clean-up, as well as the cooking, is more interesting if you're not doing it alone. Anyone can load a dishwasher and put the leftovers away, but it takes someone involved to be part of the post-party analysis, the late-night debriefing during which you hash over the food, the guests, and the most outrageous or revealing things that were said. It's inevitable that now and then one of you was in the kitchen, so it's also a chance to hear what you may have missed.

20

GIVING A DINNER PARTY (VI)

Keep in mind: attitude is everything. As Horace says, "a host is like a general; adversity reveals his genius."

FOOD

Sometimes a guest has special dietary rules: they're allergic to shellfish, cannot digest tomato seeds, or they're vegetarians. If you know ahead of time, it should influence, though not completely dictate, the menu, unless they're the guest of honor. But you're not running a restaurant, and the cocktail hour is no time to try to prepare something special.

EXTRAS

This happens so often it hardly qualifies as unexpected. A guest calls with the news that a friend or relative has appeared and asks if they can be included. Yes, if at all possible, and especially if it's only one. One of our best extras appeared on a night that John Irving called to say he thought he was in love, but he hadn't introduced her to anyone yet and could he bring her along? You bet. They married the next year.

SCHEDULE

It is rare but not unheard of for guests to show up on the wrong night. There are four choices: send out for pizza; give them a drink while you change and then go out to eat; urge them to stay and serve whatever you were going to have anyway or make a simple pasta; or, if the night is impossible, as a last resort, send them home.

ACTS OF GOD AND MAN-MADE DISASTERS

This requires a similar approach. People show up in a downpour or a blizzard when the storm has taken out the stove and refrigerator. One night, in the middle of an elaborate meal, there was a pounding on the door by two men who announced that their car, at the end of the driveway, was on fire, and could we call 911? It must have been a slow night at the firehouse, because five engines and trucks showed up. The two men, who had rescued their pizza from the backseat, joined us for the meal. But then, we're in favor of memorable dinner parties, aren't we?

21

JANUARY

JORIE GRAHAM ON LOVE

"Things taste better in small houses," Queen Victoria once said. At our house in Aspen, the kitchen and dining room are together and there's also a fireplace. The table sits six, eight at most. Jorie Graham, the poet, and several others came to dinner one January. We began talking about love and the period of the 1960s and '70s, when new and improved contraception and the nonexistence of AIDS made for openness and great sexual freedom.

Overwhelming passion, Jorie observed, when one is literally unable to breathe, had been central to and written about in Western literature for more than fifteen hundred years. "It is the signature element," she said.

There began a recalling of passionate firsts: seeing someone on a neighboring boat and in an instant falling in love, later marrying; sexual awakening on a trip through the country with a boy of twenty. "Twenty . . . how old were you?"

"Fifteen."

Stilton and pears and the almond toffee (Enstrom's) made down in Grand Junction, as good as any in the world, we all agree. Snow all around. Starry night. Everyone reluctant to leave.

22

JANUARY

NEVER TOGETHER

Part of the pleasure of giving a dinner party is inviting people who do not know but might like each other. Like Babe Ruth, who did it some thirteen hundred times, it's inevitable that you sometimes strike out. As a reminder of what definitely didn't work, we have at the back of our dinner book a page called "Never Together."

There are obvious mismatches to be avoided: guests with intensely different views who tend to speak their minds on politics, abortion, or gun control. Also those who were once romantically involved and now decidedly not.

Then there are the antipathies one might forget over time but which the participants never seem to: Gloria, once enraged by a man at a poker game and who said of him, "He's a shit, and I don't care if he knows I think so." Or potentially even more serious, a writer who's been panned by a critic we also know.

Most entries of "Never Together," however, result from a comment regarding a person such as, "I can't stand him," or the seemingly offhanded observation during a thank-you call the next day along the lines of:

"I certainly learned a lot more than I ever wanted to know about . . . ," or,

"She does seem to get repetitive after a couple glasses of wine," or,

"Doesn't she ever let someone else have a turn?" or,

"Doesn't he ever stop talking about himself and ask a question?" or even,

"Is he the world expert on everything?"

On the other hand, who wants an evening that turns out to be bland because everyone there was?

23

JANUARY

GRAND DICTIONNAIRE
DE CUISINE

The idea of writing a cookbook had been in Alexandre Dumas' mind for years. He would begin it, he said, when he caught the first glimpse of death on the horizon, and in 1869 he retreated to Normandy with his cook to have the necessary tranquility. He was sixty-seven years old.

A man of immense energy and self-esteem, with a childlike vanity, he was among the most famous French writers of his time. *The Three Musketeers* and *The Count of Monte Cristo,* among many other novels, plays, and stories, usually written with and by assistants and collaborators, earned him great sums of money, which he spent lavishly on houses, friends, food, and mistresses. Largely self-educated and with a penchant for love affairs, he was described as a kind of mulatto giant—his grandfather had been a French marquis and his grandmother a Haitian slave—with the tiny but bright, watchful eyes of a hippopotamus, and features set in the middle of an enormous face. If he were locked in a room with five women, pens, paper, and a play to be written, Dumas boasted, by the end of an hour he would have finished the five acts and had the five women.

Six months after settling down in Normandy, his huge *Grand dictionnaire de cuisine* was completed. More than 1,150 pages long, sprawling, inaccurate, filled not only with recipes, but with vivid reminiscences and far-fetched stories, it was published in 1872 and remained in print in its original form until the 1950s. It had been published posthumously. Dumas, true to his vision, had died of a stroke in December 1870.

24

AL DENTE

Pasta should be cooked in plenty of fast-boiling, salted water. Boiling water "seals" the pasta and allows it to move freely and swell. A bit of olive oil added to the water helps prevent sticking. Timing should begin only when the water returns to the boil, and the pot should be uncovered. Do not break the long strands but push them slowly in as they soften and bend.

Test the pasta as it cooks—don't merely time it. The time can vary, usually eight to ten minutes for dry pasta and about three for fresh. Drain it when it is still a trifle undercooked or al dente.

The business of al dente or "bitey," shows up in every knowledgeable text. It is the way Italians eat it—or so they say. Since pasta continues to cook after it has been drained and all the way to the mouth, the advice often given is to stop its cooking in the water when it is just soft enough to be bitten through without its snapping, very "bitey" indeed. Once you're accustomed to pasta being somewhat stiff and not soggy, you are told, you will want it no other way. Perhaps this is true, though in Italy you will find it is often served long past al dente, and it is also true that elsewhere it is commonly overcooked to an unpleasant softness.

25

APHRODISIACS

The word "aphrodisiac" comes from Aphrodite, the Greek goddess of love. Throughout history, men have eaten oysters, spices, and other foods to increase their potency, and though they are probably of limited physical benefit, the belief in their powers may be enough to do the trick. Brillat-Savarin wrote that truffles were "believed to rouse certain powers whose tests of strength are accompanied by the deepest pleasure," and Casanova, the Marquis de Sade, and Napoleon relied on them, while the Aztec emperor Montezuma was said to have drunk fifty cups of chocolate to prepare for lovemaking.

Chocolate, in fact, does contain phenylethylamine, a natural mood enhancer. Louis XV's mistress, Mme de Pompadour, drank it hoping to increase her passion for the king, who called her "cold as a stone." Years later he turned to Mme du Barry, ardent to a fault, who—before she was introduced to the king's bed—had offered chocolate to her lovers to help them keep up with her.

Spicy foods, including chilis, hot peppers, or curries, raise the heart rate and help release endorphins that produce a natural high. Asparagus, with its phallic shape, provides vitamin E, which can stimulate sex hormones. And a dozen oysters supply more than the daily requirement of zinc, a mineral that can help raise a man's testosterone level and sperm count.

While not aphrodisiacs, foods chosen for their resemblance to body parts or for their association with love have included figs, caviar, sweetbreads, and strawberries. The Aztec word for avocado was *ahua-catl,* or "testicle," and young girls were forbidden to go outside while they were being harvested.

26

JANUARY

JASON EPSTEIN'S KITCHEN

2003. A cold January day and sitting in Jason Epstein's kitchen in Sag Harbor, a smallish room barely twelve feet square, talking about food. The kitchen—its layout—is much the same as when he bought the house thirty or forty years ago. The stove is in the same place, though it is not the same stove. The dark, round table we are sitting at was there, even the rickety chairs.

This house, large and on a wide plot that runs all the way between two streets, is the house you have always wanted, deeply comfortable and civilized. Books and bookcases, wide board floors with Oriental rugs, pictures, places to sit and read or write, and a broad garden on two levels with trees and random stone pathways.

An important editor nearly all his life—one of the great Brahmins— Jason Epstein is also a remarkable cook and writer about food. He has liked to cook for as long as he can remember, perhaps resulting from the visits to his grandmother's in Maine. It was a big, unheated house where they all sat in the kitchen in the winter, the woodstove going, and Jason, a boy of six or seven sitting in the blue wood box next to the stove, would watch his grandmother carry soup and pies she had baked to the table.

In his own kitchen, there's a fireplace with a knee-high hearth, an upholstered armchair, and only about two or three feet of workspace on a butcher-block counter. The other couple of feet are taken up by an elaborate espresso machine. Doesn't he need more space than this to work? "No, the more space, the more mess you make," he says. The first rule is to clean up after yourself as you go. He's cooked dinners for as many as fifty people here without any problem.

There's a refrigerator with photographs stuck to it, an old white sink, and pots and pans hanging from an overhead rack. A long magnetic strip on the wall has twenty or thirty knives in graduated sizes on it. There are no cookbooks. These are in an adjoining room, but Jason rarely uses them. As an editor he published many, and he sometimes reads one to relax. It's a kitchen where one can read, have drinks or hors d'oeuvres before dinner, or sit and talk. The kitchen is the real heart of the house and the life.

27

JANUARY

COOKBOOKS

In early cookbooks, quantities of ingredients were designated as "a little of this and a bit of that," and directions for preparation might be along the lines of "cook it until it is done." Most recipes were never written down at all, and when they were, assumed a certain experience and expertise on the part of the cook. That changed in 1863 with Isabella Beeton's *Book of Household Management*, in which she specified amounts and urged her readers to use measures and scales to ensure that the dish would not only turn out as they expected, but that they would be able to get the same results if they made it again. Fanny Farmer, known as the mother of the level measure, published her famous cookbook in 1896.

Since then, thousands of cookbooks have been published. In the U.S., the biggest seller since its publication in 1930 is the *Better Homes and Gardens New Cookbook,* followed by *Joy of Cooking,* which first appeared the following year. Like many brides or young women setting out on their own, Kay was given a copy of *Joy,* which has been through everything, including a kitchen flood, and is still consulted despite swollen pages and a missing front cover.

Our favorite cookbooks are those with consistently good recipes and ingredients that are easy to find. They include Patricia Wells's *Bistro Cooking,* the original *Silver Palate Cookbook,* and, in addition to the *Joy of Cooking,* a couple of other fairly basic collections including Craig Claiborne's *New York Times Cookbook* and *The James Beard Cookbook,* "newly revised" in 1966 and now out of print. Our copy is held together with rubber bands. There are also those we dip into less often but always with success: *The Loaves and Fishes Cookbook* and the *Union Square Café Cookbook.*

Then there are those that are great to browse in without ever intending to use them.

The painter Toulouse-Lautrec loved to cook, and compiled and illustrated his own recipes. Unforgettable is the one for chicken, which starts by detailing the size of shot to be used in the gun and the importance of chasing the chicken around the yard first to make its meat more tender.

28

JANUARY

DE GONCOURT

"When intelligent men drink and dine together," Edmond de Goncourt wrote in the famous journal he and his brother kept for forty-five years (1851–96), "the subject of conversation is always women and love."

At dinner with de Goncourt and others in Paris in 1878, Turgenev was asked to tell them the most powerful amorous event he had known. After thinking a bit, Turgenev, who came from a well-to-do landowning family, said it had been at the age of fifteen. He'd had no experience of sex. There was a pretty chambermaid in the house, a serf girl without much in her face except a kind of stupid grandeur, and one rainy day at around dusk when he was walking dreamily in the garden, she came up to him, took hold of him by the hair, and said a single word: "Come!" That was how he'd been introduced to love. Whenever he remembered it, Turgenev said, it made him feel happy.

29

JANUARY

SPAGHETTI ALLA CARBONARA

Until the 17th century, pasta, boiled and plain, was a food of the poor, although Catherine de' Medici's wedding banquet included it in 1533.

Jefferson was introduced to it in Paris in 1784–89 and liked it so much he brought two crates of it home with him. Its real introduction to America, however, came with the great Italian immigration wave in the late 1800s, when it was known as macaroni, still the word Italian-Americans use for pasta.

A sauce should only lightly coat pasta; too much sauce is a common mistake. With a sauce that has olive oil in it, add a little more olive oil at the end to give it spirit. The bowl in which the pasta and sauce are combined should be warm—it can be warmed with some of the boiled water. Add the pasta to the sauce in the bowl, folding it in as you might gently toss a salad.

When cheese is called for, mix the freshly grated cheese into the pasta first, before adding the pasta to the sauce. Use genuine Parmigiano-Reggiano. Grated, packaged cheeses are a poor substitute.

There are countless recipes for sauces apart from simply butter and salt. A spaghetti we have made for years that is unfailingly good is *spaghetti alla carbonara,* or "charcoal worker's spaghetti." Using only simple ingredients, it can be made on the spur of the moment. The recipe is from an Italian friend, Franca Tasso.

SPAGHETTI ALLA CARBONARA

3 large, fresh eggs	*2 tablespoons extra virgin*
½ cup or more grated fresh	*olive oil*
Parmesan cheese	*1 pound dried spaghetti*
Salt to taste	*(De Cecco is very good)*
Freshly ground pepper to taste	
6 slices thick bacon or pancetta	

In a good-sized salad bowl, combine eggs, cheese, salt, and pepper to form a mixture heavier than cream but lighter than pancake batter. Cut bacon or pancetta into small pieces and fry slowly in olive oil. Meanwhile, cook pasta in three or four quarts of boiling salted water. When pasta is al dente, drain and quickly add to the bowl with the cheese and egg mixture and toss. Add the hot bacon and olive oil in which it was cooked, and stir to cook the eggs. Serves four.

30

JANUARY

WINE

The subject of wine in all its aspects is a great, complex field. There are experts as well as true experts and people who know much more than one needs to know. If you like wine, as with anything else, you will learn about it.

There are some simple, fundamental rules that, at the start, are good to know. In general, during a meal, serve white before red, serve a young wine before an older one, and serve a dry before a sweet wine. The rule of thumb—red with meat and poultry, white with fish—may have been useful in the past, but is of less use today with the countless blendings and varieties. Rust Hills, the writer and long-time editor at *Esquire,* had a rule virtually as good: white wine at lunch, red at dinner.

There are also all sorts of wine sellers, from supermarkets to distinguished merchants. If you are not dealing with the latter, remember that good wine, while not fragile, should not have been mistreated in shipment or storage, or subjected to extremes of temperature. One way to judge this is by the cork. If, beneath the foil or plastic, it protrudes slightly above the lip of the bottle, it means that the wine has been exposed to too high or too low a temperature. Select something else. Also, don't worry about sediment. In mature wine, it is not a bad sign; in fact, it is the opposite.

If you're lucky enough to deal with a good wine merchant, you may get some valuable advice. Wine merchants in the past often had a respected position in society. In one twenty-year period in medieval England, 1307–27, four mayors of London were vintners.

31

JANUARY

WHAT WITH WHAT

There are hundreds of wines from many different countries and regions, and the average person can expect to know only a small portion of them, and with that scanty knowledge answer the eternal question of which wine with which dish.

It is true that white wines are generally more acidic than reds and thus go well with seafood dishes that need lemon. It is safe to say that most chardonnays are good with most fish dishes. Most meat—beef and lamb, particularly, though not veal—marries well with a red wine of medium or full body.

A few bits of wisdom that are helpful:

• Rosé and dry champagne go with anything.
• Red wine is usually not good with cheese, especially fresh cheeses. A dry white is better, especially with goat cheese.
• No wine goes well with chocolate desserts or with salads dressed with a vinaigrette.
• Wine tastes metallic with artichokes or asparagus.
• A simple wine is best with complex dishes. Conversely, a complex wine goes best with simple dishes; certainly the very best wine does.

Among the foods and flavors that may interfere with a proper appreciation of wine with a meal are vinegar, onions, garlic, spices, curry, and mustard.

FEBRUARY

1

OUR COOKBOOK

The recipes we like best, taken from friends, restaurants, and cook-books, are all in a book of our own, mostly handwritten and organized by categories, although over the years the salads have drifted into the pastas, and there are hors d'oeuvres among the soups. Only we know, more or less, where to find each one. There are comments in the margins—how many helpings someone had who really loved it, or changes in ingredients or preparation learned from experience.

As a teenager, our son started one of his own. At eighteen, it included his aunt's pot roast, Caesar salad, homemade pasta sauce, an artist friend's apple crisp, and for the future, the dry martini.

2

FEBRUARY

NELL GWYN

1650. Nell Gwyn, the daughter of a bawdy-house keeper, was born this day in London. She grew up, according to diarist Samuel Pepys, filling the glasses of the patrons and at an early age became an actress under the affectionate wing, so to speak, of a leading actor, Charles Hart. She rose to become the mistress of a lord and then at nineteen, of the king himself, Charles II. Witty, generous, shapely, and illiterate, she was the only one of the king's mistresses adored by the public, and remained in the royal bed for sixteen years until his death in 1685. She bore him two sons, both of whom became lords, and entertained the king and his friends while living extravagantly. She died at the age of thirty-seven, two years after the king.

Nell Gwyn had begun as an "orange girl," one of those who sold that fruit in theaters and, as Waverly Root observes, at a somewhat higher price, themselves. The oranges were less for eating than for holding to one's face to mask the stench of the audience.

It seems fitting that the orange, along with the apple and grape, is one of the world's most venerable fruits. Probably originating in China, it has the distinction of not being mentioned in the Bible, and its color is not an indication of ripeness, but rather of the temperature to which is has been exposed during growth. The familiar, rich color is frequently the result of dyes or degreening.

3

FEBRUARY

OLIVES

Legend has it that in ancient Greece, two Olympian gods competed for the honor of having a newly founded city overlooking the Aegean Sea named for them. They decided on a competition in which each would give a gift to the people, who would then decide which gift was more valuable. Poseidon gave the horse. Athena struck the earth with her lance, and an olive tree appeared. The people named the city Athens.

Olives were a dietary staple of the ancient world and are still central to the cuisines of the Mediterranean region. A true Athenian, Plato called olives his favorite food. There are dozens of varieties of different sizes and shapes, but with only a few exceptions, green olives are unripe olives, harvested early and bitter. Most, including those from Italy and the prized Kalamata from Greece, are allowed to ripen on the tree, where they turn black, deep purple, or brown and become softer and more oily.

The majority of olives are crushed for oil, which in ancient times was used not only for cooking and to flavor other foods but as fuel for lamps, as a lubricant for moving objects as heavy as building stones, and even as a perfume. It was also a medicine and thought to give health and longevity when rubbed into the skin.

Both the fruit and oil provide "good" fats—the monounsaturated kind—having no cholesterol. Those not used for oil are often cured in brine, oil, water, or even lye—the method favored in Spain—or a combination of these, and then are preserved in oil, brine, or vinegar, sometimes pitted and stuffed, or flavored with herbs. They can also be cured in salt, which dries and shrivels them, intensifying their flavor.

4

FEBRUARY

TIMING

Timing, they say, is everything, and nowhere more so than in cooking. As English writer Launcelot Sturgeon wrote, "The critical minute is less difficult to be hit in the boudoir than in the kitchen."

Every culture has its expression for something cooked exactly the right length of time and no more. In Italy, pasta is done when al dente, not cooked through but with some remaining resistance when bitten. Chinese use *ts'ui* to indicate either an ingredient at its peak or something perfectly cooked. In France, it is *à point,* "at the right moment," meaning "perfectly ripe" when referring to fruit and "done to a turn" in regard to meat, which is approximately "medium."

ONION SOUP

Samuel Beckett and Harold Pinter, after a night of drinking in Paris in the 1960s, ended up at Les Halles at 4 a.m. for onion soup. Pinter fell asleep at the table, exhausted and suffering from stomach cramps. He woke to find Beckett had scoured the town and come back with bicarbonate of soda. "It was then I knew," Pinter wrote, "that this was a man who understood everything about the human condition."

5

CAVIAR

Even in the 1890s, when caviar from American and French sturgeon sold for next to nothing, Russian caviar was on a different level, both in price and in quality. Today, sturgeon have been nearly obliterated by pollution, except in the region of the Caspian Sea. Caviar is rare, there have been importation bans, and prices have soared. The czars and later Stalin got around the price by simply appropriating tons of the stuff.

Dostoyevsky's wife, Anna Grigorievna, in a less-powerful position, was nevertheless able to buy this delicacy, known as an aphrodisiac. After her husband finished writing each chapter of *Crime and Punishment,* she was said to have rewarded him with caviar and sex.

The different types of caviar are named for the species of sturgeon that produce them: beluga, oestrova, and sevruga. The tiny eggs are salted to preserve them, but the less salt used, the better the taste. Top-of-the-line caviar is called *malassol,* Russian for "lightly salted." The heavily salted variety from the Hudson River used to be so plentiful that it was served free at bars in New York to induce thirst.

6

ROOM SERVICE

Waiters are one thing, a face-to-face matter; room service is another. You are on the phone talking to someone unseen and located who-knows-exactly-where.

Irving Lazar, better known as Swifty, diminutive and aggressive, a famous literary and movie agent for more than four decades, from the 1940s on, once was staying at a hotel in the American West and in the morning called down to order breakfast.

"Yes, sir, what would you like?"

He wanted toast, he said. He'd like it burned on one side, in fact, but untoasted on the other. He would also like a soft-boiled egg, but not completely cooked, a little mucous-y on top. And coffee—not hot, however, just tepid. How long would that take?

"I'm sorry, sir," was the answer, "but we're not equipped to do that."

"You were yesterday," Lazar replied drily.

CAESAR SALAD

There are few people who aren't enthusiastic about a good Caesar salad, especially when made as it was by Caesar Cardini, an Italian immigrant and chef who created it at his restaurant in Tijuana in 1924. The story is that when customers appeared late one night, he gathered the few remaining ingredients in the kitchen and instructed a waiter to combine and toss them at the table, as if the salad were a house specialty.

Countless variations have developed since then, and most claim to be the original recipe, which, in fact, included only romaine, garlic, olive oil, croutons, Parmesan cheese, and Worcestershire sauce, but no anchovy or egg. We had eliminated those two ourselves when many guests objected to anchovies, and also raw eggs, as they could be carriers of salmonella.

The croutons are better if homemade, and the cheese, if grated by hand from a block of real Italian Parmesan. The tougher, dark green outer leaves of the romaine should be thrown away and only the crisp, paler interior leaves used, torn into bite-sized pieces.

Our own version of the classic dressing is:

CAESAR SALAD

1 teaspoon Worcestershire sauce	5 tablespoons good olive oil
1 clove crushed garlic	Romaine lettuce
2 tablespoons freshly squeezed lemon juice	Parmesan cheese
	Large pinch of salt

In a jar with a lid, combine the first four ingredients and shake until mixed. Taste and adjust as necessary. Pour over the romaine, then add the grated Parmesan and the croutons that have been made earlier by cutting into crustless cubes of about ½ inch any genuine white bread, such as sourdough or country, tossing them in olive oil and a little crushed garlic, and browning them in the oven or a frying pan. The French would specify bread that was staling and of no better use. Toss and serve immediately. Serves about six.

8

FEBRUARY

RUSKIN

On this day in 1819, in a house on Brunswick Square in London, John Ruskin was born to wealthy parents. It was the same year that Queen Victoria was born, and they would rule the century together, Ruskin in the realm of the aesthetic. He was England's preeminent art critic—dictator, in fact, of artistic opinion. His *Modern Painters* alone comprised five volumes and took seventeen years to write. He was also a major social theorist, proposing such radical ideas as old-age pensions and a nationalized system of education.

Although he knew the Bible intimately and painting and architecture as well, he was perhaps less confident, or at least conflicted, with regard to women. It is said that the sight of a woman's naked body made him uneasy or even physically ill. He married just once. It lasted six years and was apparently unconsummated.

He advised young women to combine "English thoroughness, and French art, and Arabian hospitality" in their homes. There were three feminine virtues, he declared. The first was to be intensely happy. The second was to dress beautifully and to extend this beauty to the home. The third virtue, he said, was to cook.

9

FEBRUARY

FORESTIERE

It was probably medallions of veal forestiere—small, oval-shaped pieces of veal with mushrooms and blanched bacon bits together with a gravy—eaten for the first time in Chamonix or Megève—that acquainted me with what was a very honest-sounding word. "Forestiere" seemed to stand for something prepared by a woodsman or a family that lived simply and virtuously. My eye never goes much further when I see it on a menu. With potatoes, carrots, or even a soft-boiled egg and mushrooms cooked in butter along with the bacon. Worth a detour.   J.S.

HOSTESS GIFT

The easy thing is to take a bottle of wine as a gift when you go to dinner. However, it is not so easy for the hosts. If the wine is not right for the meal, there's the awkwardness of deciding whether to go ahead and open it anyway since, if it is a good bottle, the guest may expect to drink some of it. The other possibility is to put it away. You can write the guest's name on it as a reminder to bring it out next time he or she comes.

In Europe, guests assume that the hostess has already carefully chosen the wine to go with her menu, and it would be almost an insult to bring wine. The same goes for anything that might be intended as part of the meal, including candy. Flowers are frequently the choice, though requiring the hostess to interrupt what she's doing to put them in water, arranged and displayed.

Higher on the social ladder, guests are less likely to bring a gift, under the assumption, presumably, that the hosts already have everything.

10

FEBRUARY

BOUQUET

There are some beautiful words that belong to wine, probably because of the place it has long held in human affections. "Robe" is a word for the color of a wine. "Bouquet" is a less precise word for the smell. There are actually two words for this, "aroma" and "bouquet." Aroma is used for the uncomplicated smell of grape and fermentation, usually in young wine, while bouquet is something more complex, the property of a wine that has matured in the bottle—the perfume, so to speak. It's a good indication of quality, of the wine's character and depth. Young wines and white wines normally do not possess it.

To appreciate the bouquet of a good red, it should be served at 60–65 degrees F, which is also best for taste. This is well below the temperature in a typical American room. At low temperatures there will be little smell, and higher than 65 degrees F, the smell of alcohol begins to be included. So, when it is recommended to be served at room temperature, that means somewhat cooler than most rooms. Thirty minutes or so in the refrigerator will bring a red wine that has been in a normal room down to 60 degrees F.

The correct temperature for white wine is only slightly lower—not really chilled but 55–60 degrees F, according to most authorities, no more than an hour in the refrigerator. The taste begins to vanish if it becomes much colder.

11

FEBRUARY

PERFECT DIET

The heroes of the Trojan War seem to have feasted mainly on mutton and roast pork. Actually, the ancient Greeks ate a great amount of fish, the sea being on every side: sole, turbot, tuna, octopus. There was also abundant game.

There is no single food that can supply all the nutrition humans need, though this is not the case with animals. Diets vary from country to country and through the ages, but most of them tend to supply, in one form or another, what is necessary. For the citizens of Athens, Socrates recommended a diet of bread, cheese, vegetables, olives, and fruit. They would, as a result, lead healthy lives and die at a ripe old age. Galen, the great Greek physician who stamped his ideas on medicine for several centuries, regarded fruit with suspicion, however. His father, he stated, had lived to be one hundred because he never ate any.

In the Middle Ages, the concept that the right diet was of greater importance than medicines and cures—an idea that still has its power—dominated Western medicine. The question of the right diet was another matter. It was accepted that all things were made up of four elements: air, fire, water, and earth. In humans, this took the form of four corresponding "humors": blood, bile (anger or choler), phlegm (calmness or apathy), and black bile (melancholy). Thus, a man of choleric temperament (fire) should avoid "hot" foods, while "cold" foods, such as fruit, were suitable.

Conversation at dinner, one can speculate, might be thought of as hot or cold also. Religion, politics, and sex could be called hot, although George Bernard Shaw once observed that they were the only topics of interest to an intelligent person.

12

FEBRUARY

SOFT-BOILED EGG

The greatest dishes are very simple dishes, Escoffier said.

What could be more simple and pure than a single soft-boiled egg on the breakfast table in an egg cup along with some buttered toast? The egg cup is essential. It is an altar enhancing the egg's beauty as well as holding it, still too hot to touch, while the crown is gently removed. A bit of salt, perhaps a touch of butter, and a spoon small enough to fit inside—one of life's feasts is before you. No omelet or elaborate egg dish—poached, sauced, scrambled, whatever—can surpass it.

To soft-boil, put an egg that is at room temperature into slowly boiling water for approximately six minutes. Remove and serve immediately.

For a hard-boiled egg, leave in for ten to twelve minutes, then place in cold water for six to seven minutes to stop the cooking and make the shell easy to peel. Eggs cooked too long have rubbery whites and yolks that tend to crumble.

13

BEING EARNEST

1895. The eve of the opening of Oscar Wilde's *The Importance of Being Earnest* in London. In the play, at teatime in Jack's garden, Jack and Algernon are caught in lies by their fiancées, who have stormed off.

JACK: How you can sit there, calmly eating muffins, when we are in this horrible trouble, I can't make out. You seem to me perfectly heartless.

ALGERNON: Well, I can't eat muffins in an agitated manner. The butter would probably get on my cuffs. One should always eat muffins quite calmly. It is the only way to eat them.

JACK: I say it's perfectly heartless your eating muffins at all, under the circumstances.

ALGERNON: When I am in trouble, eating is the only thing that consoles me. Indeed, when I am in really great trouble, as anyone who knows me intimately will tell you, I refuse everything except food and drink. At the present moment I am eating muffins because I am unhappy. Besides, I am particularly fond of muffins.

14

FEBRUARY

CHOCOLATE

It is not surprising that chocolate, with its reputation as an aphrodisiac, is a favorite gift on Valentine's Day. Celebrating love and romance, one legend says the holiday is named for a martyred Roman priest who secretly performed marriage ceremonies in defiance of Emperor Claudius II, who believed unmarried men made better soldiers.

Modern science tells us that chocolate is a natural mood booster, though unlikely to promote sexual interest. The word comes from the Mayan *tchocolatl*. Cacao beans were valuable enough in Central America at the time to be used as currency. Four bought a pumpkin, ten a rabbit, and twelve the favors of a prostitute.

Columbus was the first European to taste chocolate, on his fourth and last voyage to the New World in 1502. He was not impressed, but eventually others were. Once available only to royalty, chocolate eventually found its way into middle-class houses. Brillat-Savarin, who recommended it as a cure for lethargy and even hangovers, remarked, "People who habitually drink chocolate enjoy unvarying health and are least attacked by a host of little illnesses which can destroy the true joy of living."

Consumed for the mildly stimulating effect of its caffeine, as well as its taste, it was served in liquid form until the art of solidifying it was perfected in the 19th century. Americans, on average, each now eat almost twelve pounds a year, but the United States ranks only eighth in the world. Switzerland leads with more than twenty pounds per person.

It has around ten grams of fat per ounce, but of a kind that doesn't add to cholesterol. For those in need of a further excuse, dark chocolate has fifteen times the antioxidants found in broccoli.

15

FEBRUARY

LE GRAND VEFOUR

We rarely go to three-star restaurants. The prices and the reverence of the diners speaking in near-whispers dilute the pleasure. One February, however, at the end of a week in Paris spent largely at the Louvre, we decided, as a finale, to have lunch at Le Grand Vefour, "celebrated throughout the world," as the Michelin put it, for its sumptuous late-18th-century decor as well as its food and service.

What else but a great monument could afford to close for all of August, from before Christmas until after New Year's, and for a week in April, not to mention Thursday evening and every weekend of the year?

At the northern end of the Palais-Royal, its first incarnation was as the Café de Chartres, which became a meeting place for the French revolutionaries. Embracing the times as they changed, its clientele eventually became Bonapartists, and Josephine dined here with Napoleon. In 1820, after a number of owners, it was taken over by Jean Vefour, who gave it his name. Victor Hugo was one of the early patrons, followed, among others, by Colette more than a century later who, when her rheumatism made walking impossible, was carried downstairs to it from her Palais-Royal apartment.

A two-course prix fixe lunch is about eighty-five dollars, when the dollar is strong. It is well worth it. The combination of the rich cuisine and the midday wine made the coat check girl ask Jim as we left whether, given the purplish hue of his face, he was well. Nothing a stroll in the gardens wouldn't cure, he managed to assure her.

He was reminded of hearing the late Warner LeRoy, the vivid, well-fed owner of Tavern on the Green and the Russian Tea Room in New York, describe an experience at Le Grand Vefour. Having eaten a superb meal from appetizer through chateaubriand and its trimmings and on to dessert, coffee, and cognac, he was asked by the waiter, "Sir, is there anything else I can get for you?"

To which LeRoy answered, "Yes. Bring it all again." It was not only delivered but also consumed.

16

FEBRUARY

RICE

The Japanese have the longest average life span in the world: 79.9 years, compared to 76.7 in the United States. And until the end, their bones are stronger, they have fewer strokes and less heart disease, and few are overweight. Genetics may play a role, but their diet certainly deserves some of the credit. Consisting mainly of rice, fish, and vegetables, it is low in calories, fat, and cholesterol.

A good source of carbohydrates and protein, rice not so long ago was eaten at every Japanese meal. Though now it is closer to two meals out of three, rice is still at the heart of Japanese cuisine. The word for rice, in fact—*gohan*—is the same as that for a meal. As a crop, rice came to Japan some two thousand years ago by way of China. In feudal times, it was used to pay wages, including those of the samurai, and a property owner's worth was reckoned not in terms of acreage, but by how much rice it produced.

Agricultural land is limited in Japan, but rice continues to be grown wherever it is possible to establish a paddy, despite the enormous amount of hand labor involved in transplanting the seedlings. The yield is great, however, and rice is used not only as a source of food but also drink. There are over six thousand brands of sake today, all brewed from rice but differing slightly in odor, taste, and alcoholic content; most are about fifteen to twenty percent, comparable to wines made from grapes. Whether sake is served hot or cold, the rule is never to refill your own glass, but if dining with Japanese, you won't have to wait long for someone else at the table to do it.

17

FEBRUARY

MOLIÈRE

In 1673, Molière, fatigued and ill on this day but performing nevertheless in *Le malade imaginaire,* the last play he ever wrote, began coughing fiercely. He was taken home after the final curtain, and it is said that in bed he refused broth and asked instead for Parmesan cheese, the last thing he would taste on earth. He died not long after from a hemorrhage caused by the violence of his cough.

DESSERT

The word "dessert" comes from the French *desservir,* meaning "to clear the table" or take away what has been served. It has come to mean what is offered after a meal. In ancient times, this was fruit or cheese, still a very good choice, Platonic in its simplicity and difficult to pass up.

In restaurants, the display of a variety of desserts on a cart is said to have originated in Italy to tempt young women to remain at the table during family gatherings.

18

FEBRUARY

SENSE OF TASTE

Human beings have an average of ten thousand taste buds, mainly on the tongue but also on the palate and even as far back in the throat as the larynx. Cows have more than twice as many, which seems a bit of a waste.

Our taste buds are a kind of modified skin cell, and in their general arrangement register sweet (on the tip of the tongue), sour (along the sides of the tongue), salty (on the surface of the tongue), and bitter (at the back of the tongue). Some individuals have a more acute sense of taste than others, but all humans seem to be born with an inherent liking for sweetness, evident even in infants, while appreciation of spicy or sour flavors is learned. Taste buds are replaced every ten days or so and less frequently with age, accounting for a diminishing sense of taste as people grow older. The complex wiring of the brain incorporates smells into our sense of taste, which is why the taste of food becomes flat or even nonexistent when you have a head cold.

19

FEBRUARY

PEPPER

Black pepper, white pepper, and green peppercorns are all berries of the same plant, a vine that twines itself around trees growing in equatorial heat. Red pepper, also called cayenne, isn't pepper at all but a chili, misidentified by Columbus when he thought he'd reached India instead of the Caribbean.

In ancient Greece and Rome, pepper arriving by caravan from India was considered so valuable that it was preferred to money, which fluctuated wildly in value. Rents were paid in peppercorns, as well as taxes, dowries, and even bribes. Still the most widely used spice in the world, pepper was valued first as a medicine to help gastric problems and gradually evolved into a seasoning to enhance other foods. Venice grew rich importing it during the Crusades, and later Portugal, the Dutch East India Company, and the British East

India Company did the same, spreading their culture while dominating the pepper trade.

If left to ripen naturally, pepper berries turn red. Green peppercorns result from harvesting before they begin to redden. For black pepper, the berries are allowed to ripen a bit more, then are picked and dried in the sun until they turn black.

Berries to be used for white pepper ripen even longer on the vines before being harvested. They are then soaked in water to loosen the outer skin, which is then rubbed off. White pepper tends to be more expensive since more berries are needed to produce the same amount of the spice.

20

FEBRUARY

TOOTHPICKS

On this day in 1872, Silas Noble and J. P. Cooley were awarded the patent for a machine that manufactured toothpicks. It was a long time coming. Toothpick marks have been found on the teeth of prehistoric man, and chewing sticks, mentioned by the Chinese as early as 1600 B.C., had been used in Babylonia more than three thousand years earlier.

The first toothpicks were twigs, taken from trees, with a pleasant taste and scent and were used to help clean the teeth. The twigs evolved into rudimentary toothbrushes, with a pointed end and a softer, mashed one that eventually developed into a brush made of the bristles of pigs. Nylon replaced natural bristles in the late 1930s, and electric toothbrushes followed soon after.

In 1941, while on a boat bound for Brazil, Sherwood Anderson, the novelist and short story writer who had been an influence on Hemingway, died of peritonitis after accidentally swallowing a toothpick at a cocktail party. He was sixty-five years old.

21

FEBRUARY

BEAUVILLIERS

Until the end of the 18th century, a visitor to Paris could not dine except at the home of friends. There were places to stay—inns and hotels—that served some food, but only to guests.

The first actual restaurant in Paris was opened by a former chef and steward to royalty, Antoine Beauvilliers, in 1782. It was called Grande Tavern de Londres and was located at 26 rue de Richelieu. The decor was elegant, the waiters well-trained, and the food excellent. Beauvilliers dressed fashionably and carried a sword. More than 170 dishes were on the menu, including partridge with cabbage, veal chops grilled in buttered paper, and duck with turnips. By the year 1800, over five hundred restaurants had opened in Paris, and being served was a luxury that belonged to the masses, at least those with some money.

Beauvilliers' great success was due in large measure to his knowledge and style. He understood how to cater to and flatter rich patrons. He attended to them personally; he would point out something on the menu to avoid, recommend another thing, and then order for them still a third dish not listed, at the same time calling up choice bottles from the cellar. He had a prodigious memory and could greet by name customers who had been in twenty years before.

The restaurant survived the Revolution, the Reign of Terror that followed, the empire of Napoleon, and the occupation of Paris in 1814 and 1815. In these latter years, in fact, Beauvilliers especially prospered. He knew heads of state and generals of foreign armies by name and could speak, when necessary, their languages. The Grande Taverne lasted until 1825, and the name Beauvilliers did not disappear for one hundred more years.

22

FEBRUARY

LUIS BUÑUEL

1900. Luis Buñuel, the inimitable film director, was born in Calanda, an old Roman town in Spain, having been conceived during one of his well-to-do parents' trips to Paris.

All his life Buñuel was fond of bars—dark, quiet places where he could muse and drink. He was especially devoted to the dry martini. Although he drank other things—wine, vodka with his caviar, aquavit with smoked salmon—he attributed to gin a stimulating effect on his famous imagination, and rarely, if ever, missed his daily drink.

At home, his formula, reminiscent of Richard Nixon's, was: the glasses, shaker, and English gin in the freezer the day before; "a few drops" of Noilly Prat vermouth and half a demitasse spoon of Angostura bitters poured over ice he specified as too cold and hard to melt, then shaken, and poured out, the ice retaining a faint flavor; and finally, cold gin poured over the ice, shaken, and served.

Buñuel once half-planned to open a bar in New York, intended to be the most expensive bar in the world with the finest liquors from all over and a cannon by the door to be fired whenever a customer spent one thousand dollars.

I never met Buñuel in any of his favorite bars, like the Oak Room at the Plaza in New York, but for several months in Paris—where he said he had never been able to *find* a decent bar—I stayed in the same hotel as he did. He was in the next room. His lizard shoes, left outside his door to be polished, were like a nameplate, but I never saw Buñuel, unaware until later of the affection we both had for his favorite drink.   J.S.

23

FEBRUARY

BANANA

Indian legend, as well as the Koran, says the forbidden fruit in the Garden of Eden wasn't the apple but the banana, whose enormous leaves would have been far more effective than those of a fig in covering nakedness. The present variety has been cultivated to be seedless and therefore sterile, and so, unlike Adam and Eve, needs help to reproduce.

Originally from Southeast Asia or perhaps India, where Alexander the Great found them in 327 B.C., bananas are, botanically speaking, the largest herb, with leaves big enough to be used for thatching roofs and wrapping food for cooking. They grow in the tropics, and their name is from the Guinean word *banema* or *banana*.

For export, they are shipped while still green but continue to ripen after picking and can be sold in the United States at any of seven stages, from mostly green to spotted with brown. They should not be refrigerated, since at low temperatures they turn black, though this does not affect the fruit itself. As they ripen, they give off ethylene gas, as do most fruits, which further speeds ripening. But bananas produce an unusual amount, so that they're especially effective in helping other fruits enclosed with them ripen and develop color, including tomatoes and avocados.

LEMON JUICE

Peeled potatoes and sliced apples can be kept from turning brown by sprinkling them lightly with lemon juice, which is acidic and prevents oxidation. This also works with bananas, Belgian endives, and avocados.

24

FEBRUARY

HAUT BRION

Among the other things on the kitchen counter, there was an empty bottle of Haut Brion, left there more or less as a reminder and also to hint at our standards, so to speak. Kay wondered about it, "They'll be asking, but why aren't you giving that to us? What are we going to say?"

"You give me what my wife gives me, and you'll get Haut Brion," Jim said.

25

FEBRUARY

FISH

Peter Matthiessen used to stop by with bluefish he'd caught an hour earlier surf-casting in the Atlantic off Long Island. That kind of freshness is rare even at the best seafood shops along any coast. It is far more likely that by the time you sit down to a fish dinner at home or at a restaurant, what you're eating has been out of the water for at least two days and sometimes as long as a week.

The shortest route to the table is always the best. Mongers prefer fish from day trips or from the last day of the four- or five-day trips needed for bigger deep-water fish like tuna and swordfish that are caught far off shore. Ocean fish can sometimes be contaminated and so can farmed fish, such as trout and salmon, which usually reach the markets within a couple of days.

Fish will be fine if it has been flash frozen or well iced the entire time and not in contact with anything that might contaminate it. Even the freshest local fish have to be kept on ice for six to eight hours before they're firm enough to properly scale and fillet. With prewrapped fillets of fish, you have to depend on the standards of the store. When buying whole fish, you can usually see or smell freshness. The eye should be clear or, if cloudy because of contact with ice, not sunken. The gills should be red, not brown. The belly should be firm, and the skin should spring back to the touch.

As for preparation, fish served raw, as in sushi or ceviche, must be of the highest quality and purity. The flesh of cooked fish should be opaque and flake with the touch of a fork. Overcooking makes it tough and dry. On the other hand, you'll probably prefer it more done than Captain Ahab's orders in *Moby-Dick*: "When you cook another whale-steak for my private table here, I'll tell you what to do so as not to spoil it by overdoing. Hold the steak in one hand, and show a live coal to it with the other; that done, dish it; d'ye hear?"

26

FOOD AND MEMORY

The classic case of memory evoked by food, of course, is Proust's—the taste of a madeleine dipped in tea vividly recalling his childhood. But the one we like best is of an English friend whose pantry holds hundreds of jars of jam and marmalade.

She grew up eating the homemade variety. As an adult she turned to the Tiptree brand, which has the ingredients, texture, and taste of homemade. After moving to the United States, she was able to find it here and always had a number of flavors at hand. Soon after their meeting, the man who was to become her husband scolded her for the wastefulness of having several jars open at once. She rather crossly let him know that her habits regarding jam were not his concern. And as for the few jars she had in reserve, being properly sealed, they could keep for years.

He never mentioned it again, though in the 1970s, while they were traveling in England, he suggested they stop at the Tiptree factory in Essex, northeast of London. There, in a room that looked more like a huge kitchen than a factory, women chatted as they chopped fresh fruit, and an eighty-year-old man with a lifetime of experience tasted each batch of the double-cooked, extra special tawny orange marmalade they were making that day.

A decade later, her husband, in his early sixties, was dying of heart disease. One afternoon, a Tiptree van pulled up in front of their house, and the driver unloaded six hundred jars of her favorites—raspberry, apricot, and, of course, tawny orange. It was a farewell gift to her from her husband who, after he was gone, wanted her to remember him every morning at breakfast.

FEBRUARY

BREAKFAST

My wife and I tried two or three times in the last forty years to have
breakfast together, but it was so disagreeable we had to stop.
—WINSTON CHURCHILL

Our first breakfast together was huevos rancheros in Santa Fe. Later, there were romantic breakfasts in Paris hotel rooms—croissants, bread, and unsalted butter delivered on a tray with heavy silverware and a separate pitcher of warm milk for the tea and coffee. When shared breakfasts became more frequent, we often had tea, toast, oranges, and chocolate. There was a time when we included halva. We had a phase of soft-boiled eggs and another of Irish oatmeal that took half-an-hour to cook. Not long ago, we rose at 5 a.m. and staggered onto the lawn to see a spectacular meteor shower. An hour later, we sat down to some scrambled eggs and went back to bed.

It can be practical, as with the now popular power breakfast before the regular workday begins. It can be pleasantly solitary and was the only meal at which Emily Post said it was permissible to read a newspaper or book (television at that time wasn't a consideration). Whatever its form, medical experts agree that breakfast is essential for kick-starting the metabolism after its overnight slowdown. For physical energy, mental alertness, and even weight loss, breakfast continues to be the most important meal of the day.

28

FEBRUARY

AGED BEEF

Like wine, beef improves with age, though the time needed is measured in days instead of years. Meat gains tenderness for about ten days after slaughter, and the flavor increases for up to three weeks, all the result of natural processes. Most beef sold in grocery stores has been aged for five to seven days, generally long enough to have most of the benefits. Good restaurants may use beef that is twenty-one days old and pass the extra aging costs on to the customer.

There are two methods for aging. In "dry" aging, the meat hangs in a humid room of circulating air cooled to 34–36 degrees F. The "bag" method, used now by about ninety percent of wholesalers, involves vacuum packing and refrigerating the beef. It is preferred because the meat shrinks less and is less likely to pick up odors or flavors from its surroundings.

29

FEBRUARY

ROSSINI

"To eat, to love, to sing, to digest: in truth, these are the four acts in this opera buffa that we call life and which vanishes like the bubbles in a bottle of champagne," said Gioachino Rossini. Son of a singer and a horn player, he was born in Pesaro on leap year day, 1792. His most popular comic opera, *The Barber of Seville,* opened when he was twenty-four, and he wrote thirty-seven others before suddenly giving up composing them in 1829.

For the next quarter of a century, one of the things he substituted for music was his passion for food. Living in Paris, he nevertheless had Italian specialties sent to him, including favorites like *zampone,* a sausage of stuffed pigs' feet, and another sausage called *cappelli da prete,* named for the priests' hats it resembled. Once, on receiving a shipment of *sardone,* large sardines he was especially fond of, Rossini asked an invited dinner guest not to come after all. He liked to enjoy them in solitude and quiet, he explained. Unwilling to share them, he made an exception for his mistress, for whom he saved a single sardine.

He also created his own recipes, relying heavily on two ingredients: foie gras and truffles. Though he called the white truffles of Alba "the Mozart of mushrooms," he usually made do with the black variety, used, along with goose liver, to garnish his tournedos Rossini and eggs Rossini. The recipe for his macaroni was said to have rivaled his most dazzling music. Dumas asked to include it in his thousand-page work on food, and Rossini invited him to his house to taste it. Dumas accepted, but when he arrived, he explained to his host that he never ate macaroni. Rossini, who had made a great effort over the meal, refused him the recipe. No record of it survives.

MARCH

1

LA QUINTINIE

Born this day in 1624, Jean-Baptiste de la Quintinie gave up practicing law after discovering the pleasures of gardening. His reputation
impressed Louis XIV, who brought him to Versailles to oversee the
fruit and kitchen gardens that supplied the table at court. La Quintinie's epic book, *Instruction pour les jardins fruitiers et potagers,* detailed
not only the planting and raising of vegetables and fruit but also the
aesthetics of creating a beautiful garden.

Nearly every fruit was represented at Versailles, including a grove
of five hundred pear trees. La Quintinie wrote rhapsodically about a
variety called the Bon Chretien, imported from England and called
the Williams there, as being "of a yellow color and with a pink blush
on the side which gets the sun, rejoicing the eyes of those who come
to look at it as they might a jewel or a treasure." It was sweet, as all
pears are, and like any pear had more fiber than a serving of prunes.

It was renamed for a local nurseryman after it crossed the Atlantic
to the United States: the Bartlett.

2

TURGENEV ON LOVE

At a dinner with Flaubert and others on this date in 1872, Turgenev talked about love. There was not a book nor anything else in the world that could take the place of a woman for him, he said. Love produced a flowering of the personality that could be brought about by nothing else.

He then recalled a story from his own past. When he was young, he said, he had a mistress, a miller's daughter he used to see when he went hunting. She was delightful, pale, with a cast in one eye, but she would never accept anything from him, money or gifts.

One day she asked for a present. She wanted him to bring her some soap. When he came with it, she took it and disappeared, to return blushing and holding out her now scented hands. She wanted him to kiss them, she said, the way he kissed the hands of the ladies in the drawing rooms in St. Petersburg. He fell to his knees before her. There was not a moment in life to equal that one, he said.

3

MARCH

FIRST TASTES

Moderation in all things, the ancient Greeks believed. But not at all times. When you're young and discovering the world, food has the ability to amaze. Baklava: impossible not to eat five at a sitting. Prosciutto and melon: an astonishing combination. Peach Bellinis: unforgettable. One learns, of course, that it's as much the place, the company, one's age that transform a particular taste into an indelible memory. Baklava on a deck above the Aegean. Prosciutto and melon at the Rainbow Room looking out over Manhattan before seeing a first Broadway show. Champagne with puréed peaches in Venice. Years later, the first taste remains.

4

MARCH

CHEFS

The word "chef" is now a common term for almost anyone who cooks, but it was formerly a designation of rank. The chef ruled the kitchen and those who worked in it.

In ancient Rome, the head chef sat on an elevated seat in the kitchen to supervise. The waiters were young boys in flimsy tunics open in back to make them accessible. There were special slaves who kept flies away from the table and others who set and cleared it. Some chefs were rewarded for their excellence by being freed—virtually all servants in a Roman household were slaves. In later times, some renowned chefs were even raised to the nobility.

It was Marie-Antoine Carême, in his dazzling career as founder of French grand cuisine in the early nineteenth century, who defined the modern chef as someone who devised the menu, ordered all supplies, and oversaw the cooking—duties that once had been the concern of a number of others. The artist chef was born.

Thackeray, in his novel *Pendennis,* describes one such: "It was a grand sight to behold him in his dressing gown composing a menu. He always sat down and played the piano for some time before. Every artist, he said, had need of solitude to perfectionate his works."

5

KING'S GLASS

During the Middle Ages and after, the fear of being poisoned was very real among kings and their rivals. At the French court, the royal knife, fork, and napkin were kept under careful lock and key. Before use, all implements and dishes were rubbed with balls of bread-crumbs, which the servants were then obliged to eat.

Wine for the king and queen was tasted first by both the cup-bearer and wine steward, and the glasses were served covered until the moment of drinking.

This strict ritual lasted until the French Revolution and began again under the Empire.

6

MARCH

DIET

Every diet has its advocates and hour of popularity, but the iron rule of weight loss, like the advice of Mr. Micawber in *David Copperfield,* remains the same: Calories in must be less than calories burned, else misery.

Easier than a diet but with comparable results is a trip to Japan, where overweight people are nearly nonexistent, and where two weeks of Japanese food—soups, sushi, rice, soba, and udon noodles, and no sweets—can result in a weight loss of six or eight pounds.

The Japanese also eat seaweed, the brown Pacific kelp with long fronds rich in potassium and iodine. No marriage banquet is complete without it since it also symbolizes fertility.

7

MARCH

BUTTER

Butter is made from churned cream that has generally been ripened by lactic acid–producing bacteria. Its taste may vary according to the locale and the feed of the dairy cows. In France, for example, butter from Normandy is highly regarded. The Greeks and Romans used butter mostly medically, as a dressing for wounds. By the Middle Ages, it was being sold as food in local markets and preserved in cool salt water.

Food cooked in butter tastes better and, browned, has a nicer color. Butter will blacken when heated too much, however, giving a burnt taste. Clarified butter will not and is sometimes called for in recipes that involve sautéing delicate things, such as skinned chicken breasts or fish.

Clarified butter is effortless to make. In a pan, gently heat a stick or two, perhaps cut into pieces, and skim off the foam that forms. Then carefully pour off the clear liquid which is the clarified butter, leaving the milky residue in the pan. In small crocks, it will keep in the refrigerator for weeks.

Butter in the refrigerator should be covered, since it absorbs odors. It also contains a large amount of saturated fat, not particularly healthful.

CÉZANNE

Manet, Utrillo, and Toulouse-Lautrec, among others, painted scenes of restaurants and eating, and painters sometimes sought to pay for meals with their work. The Kronenhalle in Zurich and the Colombe d'Or in Vence profited fantastically in the end by accepting paintings, but in another case, M. Bise, proprietor of a small restaurant on Lake Annecy, near Geneva, refused to accept one. He perhaps should have. It was offered by the then little-known Paul Cézanne.

8

MARCH

SYRUP

Maple syrup is perfect on pancakes, if you can get it on them. What you assumed was maple when you took syrup from the grocery shelf is nothing of the kind. A quart of it is made of 2 cups of water, a cup of sugar, 2 cups of dark corn syrup, ¼ teaspoon of salt, and 1 teaspoon "maple flavoring." The word "maple" doesn't appear in the name, nor should it.

The real stuff is called exactly that, maple syrup, on the label. You can also tell by the price, which is justifiably much higher than the corn syrup variety. Maple syrup is made in the Northeast and Minnesota from the sap of sugar maple trees during the very early weeks of spring, when the days are warming but the nights are still below freezing. It's the alternating temperatures that make the sap flow in the tree, and when tapped, into a bucket. The tree must be mature enough—usually at least forty years old—to be able to recover from the half-inch tap driven three inches into its trunk. Each tap finally produces about ten gallons of sap, only a fraction of that in the tree, and from those ten gallons, only about one quart of maple syrup is produced once most of the water has been boiled out of the sap. Large, healthy trees can provide sap for one hundred years or more, often from more than one tap each year.

9

MARCH

TOASTS

In 16th-century England, water was too dangerous to drink, and Queen Elizabeth I had beer or wine with breakfast. Even wine could be tainted, and the favorite remedy was to float a piece of spiced bread in the cup to improve the flavor, as well as provide a bit of nourishment. Raising the glass eventually came to be named for the bread: a toast.

MARCH

THEO'S BIRTH

1985. In Paris, the labor pains began in the morning as we drove out to Versailles to walk the splendid grounds and take the tour. "Don't go to the hospital too early and end up just waiting," the Lamaze teacher had advised. "Keep busy." So it was late afternoon in the Great Hall of Mirrors when I told Jim to skip the postcards this time; we had to get back to town.

Experienced friends had strongly advised that we stay close to home for the birth, both for the advantages of cutting-edge medicine and to encourage what they called my nesting instincts. Instead, we chose Paris as the perfect place to begin life as three. The first faint green was appearing on the chestnut trees. Confectionary shop windows were filled with chocolate animals as Easter approached. We'd found a French obstetrician, Dr. Bazan, graying and distinguished-looking, from Brittany, as it turned out, where they are traditionally more laconic. And we'd visited the American Hospital in Neuilly, where it would all happen.

Jim had once read that the lips of the future kings of France were moistened at birth with a good French wine, so they would always remember the taste. He'd carried with us a bottle of Château Latour, chosen for its quality and perhaps also its history, built as a fortification to defend against pirates and later occupied in turn by the English and French during the Hundred Years War. The ruined tower is all that remains and is the centerpiece of the vineyard today.

As the orderly was wheeling me into the delivery room, Jim took a moment to speak to Bazin, who had been summoned from a dinner party and was still wearing evening clothes. There had been a few complications—Bazin wanted to get going without delay, he said, but didn't want us to be alarmed.

"We have all the confidence in the world in you, Doctor," my husband told him. "There's just one thing."

"Yes?" said Bazin.

"When the baby is born, we'd like to wet its lips with a good French wine."

Bazin, whose English was all right within normal confines, took a few seconds to comprehend, his glance wandering a little until it fell on the bottle of Latour on the shelf over the sink. He went over and picked it up.

"This is the wine?"

"Yes."

"It's not entirely a bad wine," he commented, and joined me in the delivery room.

Things proceeded pretty much as expected and at one in the morning, Jim, standing outside the delivery room, heard the robust cry of an infant, and soon after, one from Bazin.

"Pull the cork!" he called.

A few drops of the wine were applied to Theo's lips, and then the rest of us—doctor, nurses, Jim, I, and a friend who had rushed to the hospital when he learned the event was imminent—shared the bottle in celebration. It matched its reputation.

We returned to the States seven weeks later, and when it appeared a couple of years after, bought a case of another Bordeaux, Château Leoville-Barton, 1985, the year of Theo's birth, which proved to be

one of the great vintages of the last quarter-century. When he was
old enough to drink some, we asked hopefully,

"Recognize the taste?"

He looked as if he did. K.S.

11

MARCH

BEES

1989. Last dinner party in Aspen before leaving town late in the season. Corned beef with turnips, carrots, and cabbage, horseradish
sauce. There were nine at the table. Two of the men were talking
about bees, saying they have an ideal society—only the females work.
The males, far fewer in number, care for the queen.

If stung, *brush,* don't pull, the stinger out of your skin, as the venom
sac and a pulsating muscle are still attached to it. Only females sting,
they say, and queens only sting queens.

EGYPTIAN AFTERLIFE

Ancient Egyptians believed in sending the dead into the afterworld
with everything they needed to mirror their life on earth, especially
food and drink.

During the Old Kingdom, some 4,500 years ago, those wealthy
enough to have tombs were provided with alabaster replicas of

roasted geese and statues of servants making bread. By the time of
the New Kingdom, 1,500 years later, internal organs of the dead that
might cause hunger were removed from the body and placed in
funerary jars guarded by magic animal spirits.

Even the poor, buried in only three feet of desert sand, were given
bowls of meat and drink in their graves. But they were not honored
by the sacrifice of an ox or bull as the rich were, when the heart and
legs, considered the best parts, were offered to the gods, and the rest
was cooked to feed the mourners.

12

MARCH

FLATFISH

Flounder, sole, turbot, plaice, and halibut are among the fish that lie
flat on the sea bottom and have both eyes on the same side of the
head. They are not born this way. They begin life swimming verti-
cally with an eye on each side, but one eye gradually migrates to
either the right (flounder and sole) or left side (turbot), and the fish
begins to swim lopsided and finally flat. It lies camouflaged side up,
eyes visible above the sand looking for food or, as may happen, danger. The flounder, a continuous fin almost all around it, is described
as seeming to ripple through the water and glide to the bottom,
where it buries itself.

The largest fish of this type, the halibut, can be as much as eight
feet long and weigh more than six hundred pounds.

Flounder, sole, and the others cook easily, being of uniform thickness and readily de-boned. As a matter of interest, it does not take twice as long to cook a two-inch-thick fillet as a one-inch, but *four* times as long.

One day we watched Pierre Franey and Craig Claiborne, who both wrote on food for *The New York Times,* testing a recipe, if it can be called that, for cooking flatfish—in this case, flounder. They made Flounder à l'Anglais: dab flounder fillets with bits of butter, sprinkle them lightly with breadcrumbs, and broil them for five minutes, without turning, fairly close to the flame. They will come out beautifully browned and about as delicious as fish can possibly be. A squeeze of lemon perfects them.

13

TAILLEVENT

The most famous cook of the Middle Ages was Taillevent, a name that has gone down in history when even the architects and builders of great cathedrals were anonymous. Born around 1310, his real name was Guillaume Tirel, but he has always been known by his nickname, probably derived from his long nose. He began as a kitchen boy with the hellish task of turning the big roasting spits in the service of Jeanne d'Evereux, who was to become queen of France. He advanced steadily, employed in the households of the great, reaching his highest position under Charles VI, who granted him nobility.

His immensely influential cookbook, *Le viander,* was a collection of recipes and descriptions that remained important for two hundred years and still provides a look at eating habits in the 14th century, when foods were highly spiced and the principal methods of cooking were roasting and boiling. Very few green vegetables were consumed, but fowl included swans, storks, herons, comorants, and turtledoves.

14

MARCH

HONEY

Honey, esteemed as a food since deepest antiquity, is mentioned in Egyptian writings from 7,500 years ago. It is thought to be superior to sugar, both because of its mineral and protein content and because the simpler sugars it is composed of—dextrose and fructose—are absorbed more readily into the bloodstream than processed sugar. In *The Iliad,* the weary heroes revived themselves with honey, and Plutarch remarked that the ancient Britons, great consumers of it, only began to grow old after 120 years.

The flavor and color of honey depend on the flower the nectar comes from. The wax of the comb, sometimes present, is not nutritious.

A single bee may make more than five hundred flights to carry back one ounce of nectar, about a teaspoonful. Though pollen content can make honey cloudy, all honey is pure, but it may darken over time. If it crystallizes, its container should be warmed gently in water to restore it. Honey keeps indefinitely if tightly covered and cool. It need not be refrigerated.

Mme du Barry and others used honey in beauty preparations, and when Sherlock Holmes retired, his creator made him a beekeeper— they are said to be long-lived—on Sussex Downs.

15

ANNA KARENINA

There are meals that make you forget other meals, restaurants that erase other restaurants, and books that stand above others. *Anna Karenina,* Tolstoy's great masterwork, written and rewritten as many as six times from April 1873 until 1877, has remained towering for more than a century and even into an age of images, vulgarity, mobs, and noise. Tolstoy was forty-five years old when he started it, having thought of the idea three years before, and by the time he was deeply involved in the writing, he had lost all interest in it. "If only someone would finish *Karenina* for me," he wrote to a friend midway.

The novel opens with an infidelity. Oblonsky, who has deceived his wife and doesn't know how to make things right, has dinner with Levin, his friend, who is hopelessly in love with Oblonsky's lovely young sister-in-law, Kitty. Oblonsky, a prince, is sleek, handsome, and well cared for. Levin is earnest, intensely idealistic, and unfashionable. Attendants with napkins over their arms welcome them in the restaurant, and a fresh tablecloth is immediately spread over another. A private room ("Prince Golitsyn and a lady") may shortly be available, if they prefer.

The dinner begins with fresh Flemsburg oysters and champagne, then Parmesan cheese, vegetable soup, turbot (of which Levin is tremendously fond), roast beef, capon, and to finish, stewed fruit. The wine is Chablis. It is a world of aristocracy and wealth, doomed to vanish forever in less than fifty years, though none of them, including Tolstoy, who modeled Levin upon himself, foresaw it.

Anna, the beautiful and heartbreaking heroine—Oblonsky's sister, as it happens—dies at the end, but it is she, nevertheless, who has survived the Russian revolution, the bloody civil war that followed, and the nightmare of Stalin and his successors.

16

MARCH

WATER

About two-thirds of a person's weight is water. Even mild dehydration from sweating or fever can make the body function less efficiently, making it feel tired. The brain is especially susceptible, and lack of water can cause headaches, dizziness, and mental confusion. The sensation of hunger is often really just unrecognized thirst, curable with a glass of water.

Water is cheap. The hundred gallons the average person uses each day cost only about twenty-five cents. Water is perfect for bathing, for doing dishes, or washing the car—the questions come when you're going to drink it. City water is frequently and rigorously tested, so there's very little danger of it ever making you sick. Water may be safe and yet unpalatable, however. It's hard to get enthusiastic about the recommended eight glasses a day if the water you're drinking has a noticeable odor or unusual taste. Filtration, the addition of chlorine or potassium permanganate, or other remedies, may be necessary.

Bottled water can be artesian, spring, mineral, sparkling, or purified, which includes water that has been distilled or deionized.

There's also seltzer and club soda, though they are technically not water but soft drinks, since they are artificially carbonated and, in the case of club soda, have minerals added and sometimes flavoring and sugar.

The testing, bottling, and labeling of bottled water are governed by the Food and Drug Administration, reinforced by state regulations, and imported waters have to meet the same standards. The water must be calorie-free, sugar-free, and have the same qualities it has at its source, including any minerals or carbonation. Most bottled water is safe, though it is not tested, as tap water is, for certain bacteria such as e-coli, for the parasite giardia, or for arsenic, and any that is sold in the same state where it is bottled doesn't have to be tested at all.

17

MARCH

AVOCADO

The slow sale of avocados in the 1920s, it is said, immediately shot upward when the growers began to deny indignantly that they were aphrodisiac.

Avocados are ripe when they give slightly under the pressure of a finger. They will ripen by themselves in a few days at room temperature or in a paper bag and can then be kept in the refrigerator. When cut they will quickly turn brown, though some lemon juice and plastic wrap prevents that. They are extremely nourishing, having the highest protein content of any fruit, as well as the highest number of calories, about five times that of an apple.

18

MARCH

GROVER CLEVELAND

Grover Cleveland was born in Caldwell, New Jersey, on this date in 1837. In 1885, he was elected president, the first Democrat to win since the Civil War. A bachelor upon taking office, the luxuries of the White House made him uncomfortable. "I must go to dinner," he wrote to a friend, "but I wish it was to eat a pickled herring, a Swiss cheese, and a chop at Louis' instead of the French stuff I shall find."

A year into his term, he married his twenty-two-year-old ward, Frances Folsom, the youngest First Lady in history and the first to be married in the White House itself. Daughter of Cleveland's law partner, who had died when she was eleven, Frances became enormously popular.

Cleveland was defeated by Benjamin Harrison in a bid for re-election, but returned to office in 1893, becoming the only president to serve two nonconsecutive terms. Just before that election, he received a gift of apples from a friend, F. J. Parker, in Walla Walla, Washington. In his letter of thanks, Cleveland said, ". . . a state that can produce such fruit as that which has decorated my table since the apples reached me ought to be able to produce anything—even a Democratic majority."

19

MARCH

BOILING WATER

Water boils at 100 degrees C at sea level. In fact, the Celsius scale, 0–100, is based on the freezing and boiling points of water (32 degrees and 212 degrees, respectively, in Fahrenheit). Water boiling violently is no hotter than water gently boiling; it is only turning to steam more quickly. Salt added to water doesn't significantly affect the boiling point, although sugar raises it.

Altitude lowers the boiling point and increases cooking time. For every thousand feet above sea level, water boils at 1 degree C and about 1.5 degrees F lower, so in the mountains, your tea will be cooler.

20

MARCH

PASTA

The origins of pasta are obscure. Contrary to popular belief, pasta was not brought back from China by Marco Polo but probably originated in Sicily, which was the granary of the Roman Empire in its later days. It is mentioned in literature as early as the 12th century, and by the 15th century, various recipes were in print. Most likely, it came into being as a method of preserving milled wheat by mixing it with water and drying it in the sun.

Pasta is made from semolina flour—the product of hard, high-gluten wheat (durum wheat) that allows the dough made from its flour to have a strong, elastic structure—and water. It is low in calories and has nearly the same protein content as beef. With some butter or fresh tomato sauce and grated cheese, it makes a complete meal.

The commercial manufacture of pasta became possible in the early 1800s when machinery was devised to force the heavy semolina dough through a die, creating long strands of various shapes and thicknesses: round forms like spaghetti, flat like fettucine, star-shaped, and so on. The early machines could extrude a five-foot length of pasta that in Naples, in the old days, was hung on racks in the back streets and courtyards to dry. Afterward, it was broken in two where it had been folded and thus for a long time had a characteristic curved tip. Today almost all dried pasta comes in shorter lengths to fit on supermarket shelves. Italian-made pasta is judged superior to others.

The area around Naples originally provided the durum wheat necessary for pasta; then Ukraine became the biggest source until Soviet times. Today much of the wheat necessary for pasta comes from North and South Dakota.

Besides the dried variety, made to have an indefinite shelf life, there is fresh pasta, made with various kinds of flour, eggs, and vegetable flavorings, which must be used quickly. Fresh pasta is most suitable for mild cream or butter sauces. It is not superior to dry pasta, merely a different form, and its quality will depend entirely on who is making it.

21

NIP

"Nip" probably originated with the Dutch *nippen,* which means "a sip," or from *nipperkin,* meaning "a small measure." However, it's possible that it comes from the name of the Greek nymph Aganippe, whose spring on Mount Helicon was sacred to the Muses because it was believed that those who drank from it were given poetic inspiration.

LUCULLUS

In 66 B.C., at the age of sixty, Roman general Lucullus won a glorious victory for Rome over Mithridates, the ruler of Asia Minor. Nevertheless, his army, which had never been devoted to him, threatened mutiny almost daily, and Lucullus was forced to retire to his country villa, where he consoled himself by hosting lavish entertainments and feasts, sometimes featuring the fruit he'd discovered on a campaign years before in Armenia and brought to Rome for the first time: the cherry.

Wishing to test his reputation for opulence, Cicero and Pompey appeared unannounced one night but would not let Lucullus give any special orders to his servants except to say two more places should be set at the table. They didn't know that his dining rooms were designated by the amount to be spent on each guest. Determined to impress them, Lucullus told his chief steward there were to be two extra places in the Hall of Apollo, where, as his staff knew, the lavish meal served always cost the equivalent of over one thousand dollars per person.

On one rare occasion, Lucullus told his chef that no guest would be coming to dinner. The chef interpreted this to mean that a meal costing a mere five hundred dollars would do. Afterward, Lucullus expressed extreme annoyance: "On those days when I am alone, you must make a special effort, for that is when Lucullus dines with Lucullus."

22

MARCH

EGG

The 20th-century sculptor Constantin Brancusi, known for the simplicity and purity of his own work, called the egg "the most perfect form of creation." In ancient Egypt, it symbolized resurrection into a future life, as it did later in Christianity. It has even found its way into the language to describe human qualities: bad egg, good egg, egghead.

The word "egg" by itself almost always means a chicken's egg, the most widely eaten by far. An ostrich egg may weigh three pounds and make an omelet big enough for a dozen people, but it is the hen's egg that is used so often in cooking that a French gourmet once described it as being to cuisine what the article is to speech.

Nearly perfect in both nutrition and form, the egg is the food against which all others can be measured for efficiency. Loaded with protein, one egg contains about seventy-five calories, as well as all the amino acids; vitamins A, B, D, and E; and most of the minerals, including iron, essential for human life. The shell, because of its shape, has immense strength for its size, able to protect its contents yet breakable by the chick inside.

The color of the shell and of the yolk have no bearing on the taste, nor is a white or brown shell or a dark or pale yolk any indication of an egg being more "natural." What can make a difference to its taste is what the hen eats. The best-tasting eggs result from a diet of grain with the addition of such odds and ends as insects and worms that the hen finds in her wanderings.

The other factor is freshness. The test is basically the same today as it was two hundred years ago, recorded by Amelia Simmon in the first American cookbook: "Put them into (salted) water. If they lye on their bilge, they are good and fresh, if they bob up on end they are stale, and if they rise (and float horizontally) they are addled, proved, and of no use."

Eggs should be stored unwashed with the narrow end down in the least cold part of the refrigerator. Generally, they'll last for a month. Refrigerated raw egg whites keep for up to twelve hours; a yolk for twenty-four hours.

The white of the egg, or albumen, contains no cholesterol or fat. The yolk, which makes up about a third of the weight, has both. Thirty years ago, medical experts decided that eating too many eggs could increase cholesterol and contribute to cardiovascular disease. However, a recent study in the *Journal of the American Medical Association* indicates that eating an egg—or even two—a day has no negative effect on the health of a person with normal cholesterol. The cholesterol level rises slightly, it is reported, but is compensated for by the beneficial nutrients in the egg. Most doctors, along with the American Heart Association and the National Institutes of Health, still recommend eating only three or four eggs a week but at present agree that there's no reason to give them up entirely.

23

MARCH

HOUSE DRESSING

Salad dressing is better made than bought. Occasionally a recipe suggests a special ingredient—lemon juice or balsamic vinegar—for a particular flavor, but for nine out of ten salads, this classic vinaigrette is the one.

HOUSE DRESSING

3 tablespoons extra virgin olive oil	*Dijon mustard, the amount that can be held on half an*
1 tablespoon red wine vinegar	*inch at the end of a dinner*
Salt and pepper to taste	*knife or more for a sharper*
1 crushed garlic clove (optional)	*taste*

Place all ingredients in a small container with a tight lid and shake until well blended. Pour over greens and toss. The dressing should lightly coat but not drench the greens, which must be thoroughly dry for the dressing to adhere.

HUNGER AND APPETITE

The dictionary makes little distinction between hunger and appetite, but we tend to understand that hunger is the need to eat, almost entirely physical, while appetite is the desire to eat, stimulated by smell, sight, or the memory of certain foods or even the desire to satisfy emotional needs. Hunger indicates necessity; weakness is the result if it is unsatisfied. Appetite has more to do with interest and allure. When the two are combined we have someone very ready to eat. The problem is to keep them away from the bread.

This brings up another matter: what is good bread? The commercial, factory-made breads with their sugar and preservatives, soft crust, and softer interior or crumb, are pale imitations. Good bread should have a fairly crisp crust and a soft interior, generally with irregular, slightly glazed holes. Almost no bread should be served hot, and rye bread—the loaf—is best when slightly stale. Warm, freshly baked bread from the oven is one thing, but previously frozen and heated loves are not. Cool, sweet butter is the finest accompaniment.

24

MARCH

WAITERS

The vast majority of waiters don't think of the job as a career but a way station, a means of making some money on the way to something else. But there's another tradition, the professional waiter who trains for his job, performs it with style, and who, if asked about goals for the future, cites not acting but perhaps the ownership of a restaurant.

Aside from the basics—cleanliness, fluency in the language, knowing which side to serve and clear from, how to set a table, how to time the arrival and removal of dishes—what should be expected?

• A knowledge not only of the items on the menu, but their ingredients and how they are prepared.

- A memory that allows easy recitation of specials or changes in the menu. An ability to suggest items on the menu and the wine list—the vast majority of customers ask the waiter for his recommendations. He should be a salesman to the degree that the client wants help in choosing, but not to the point of trying to make a bigger tip from the cost of the meal.
- Also, a memory for the customers he serves, including the drink they like before dinner and their favorite dishes and wines. A good waiter knows this after the second visit.
- An understanding of how to move through a restaurant's crowded space with an eye for the big picture, just as a hockey or basketball player sizes up not only his own position, but also that of every other player.
- An eagerness to do everything possible to ensure a pleasant, relaxing evening for the patron. It is far more likely that customers will remember the quality of the service than that of the food when they decide where to go for dinner. A towering figure in French cuisine and chef/owner of the restaurant in Paris named for himself, Joël Robuchon once said, "I like waiters to be attentive and smiling, as if they were having good friends over to their own house."
- But that doesn't mean actual friendship. If a waiter's first words are "My name is . . . ," you can blame the owner. Still, a good waiter is sensitive to the customer and grants him the extent of conversation and its tone.
- A passion for food and wine, or as one waiter-turned-restaurateur put it, "They have to work with their hands and legs, with their brains, but especially with their hearts."

25

MARCH

PEA SOUP

In Berlin in 1928, Elias Canetti, a twenty-three-year-old writer struggling with shattered idealism, met Isaac Babel, eleven years older and one of his literary heroes, who was visiting from Russia. Babel weaned him from the "blabbering vanity" of the decadent Weimar Republic and took him to lowly restaurants where, Canetti, said, "we stood side by side, very slowly eating a pea soup. With his globular eyes behind his very thick eyeglasses, he looked at the people around us, every single one, all of them, and he could never get his fill of them. He was annoyed when he had finished the soup. He wished for an inexhaustible bowl, for all he wanted to do was to keep on looking."

Babel, falsely accused of espionage, was executed in Moscow in 1941. Canetti, who retired to London in his early thirties, lived there quietly for the rest of his life, writing the books that earned the Nobel Prize for Literature in 1981.

26

MARCH

ARCHESTRATUS

The best ingredients straightforwardly prepared is the infallible doctrine of many great chefs and restaurateurs. It is a formula that goes back at least as far as ancient Greece and the writings of Archestratus, a widely traveled Greek from Gela, in Sicily. He repeated it over and over in his epic poem, *Hedypatheia*—also known as *Gastronomy, The Art of Dining,* or even *The Life of Luxury*—which appeared around 360–350 B.C. It is written as advice to one or two cultivated friends, but unfortunately the complete work has been lost, and there remain only sections of it cited elsewhere.

27

MARCH

CAFÉ AU LAIT

Café au lait, coffee made with milk, was a favorite of Marie Antoinette and also of Mme de Sévigné, whose doctor, perhaps knowing more than we do about these things, prescribed it for her chest. Balzac, however, a man who lived on coffee, vehemently disapproved of its combination with milk, claiming that this saddened the soul and weakened the nervous system.

Coffee itself, at least when made from roasted beans, was probably first enjoyed in the 13th century in the Middle East. In Paris it was
introduced in the early 1600s but popularized only later in the century by the Turkish ambassador, Soliman Aga, whose black slaves,
dressed in dazzling Oriental costumes, served it to the French ladies
who came to call.

The best café au lait is made with freshly ground coffee beans and
brewed stronger than regular American coffee. Heat whole milk in a
pan, just to the boiling point, and add it, to taste, to a large cup of the
hot coffee. Sweeten if desired.

28

MARCH

BREAKFAST

"When you wake up in the morning, Pooh,"
said Piglet at last, "what's the first thing you say to yourself?"
"What's for breakfast?" said Pooh. "What do you say, Piglet?"
"I say, I wonder what's going to happen exciting today?" said Piglet.
Pooh nodded thoughtfully. "It's the same thing," he said.
— A. A. M I L N E , *Winnie-the-Pooh*

The 1918 edition of the Fannie Farmer Cookbook lists two dozen
"suitable combinations" for breakfast. All include cereal with sugar
and cream; all include coffee, the favorite morning beverage in the
United States even then. After that, the list cuts a wide swath: applesauce griddle cakes, creamed potatoes, fried hominy, broiled liver,

codfish hash, and minced lamb on toast, along with eggs in every configuration, matched with bacon or sausage, and many varieties of breads and muffins.

There's fruit, but no juices. Authorities on physical training today say the best antidote to having consumed too much alcohol the night before is a morning that includes plenty of fruit, along with exercise to circulate the nutrients and repair the damage.

29

MARCH

LAMB

Louis XVI referred to them irreverently as "walking cutlets," but lambs have had the dubious honor of being part of religious ceremonies for millennia. In the Middle East, sheep have been raised for over nine thousand years. They are mentioned forty-five times in the Bible, far more often than any other creature. In a dramatic story in Genesis, God tells Abraham to sacrifice his son Isaac, then at the last instant relents, spares Isaac, and allows father and son to discover a lamb in the nearby bushes to be used as the offering. Isaac's descendants, the tribes of Israel, rubbed lambs' blood over their doors in remembrance of the first Passover, to identify themselves as the chosen people, protected by God. Jesus, a Jew himself, was called the Lamb of God, sacrificed for the sins of the world, and lamb is still a traditional Easter dish, especially in Greece and Italy.

Lamb and mutton dishes are also at the heart of Islamic tradition. They are served on all important occasions, including the feast that ends the month-long prayer and fasting of Ramadan and at a celebration called Bakri-eid-el-Kurban that commemorates Abraham's willingness to sacrifice Isaac. On that day, wealthy families kill a sheep or lamb, roast it on a spit according to ancient custom, and use it to feed the poor.

30

MARCH

KNIVES

When it comes to kitchen knives, the important thing is to buy good ones. The best—high quality, stainless steel, and with a wooden handle—are worth the price. Knives last a long time and should be comfortable to hold and keep an edge, although they should be lightly honed with stone or steel almost daily.

Three knives are essential in the kitchen:

- A chef's knife, eight to ten inches long with a wide, tapering blade for slicing and chopping.
- A carving knife, thinner, for slicing and carving meat, turkey, etc.
- A paring knife, which is a small version of a chef's knife, for peeling, coring, mincing.

Also useful are:

- A bread knife with a serrated blade.
- A knife that Kay once impulsively bought at a demonstration in a supermarket, where a man was alternately slicing tomatoes and cutting nails in two with the same blade. Indestructible, he said. It turned out he was right. The knife was one of a set of three for nine dollars, the other two being unexceptional. The "best quality" rule was disregarded in this case, luckily. The long, flexible blade has very small serrations and a forked, pointed tip. It is stainless steel and is stamped "Taiwan." It will do anything, though whether you can ever find the man again is doubtful.

Knives should be kept in a wooden block holder or on a magnetic wall rack rather than loose in a drawer. They should not be put in the dishwasher.

31

MARCH

CHICKPEA

On this day in 1282, remembered as the Sicilian Vespers, being able to pronounce the name of a vegetable meant the difference between life and death. The Sicilians, in rebellion against France, murdered anyone who couldn't say chickpea—*cece*—in Italian.

APRIL

BRILLAT-SAVARIN • PLATO

CASANOVA • FOX'S HOUSEGUEST RULES

POLPETTONE ALLA TOSCANA • ROALD DAHL

COMMANDARIA • KELLOGG • BUDDHISM • RABELAIS

MANNERS • AGNÈS SOREL • HOT DOGS

YR. OBEDIENT SERVANT • TITANIC

WAVERLY ROOT • DOUGHNUT • BRIE

BRIE—POEM • SPAGHETTI AND MEATBALLS

JOHN IRVING • PEKING DUCK • LEMONS

CHAUCER • VATEL • WINE PRICE • TEA

EGYPTIAN DINNER PARTY • ALICE WATERS

JFK AND JEFFERSON • ETIQUETTE

SACHERTORTE AND BRIE

1775. Jean Anthelme Brillat-Savarin, who was to write what is perhaps the most famous book on food, *The Physiology of Taste*, was born in Belley, France. The son of a lawyer, he became a lawyer himself and eventually the popular mayor of the town. He was a cousin through marriage of the French beauty and social figure Mme Récamier, as well as a friend of Talleyrand and often a guest at his table.

He might have disappeared into a quiet provincial life, but in the wake of the Revolution, he was forced to flee the country. He ended up in America, where for three years he supported himself by giving French lessons and playing the violin in an orchestra. Music was one of his great interests, as were women, though he never married. But above all were his interests in dining and the glory of good food. Invited once to dinner with the choice of either scientists or men of letters as companions, he replied grandly, "My choice is made. Let us dine twice."

In 1797, he returned to France and, though he had lost almost everything, including a vineyard, he was reinstated. He became a judge, served for a time with the army, and spent the last twenty-five years of his life peacefully practicing law in Paris. *Physiologie du Gout,* written on the side, so to speak, over more than three decades, was published anonymously and at his own expense in the fall of 1825, a few months, as it turned out, before his death. Containing description, opinion, anecdote, history, philosophy, fact, fancy, poetry, and occasional recipes, it is remarkable both for breadth of knowledge and style, a great-hearted tribute to the civilized pleasures of the table, as well as some related pleasures. It was an immediate success, admired by Balzac, among others, who paid it the compliment of writing his own *Physiology of Marriage.* "Animals feed," is one of the many aphorisms in Brillat-Savarin's book, "man eats; only a man of wit knows how to dine."

In the icy January of 1826, already ill with the flu, he loyally attended a mass for the soul of the former king, Louis XVI, beheaded many years earlier. The prayers were long, and three distinguished men were to die as a consequence of having endured the cold, including Brillat-Savarin, who developed pneumonia a few days after. He died on February 2, leaving life, as a close friend later wrote, "like a well-fed guest leaving a banquet . . . without regret."

The rights to his great book were sold by his brother for fifteen thousand francs, the price of a good horse at the time. The first edition sold out. New editions followed in 1834, 1835, 1838, and 1839. It has never been out of print. On its spine, Balzac said, could be written, "Here lies the soul of Brillat-Savarin."

P L A T O

Plato, of whom it is said that all philosophy is merely a footnote to him, felt that conversation was by far the most important part of the meal and had little regard for cooks and cooking. He prescribed and subsisted on a simple diet. When he voyaged to Sicily, known for its abundance and its rich food, he wrote scornfully of a society where they thought that happiness came from satiety at the table, never sleeping alone at night, and the other indulgences that went along with such a life.

C A S A N O V A

1725. Giovanni Giacomo Casanova was born this day in Venice. Famous not only for his conquests but for his memoirs filled with accounts of food and meals, he often made special journeys to taste such delicacies as lark, cap mushrooms, and unusual wines and liqueurs, including one made of maraschino cherries, which he found helpful in increasing his sexual potency.

He knew, of course, the sensual importance of dining, the opening act in so many of his seductions. Prominent in his memoirs is the use of truffles or champagne as aids, and by voluptuously passing oysters from mouth to mouth, he once led two young novitiates into carnal sin. In the last year of his life, at age seventy-three, it was observed that though he was no longer a god or satyr, he remained a wolf at the table.

FOX'S HOUSEGUEST RULES

Joe Fox was from Philadelphia but lived most of his life in New York. A senior editor at Random House—Truman Capote, John Irving, and Philip Roth were among the writers he worked with at one time or another—he had been divorced from his first wife and for a time was living as a single man, with two sets of evening clothes to keep up with invitations. He had manners when they were called for and fixed rules of behavior, including six for being the perfect houseguest:

- Never arrive early.
- Bring a house present the hostess will love.
- Stay to yourself for at least three hours a day.
- Don't sleep in the wrong bed.
- Play all their games.
- Leave on time.

4

APRIL

Occasionally at dinner something—or perhaps someone—makes such an incredible impression that you simply must know more—in the case of food, this means asking for the recipe.

One night at our great friend Lorenzo's when he was living on Union Square, there was a marvelous meat dish, dense and deeply flavored, in a rich sauce of wild mushrooms. Though in slices like tenderloin, it turned out to be a kind of meat loaf, but far less ordinary than that sounds.

Meat loaf, of course, is a great favorite of almost everyone, chefs included, and there are countless recipes for it, all with strong assurances, but this version, from Marcella Hazan's *The Classic Italian Cookbook,* is easy to prepare and will reward you handsomely many times over. For us, it has never failed, to a degree that has made it a bit difficult to confess that it's only a simple Tuscan recipe:

POLPETTONE ALLA TOSCANA *(Adapted from Marcella Hazan)*

2 ounces imported dried wild
   mushrooms

1 pound very lean ground beef

1 tablespoon milk

2-inch square of white bread,
   without the crust

1 tablespoon finely chopped
   yellow onion

2 teaspoons salt
   Freshly ground pepper

2 tablespoons chopped prosciutto or (second choice)
   unsmoked ham

⅓ cup freshly grated
   Parmesan cheese

¼ teaspoon finely chopped
   garlic

1 lightly beaten egg yolk

½ cup unflavored bread
   crumbs

2 tablespoons vegetable oil

1 tablespoon butter

⅓ cup dry white wine

4 tablespoons tomato paste

Soak the mushrooms in two cups of lukewarm water for half an hour or more. In a bowl, loosen the beef with a fork. Heat the milk, mashing the bread into it until creamy and add it to the meat, along with the onion, salt, pepper, prosciutto, cheese, and garlic. Mix thoroughly by hand. Mix in the lightly beaten egg yolk. Shape meat into a firm, round ball; then roll this into a salami-like loaf about two and a half inches thick. Tap with your palm to drive out any air bubbles. Roll the loaf in the bread crumbs until evenly coated. Drain the mushrooms (save the water they soaked in) and rinse them several times in clean, cold water. Chop them roughly and set aside. Strain the soaking water through a fine sieve lined with paper towels and set aside. Heat the butter and vegetable oil in a heavy oval casserole just big enough for the meat.

Brown the meat on all sides in the casserole over medium heat after the butter foam subsides, handling carefully. Add the wine. Increase heat to medium high. Boil wine briskly until reduced to one half, turning meat carefully once or twice. Turn heat to medium low and add chopped mushrooms. Stir the tomato paste into the strained and warmed mushroom water. When smooth, add to the meat and mushrooms. Cover and cook at a simmer for thirty minutes, turning the meat once or twice. Remove meat to a cutting board. Allow it to cool slightly and settle. Cut into slanted slices about three-eighths of an inch thick. If the sauce seems thin, concentrate it by boiling rapidly for a few minutes. Pour a little sauce on a warm serving platter, arrange the meat slices, then cover with the remainder of the sauce. Serves about four.

5

APRIL

ROALD DAHL

Among all that has been written about wine—roomfuls—a short story by Roald Dahl stands out. It is called "Taste" and is about an unforgettable wager one night on whether or not a guest at dinner can taste an unknown wine and identify it as to region, year, and even vineyard. The story is dazzling in its detail, and the end of it completely unexpected.

Joe Fox, who was then an editor at Knopf, said that Alfred Knopf, the famed founder, had read the story in *The New Yorker* and had wired

Dahl, saying that he would like to publish anything he wrote. It is the equivalent of having someone whisper "I adore you."

6

COMMANDARIA

Tradition says that Aphrodite, the ancient Greek goddess of love, was born out of the seas off Cyprus. The wine poured there on great feast days in her honor is a sweet, red dessert wine, originally called Nama, and as early as 700 B.C., Hesiod, a farmer as well as a poet, described how to make it by first drying both red and white grapes in the sun for a couple of weeks, and later aging the wine in great earthen jars. Shakespeare wrote a scene in which Antony gives the wine to Cleopatra, saying, ". . . your sweetness, my love, is equal to Cyprus Nama."

When Richard the Lionhearted landed on Cyprus in 1191, he praised Nama and said he hoped to return, "if only to taste this wine again." Nevertheless, he sold the island to a military and religious order called the Knights Templar, founded in 1118 to protect pilgrims during the Crusades. The Knights already controlled an area on the island called Commandaria. It became the wine's new name and now, more than eight hundred years later, it is the oldest existing name for an individual wine. Edward III served it at a banquet in England in 1352 when he entertained the kings of France, Scotland, Denmark, and Cyprus. Two hundred years later, Elizabeth I also liked it and gave Sir Walter Raleigh the exclusive privilege of importing it.

There is no way to know for certain, of course, but it is likely that the present wine is quite similar to that of the past, though the blending of the grapes is more exact and almost all the aging is now done in oak casks instead of clay jars. Unfortunately, it is no longer credited with its miraculous healing properties.

7

APRIL

KELLOGG

On this day in 1860, Will Keith Kellogg was born in Battle Creek, Michigan, the town he was to put on the map. He had only a sixth-grade education, but with his older brother, John Harvey Kellogg, a pioneer in nutrition, he developed an entirely new approach to breakfast. They developed a method of flattening grain into flakes, then baking them to make a crunchy, convenient cereal that ended up largely replacing the traditional hot meal in the morning.

In 1906 the Battle Creek Toasted Corn Flake Company was created, soon to be renamed the Kellogg Company. Competitors sprang up, and Kellogg decided to distinguish his product by putting a copy of his signature on every box. His success was global, and from the beginning, he wanted to share his wealth. He created the W. K. Kellogg Foundation in 1930, which during his lifetime gave away almost his entire fortune—sixty-six million dollars dedicated mostly to helping children, with special emphasis on health and education.

8

APRIL

BUDDHISM

April 8 is the traditional birthday of the Buddha, who was born a prince, Siddhartha Gautama, and lived in luxury. He withdrew from the world at the age of twenty-nine to seek an answer to the suffering he saw around him, and after six years of searching, received enlightenment. The last forty-five years of his life were spent teaching and founding the religion.

Muslims eat no pork, Hindus no beef, and Buddhists nothing that has been slaughtered, since the first precept of Buddhism is that there is to be no taking of life. Reincarnation is a Buddhist belief that one's soul may have or will someday inhabit an insect or animal, giving more reason not to kill them.

The real wrong is in the killing, not so much the eating, and to some Buddhists, an animal that has been killed in an accident or by another (evidently non-Buddhist) animal or person is all right to eat. Buddhist monks, though, strictly do not eat meat and take nothing solid after midday.

Buddhism is important or dominant in Sri Lanka, Thailand, Cambodia, and Japan, but oddly has nearly disappeared in India, its country of origin. It is said that the prohibition against killing is observed by Thai fishermen through their regarding fish as not being killed when caught, but merely removed from water.

François Rabelais died on this day in 1553. Rising early was no happiness, he wrote, drinking early was far better. He was born, it is believed, in Chinon ca. 1493, became a monk and then a doctor, and his name has become an adjective for wild imagination, bawdy humor, and gluttonous feasting. His great comic novels, *Pantagruel,* 1532, and

Gargantua, 1534, were condemned by church authorities but were enormously successful. The king, François I, to whom they were read, enjoyed the books thoroughly. Even Shakespeare made reference to Gargantua's large mouth.

Rabelais's dying words were "Draw the curtain, the farce has ended."

10
APRIL

MANNERS

The place of honor at the dinner table is the seat to the right of the hostess or host, given to a man or woman. In ancient times, though, it was always to the left of the host, that being nearest to his heart. The Romans ate lying down, and belching for them was a sign of politeness, as it still is in the Middle East.

Manners have evolved through the centuries. Among the Greeks, the guest or stranger was offered a foot wash. Erasmus, in his *Treatise on Manners* in 1530, advised that it was absolutely not done to throw bones under the table or lick your plate. There are accepted rules for the use and placement of knives and forks, the removal of plates, the amount that should be poured into wine glasses, etc., but generally whatever is inoffensive is now permitted.

The true mark of courtesy is for the host or hostess to casually commit the same mistake as the guest to show that it is perfectly all right. The opposite of this once took place at the White House after lunch when President Calvin Coolidge, a taciturn man, put some milk into his coffee and slowly poured it into his saucer. His guest politely imitated him. Then Coolidge reached down and put the saucer on the floor for his cat.

11

APRIL

AGNÈS SOREL

It was said of Agnès Sorel, the first mistress of a French king to be more or less officially recognized as such, that she knew the value of satisfying the royal appetite—she found the best chefs to do so, and she was not above putting on an apron and going into the kitchen herself.

The king, Charles VII, met Agnès Sorel at a festival in 1444. She was twenty-two years old, from a family of minor nobility, and exceptionally beautiful. His love for her continued until her death, following the birth of their fourth child in 1450. The object of much jealousy and intrigue, she may have been poisoned.

12

APRIL

HOT DOGS

Its parentage was European, but the hot dog has been American since it was christened here in 1901. Previously called a frankfurter for its German hometown and then a wiener when it migrated to Vienna, it was first known in this country as a dachshund sausage, after the elongated dog.

At the Polo Grounds in New York on a chilly April day when the baseball Giants were playing, cold foods and drinks weren't selling. Concessionaire Harry Stevens told his vendors to try shouting, "Get 'em while they're hot!" Sports cartoonist Tad Dorgan captured it for the newspapers, but he didn't know how to spell dachshund. His caption called them "hot dogs."

In St. Louis at the World's Fair in 1904, they made their official debut in buns that matched their shape, garnished with George French's newly created yellow mustard, a combination that has remained popular for more than a century.

YR. OBEDIENT SERVANT

April 13, 1987, opening night of *Yr. Obedient Servant,* a one-man play about the immortal Dr. Johnson at the Lyric Hammersmith Theater in London—Kay's first produced play. The lead was played by Scots actor Robbie Coltrane, who occasionally misread his lines, which did not go undetected by an English audience steeped in Johnson.

At the small rented house in nearby Chiswick, preparations had been going on all day for the after-theater party for the producer, director, sole cast member, and friends who had come from the United States and other parts of Europe. The girls hired to help with the serving showed up in short black skirts with little aprons and caps like maids in bedroom farces.

After the buffet, dessert appeared—a huge cake decorated in icing with a likeness of Samuel Johnson. It was served with a fresh fruit salad, the origins of which are now lost but that is simple to make and that we still serve. It continues to be excellent several days later, should there be leftovers, in which case it's also good for breakfast.

FRESH FRUIT SALAD YR. OBEDIENT SERVANT

1 fresh pineapple, cut into
small chunks
3 or 4 navel oranges, peeled,
divided into sections, the
sections cut in thirds
Large bunch black or red
seedless grapes, halved

The marinade:
Dry white vermouth and
cassis, about half and half
or to the desired sweetness
½ cup sugar
½ teaspoon cinnamon
A dash of vanilla extract

Mix ingredients together and allow to marinate for several hours or overnight in the refrigerator. Serves about eight.

14
APRIL

TITANIC

On this night in 1912, passengers in the *Titanic's* first-class dining room were served ten elaborate courses, each with a specially selected wine. Oysters were followed by soup—consommé or cream of barley—and then a mousse of poached salmon. Next came a choice of filet mignon or chicken Lyonnaise. The fifth course, which included an array of vegetables, was lamb, roast duckling, or beef sirloin. Then a palate-cleansing punch, followed by squab, asparagus vinaigrette, and foie gras. Dessert was an array of puddings, peaches, éclairs, and French ice cream. Coffee and port, along with cigars for the gentlemen, concluded the evening's meal.

In today's prices, those in first class were paying more than $120,000 for the privilege of crossing on the maiden voyage of the luxurious new ocean liner. Late that night, four days out of England, the ship struck an iceberg in the North Atlantic and sank in less than three hours. Of the more than 2,220 people aboard, only about 705 lived to eat another meal.

15

APRIL

WAVERLY ROOT

1903. Journalist and food writer Waverly Root is born in Providence, Rhode Island, and named for the Waverly novels of Sir Walter Scott.

In 1927, barely eking out a living as a young writer in Greenwich Village, he impulsively decided one evening to go to Paris. The following day he boarded a boat. Paris was legendary, and his professor at Tufts had told him of seeing art students returning from a ball at dawn, carrying their naked models on their shoulders. Intending to stay for a few weeks, Root remained, apart from the war years, for the rest of his life. He prided himself on not having known Hemingway.

Among his works are an autobiography and the twin, idiosyncratic volumes *The Food of France* and *The Food of Italy,* as well as a large, informative dictionary, *Food.* The last thing he wrote was a note to his editor regarding the supposed thinning qualities of oysters. He had been off in Brittany feasting on them. "I have gained three kilos," he reported happily. It was October 31, 1982. He died in his sleep that night.

16

APRIL

DOUGHNUT

In 16th-century Holland, where they originated, doughnuts were called *olykoeks* or "oily cakes," made of round lumps of dough about the size of a large nut and fried in pork fat. The Pilgrims brought them to America, where they were called, logically enough, dough-nuts.

As to the origin of the hole, one of the most compelling versions has a 19th-century sea captain, Hanson Gregory, of Rockport, Maine, at the helm during a storm at sea. As he was eating a doughnut, the ship pitched wildly and the doughy cake was impaled on a spoke of the wheel, leaving a hole in the center. There is perhaps some question about this since Gregory was only fifteen at the time. On the other hand, his name is closely associated with the doughnut, and he may deserve credit for the hole simply by having asked his mother to remove the center of the deep fried dough, since it had cooked less completely and was soggy.

What is more certain is that by World War I, doughnuts were so popular with American troops in Europe that the soldiers came to be known as doughboys.

B R I E

Charlemagne, the great, energetic ruler who inherited a Frankish kingdom from his father and enlarged it through war into the Holy Roman Empire, died in 814 A.D. after a long reign that is now recognized as marking the end of the Middle Ages. He was a large man in many respects, with five legitimate wives and a number of "supplementary" ones. Dazzled by the monuments and ceremonial grandeur on a trip to Rome in 774, he formed the idea of making his own realm one of comparable beauty and culture. It was also the year he was said to have first tasted Brie and enjoyed it.

The real Bries, Brie de Meaux and Brie de Melun, are made from raw milk in the Ile-de-France not far from Paris. Always packed in a flimsy, round wooden box fourteen inches in diameter and an inch and a half high, Brie will carry a label reading *"Appelation d'Origine Contrôlée."* At its peak of readiness it is viscous, though not runny, with a slightly bulging, uneven white top mottled with pale brown. It is a cheese that ripens from the outside in and once cut, ceases to ripen. A wedge bought unripe will only age and grow hard.

Genuine raw Bries cannot be imported, but there are some pasteurized French Bries that are reasonably good, as well as a host of poor imitations from Germany, Denmark, and the United States, which sometimes even come in a can. These are usually chalky, firm, and not worth it.

BRIE—POEM

On a piece of paper folded to fit into a small silver pillbox, given as a gift, in the early days, when Jim had just introduced me to Brie:

My darling, you will quickly see
This tiny box contains no Brie
And, if it did, it is so small
It would be hardly any Brie at all.
But thoughts, however small or great,
No shape possess, nor size nor weight,
And thus, this box can well confine

All delicious thoughts of mine,
As, richer far than any Brie,
Are thoughts of crossing Italy,
And finer than the farms of Meaux
Are memories of things we know.
So keep it safe, my wondrous beast —
This box contains a dazzling feast.

K.S.

19

S P A G H E T T I   A N D   M E A T B A L L S

In addition to having the finest quality, Hermès in Paris based its reputation on being the most expensive shop in the city and probably anywhere—you could not, no matter where you went, pay more. The Hermès label in a coat or handbag was an announcement that the possessor was either rich or greatly loved, or wanted to appear so.

The link between quality and price is axiomatic. For the very best, you must pay a lot. It is a little like drinking grappa or *marc*—it stings at first, but warmth and a deep satisfaction follow.

At an upscale restaurant in New York, a regular, if unexpected, special on Wednesday nights was spaghetti and meatballs. Pasta was still available, but the old-fashioned meatballs were usually gone by mid-evening. For one customer, the great popularity seemed inexplicable.

"What's so special about spaghetti and meatballs?" he asked one of the owners.

"The price," she said simply.

At his house, John Irving does all the cooking, enjoying the relaxation after a day at one of his several typewriters. He's an excellent cook, easygoing in the kitchen, and likes the company of guests, drinks in hand, as he makes his favorite dishes, though he has the most fun cooking for his children.

"My kids (and my grandchildren now) like my meatballs. Sometimes I make them when there are no kids at home, because I'm missing my kids. Any good bread will do for the bread crumbs; put a chunk of Parmesan in the food processor with the bread crumbs, and a teaspoon each of oregano and basil. I use two raw eggs with a pound of lean hamburger—the meatballs should be golf ball–sized and browned in hot olive oil. Leave the meat scraps in the pan—with garlic and onion and a handful of fresh basil, if you have it. (No dried herbs in the tomato sauce.) My grown boys live in Colorado and California. Often, when I've made the meatballs in Vermont, I call them and leave pointless messages on their answering machines. 'Hi. It's Dad. Give me a call. I just made some meatballs.'"

21

PEKING DUCK

There are legendary destinations like Petra and Machu Picchu, as well as fabled dishes like *coulibiac* and Peking duck, the latter of uncertain origin but well-defined locale. It is said that the ducks fortunate enough to feed to heart's content on the spillage of grain being brought by barge to the capital designed their own fate, so to speak. In any case, it's a kind of duck prepared in a singular manner.

The duck restaurant in Peking—now Beijing—was said to be the best. This was 1948. The Red Army was advancing on the city. Inflation was rampant. The restaurant had a dirt floor and a tall brick chimney where the ducks, which had been carefully prepared—scalded, their skin separated from the flesh by compressed air, stuffed with celery, scallions, ginger, and sesame oil, and basted for a long time with honey—were roasted. Only the crisp skin, cut into small rectangles and delicious, was eaten, although—I can't recall—we may have had some of the meat as well.

We stayed in the Grand Hôtel des Wagons-Lits, owned by a Frenchwoman and doubtlessly now vanished. In the morning, a large dish of fresh strawberries and cream cost five cents, which was a couple of handfuls of money. In the dusty square, rickshaws thick as crows were parked. In the mob of drivers there was a slight agitation, and the one you had hired for fifty cents or a dollar a day would rise and trot his rickshaw up to the front entrance whenever you happened to appear, be it noon or midnight. The drivers slept and lived there in the square. Mao and the revolution freed them from all that.   J.S.

22

LEMONS

The lemon, rich in vitamin C, may be the only well-known food that is almost never eaten. Normally, only its juice or peel are made use of.

Lemons were important in the prevention of scurvy, probably the first disease known to have been caused by a dietary deficiency. A scourge for centuries, particularly among sailors, scurvy was caused by a lack of vitamin C during long voyages. Its symptoms included bleeding gums, loosened teeth, and often fatal debility. More than half of Vasco da Gama's crew on his famed 1497 voyage around the Cape of Good Hope died of scurvy.

In the 18th century, the British navy finally took measures to counter the disease that was killing more sailors than enemy action, and lemon juice was mixed with the daily rum ration. Later it was lime juice, hence the name "limey."

The ancient Romans used lemons as an antidote to poison, and in the French court of Louis XIV, they served as a cosmetic meant to redden the lips and make complexions pale. Lemon juice is still used as a rinse to lighten and highlight blond hair.

Good lemons should be heavy, with a distinctive fragrance. The rind may have chemicals on it and should be washed before use.

Lemon trees, like people, do not like too much rain and do best on coasts, where temperatures are mild and the air humid.

23

APRIL

CHAUCER

On this day in 1374, Geoffrey Chaucer was awarded a royal grant of a pitcher of wine daily. It was eventually increased to 252 gallons annually. In *The Canterbury Tales,* his masterpiece, he tells of an aging knight who drinks claret and vernaccia to give himself courage before entering the bedchamber of his new, young bride. This was effective enough to enable him to pleasure her until break of day when, dipping a sop of bread in the wine, he ate, began singing, and dallied with his wife again.

Little is known of Chaucer's life other than entries in official records. The son of a well-to-do wine merchant in London, he was sent on royal missions, given lucrative positions, and was once charged with rape, but seems to have paid to have the suit withdrawn.

A towering figure in English literature and a source for Shakespeare (*Troilus and Cressida*), he has been influential to this day. He died on October 25, 1400, and was buried in Westminster Abbey. He was between fifty-six and sixty years old.

24
APRIL

VATEL

No matter how much thought and care has gone into the planning and execution of a meal, disaster can strike. Fritz Karl Vatel, a Swiss immigrant who worked as a steward for Louis XIV's finance minister, Nicolas Fouquet, and later at the great estate of Chantilly outside Paris, took his problems perhaps too much to heart. The Prince de Condé had given him the responsibility for food and entertainment during a celebration in honor of the king, but even on the first day, things began to go wrong. There wasn't enough meat for guests who showed up unexpectedly, and then the sky clouded over for the fireworks display. Neither of these could have been foreseen or remedied by Vatel, but he felt his reputation was destroyed. The next day when the fish for the meal didn't arrive as scheduled, he gave up hope for regaining his honor and fell on his sword just as the shipments were passing through the castle gates. He was thirty-five.

Nearly three hundred years later, Vatel was scolded posthumously by Phileas Gilbet, a much-respected French cook and author of a number of books on food, as well as a collaborator on Auguste Escoffier's *Le guide culinaire.* Always ready for a scuffle with colleagues alive or dead, Gilbert wrote that every cook can recall disasters, "but recourse to the cook's knife (in the absence of a sword) would solve nothing, and it is in such difficult circumstances that firmness of character emerges in the one who commands. . . . Such a one will never lose his head and would not dream of committing suicide. An authoritative appeal to the goodwill of his team temporarily at a loss, some brief and clear orders called out over the tumult of the upset pots and pans, and the problem is resolved. The service continues. . . ."

25
APRIL

WINE PRICE

Wine maketh merry but money answereth all things.
—ECCLESIASTES 10:19

When you're paying more in a restaurant for the wine than for the food, you may ask yourself, why is the wine so expensive? The reason is a three-tier system that governs the price in most states.

Let's assume it costs a winery ten dollars to produce a bottle. The importer or wholesaler pays about twelve dollars for it and later sells it to a liquor store or restaurant for an additional five dollars to realize his profit. The liquor store adds another third or so, and the resulting price is about twenty-five dollars.

A restaurant generally charges double or triple the wholesale price, selling this same bottle to the customer for somewhere between thirty-five and fifty dollars, plus tax and tip. The sale of wine is more profitable than the cost of buying and preparing food, and most restaurants rely on wine and liquor sales to help keep themselves in business.

26

A P R I L

T E A

Except for water, more people in the world drink tea than any other beverage. The green tea of Japan is central to the Zen Buddhist tea ceremony but is also used to flavor the tea ice cream sold by street vendors. The nomadic desert tradition of the Middle East regards the serving of highly sweetened black tea to strangers as both symbolic and practical hospitality. China is the greatest producer of tea, which requires hand picking and, therefore, cheap labor.

All tea comes from the same bush, no matter where it is grown. Whether it is black, green, or the intermediate oolong depends on how it is prepared. Green tea is dried immediately after it is picked, black is fermented by wilting and rolling the leaves to encourage oxidation before it is dried, and oolong is fermented only partially before drying. Green has the lowest levels of caffeine, only about twenty-five milligrams per cup, while black has twice that, though only about half as much as brewed coffee.

Green tea is now believed to have health-giving properties and seems to help fight arthritis and some cancers, including those of the mouth, pancreas, breast, and lung. Some scientists think further study will show that all teas have such properties.

Besides these benefits, you can reduce puffiness around the eyes by placing moistened tea bags over them for several minutes.

- Most Indian teas are black. Assam and Darjeeling are among the best known.
- China produces both black and green teas—Keemun is a favored black.
- Ceylon teas are excellent. Formosa produces the best oolong.
- Pekoe or orange pekoe is only a quality designation for black tea.
- Earl Grey is black tea, oddly enough, scented with the oil of an inedible but fragrant citrus fruit, the bergamot orange, grown almost exclusively in Calabria, in the south of Italy.

27

APRIL

EGYPTIAN DINNER PARTY

The dining hall was the most important room in wealthy Egyptian households of 2,500 years ago, and the preparations for a dinner party were intended to honor both the host and the guest.

The staff included the superintendent of the storehouse, who also oversaw the slaughterhouse and the bakery where grain was ground into flour by hand and then kneaded, occasionally with the feet if great quantities of dough were required. In charge of cooking was the head of the kitchen, who also supervised the "bearers of cool drinks" and the "preparers of sweets."

The dining tables were covered with embroidered cloths and decorated with lotus flowers, and the guests also wore flowers in their hair. Boys and girls passed perfumes and wine to the sounds of harps, flutes, and less soothingly, castanets and kettledrums, while the harem women—a part of every large home—entertained with dancing and singing.

28
APRIL

ALICE WATERS

Alice Waters, born on this day in 1944, grew up in New Jersey, where she "never tasted a perfectly ripe tomato." On a trip to France in her early twenties, she experienced for the first time food straight from the garden or farm, simply prepared and eaten at rustic country tables. It changed her life.

She adopted that cooking style as her own, and the friends who gathered at her house in Berkeley often urged her to open a restaurant. The result was Chez Panisse, which opened its doors in 1971. She imagined it as a place where straightforward food prepared with fresh ingredients would be served in an atmosphere of true hospitality. This was a simple idea, but all simplifications are astounding.

Over the years, her enthusiasm, energy, and insistence on perfection changed the face of American dining, first at her own restaurant and then through the chefs who worked with her, adopted her creed, and opened their own restaurants across the country.

An early advocate of organic food, she developed a network of more than sixty farmers and ranchers who supply ingredients to Chez Panisse. She has even created a special position at the restaurant, the forager, whose job it is to make the rounds of suppliers and to seek out new ones. Rather than deciding on what will be served and then shopping for the food, the menu is determined each day based on the best ingredients that have been found.

She believes people need to renew a lost connection to the land. In line with this idea was the Garden Project: inmates at the San Francisco County Jail growing organic greens. Alice was a huge supporter and bought the produce for Chez Panisse. She herself started the Edible Schoolyard, where kids grow, harvest, cook, and eat their own food. She believes in starting early to teach children not only the wisdom but also the pleasure of eating healthful food. A close friend of hers always pauses guiltily before entering a fast-food restaurant. "Don't tell Alice," she says.

29
APRIL

JFK AND JEFFERSON

1962. The Nobel Prize winners were honored on this day at a White House dinner hosted by President John F. Kennedy, who addressed the distinguished group by saying, "I think this is the most extraordinary collection of talent, of human knowledge, that has ever been gathered together at the White House, with the possible exception of when Thomas Jefferson dined alone."

ETIQUETTE

Manners and etiquette change over time. For something more than a casual meal, there are some basics that, at present, are worth knowing:

- Never arrive early for lunch or dinner, but try not to be more than fifteen minutes late.
- The hostess takes her seat first and rises first when the meal is over.
- If you are giving the party, most of the effort should have been expended beforehand.
- Serve from the left, pour and remove from the right.
- When to start eating: In the United States, one usually waits until everyone is served. In Europe, no waiting.
- Clear plates only when everyone is finished.
- The ultimate courtesy is to make a guest feel comfortable in whatever they are doing.
- There are occasions when etiquette is pitched overboard. Then it is every man for himself.

SACHERTORTE AND BRIE

Sachertorte, literally Sacher's cake, a rich chocolate sponge cake glazed with apricot jam and covered with bittersweet chocolate, was created by Count Metternich's pastry chef at the Congress of Vienna in 1814. Metternich, the skilled Austrian diplomat whose name is often given to the period 1815–48—the Age of Metternich—had this favorite cake pronounced King of Cakes at the Congress, which had been convened to restore order in Europe after the great upheavals of the French Revolution and the Napoleonic Wars.

Talleyrand, a master diplomat himself, was the representative of a defeated France but cleverly managed to achieve an equal voice in the negotiations that were remaking the map. His response to the crowning of the Sachertorte was having a French cheese, Brie, proclaimed King of Cheeses, thus reestablishing a balance of power.

Aided in no small way by the excellence of his table, which for a long time had been one of the finest in Europe, Talleyrand preserved his wealth and position through both revolution and restoration. He was a lover of good food who disdained lunch and focused instead on splendid dinners of a traditional six courses, including two kinds of roasts, which he carved at the table himself.

Before leaving for Vienna, he had told Louis XVIII, "Sire, I have more need of saucepans than instructions."

MAY

CHÂTEAU D'YQUEM • SOLITARY DINNERS

BURAN • JAMES BEARD • MUSTARD • SPOONS

VICTORY IN EUROPE • SUN KING • RUM

VEGETARIANISM • GOSKY PATTIES

STRANGE KITCHENS • CHEESE • SALMON

BOSWELL MEETS JOHNSON • SALAD

CIGARS • NELLIE MELBA • BALZAC • CHEF UNIFORMS

SECOND WINES • SWANS • MICHELIN GUIDE

PEPYS • MONTAIGNE • ROMAN GOURMETS

FIGS • RESTAURANT SEATING

DUMAS' FAVORITE DRESSING • GARUM

EDWARD ROBERT BULWER-LYTTON

THE SIX SENSES • PRETZEL

PEPYS'S DIARY

1

MAY

CHÂTEAU D'YQUEM

Perhaps the finest tribute to a meal is, at the end of it, to drink one of the world's great wines, Château d'Yquem, brilliant and immortal, a wine that has made countless admirers, including Thomas Jefferson, praise its finesse, richness, and ambrosia-like taste. Jefferson's letter to the grower reads: ". . . I have persuaded our President, General Washington, to try a sample. He asks for thirty dozen [bottles], sir, and I ask for ten dozen for myself . . ." The wine expert Alexis Lichine commented that in every great wine area there are one or two plots that year after year somehow produce wine superior to other, even adjoining, vineyards. This is true in Burgundy, and in Bordeaux where the wine in question comes from. Château d'Yquem is a Sauternes, a dessert wine, the god of them. One taste of it is enough to seduce.

The château itself, about twenty-five miles southeast of Bordeaux, dates from the 12th century and sits atop a hill, the highest point in the vicinity. It was once an English stronghold, and its 260 acres produce 100,000 bottles a year, a small number for so esteemed a wine; it is, in consequence, expensive. Other of the greatest Bordeaux châteaus produce six or seven times as much per acre.

André Simon, the great French wine critic, defined a good wine as necessarily being of good value so as to be enjoyed by many "sensible people" who expect to have their money's worth. A great wine is so good that price means nothing. There are always people who both want and can afford it. Great wines, in addition, are limited in quantity. Château d'Yquem is so scrupulously produced that the grapes, withered and rotten looking as a result of their being attacked by a particular mold, are harvested one by one as each reaches its desiccated perfection, giving them a greater concentration of sugar and resulting in the subtle sweetness of the wine. As well as being expensive, Château d'Yquem can also last for fifty to one hundred years. Usually mentioned as the single most extraordinary vintage is 1975, but many others are close.

Fargues, a Sauternes made exactly like d'Yquem; Rieussec; Raymond-Lafon; and Suduiraut are all worthy, but there is only one Château d'Yquem, luscious and golden, beyond category.

It's not only in times of happiness that one thinks of d'Yquem. One night some years ago, Jim's editor, Joe Fox, and his wife, Anne Isaak, the co-owner of two well-known New York restaurants, came to dinner and brought with them a bottle of Château d'Yquem. It was to be their last meal together as a couple they said; they were separating, and the end of the marriage deserved commemoration. We drank the bottle together. There are nights one remembers.

2

SOLITARY DINNERS

"Solitary dinners ought to be avoided as much as possible, because solitude tends to produce thought, and thought tends to the suspension of the digestive powers. When, however, dining alone is necessary, the mind should be disposed to cheerfulness by a previous interval of relaxation from whatever has seriously occupied the attention, and by directing it to some agreeable object." So wrote a 19th-century writer, Thomas Walker.

One is not certain what was meant by "agreeable object," but solitary dinners are inevitable and, far from being avoided, can be pleasant, providing you like your own company.

When the two of us are together, we make a real dinner—something we cook together. It doesn't have to be elaborate and is sometimes only reheated leftovers and a salad. We have a drink or glass of wine, perhaps while watching the news. The table is set, and at about eight we sit down, eat, and talk. It's the event that separates the tasks of the day from the rest of the evening.

It's different when I'm alone, and I don't try to make it the same. I eat when I'm hungry; it may be at six o'clock or not at all. It may be in front of a fire with a glass of wine and music playing or with a movie on TV or a book in hand. It's always very simple, involving almost no preparation and only what I actually feel like eating: a baked potato or an English muffin with scrambled eggs or even popcorn. I wouldn't want to do this all the time, but when it's only now and then, it never seems like making do but like an indulgence. K.S.

SOLITARY DINNERS

There are periods in life when the most difficult problem is, who can you have dinner with? It seems a banishment, an exclusion from all that may be going on, to have to eat and perhaps spend the evening alone. This is especially true if you happen to be young.

When eating alone at home, I either eat very lightly or take the time to prepare a creditable dinner, not frozen or microwaved, and sit down to it feeling sorry for those who are not there. If it's winter, I have a fire. In the summer, I sit outside.

Eating alone in a restaurant, sitting at a table, is usually tedious. First there is the wait for the menu, then to give your order, then a longer wait for the food itself, etc. You are marooned at the table with a rarely seen waiter as the only possible rescue, the light is probably not good enough to read by, and also you haven't brought a book. If it is a decent restaurant, there is usually service at the bar, the best solution. There is no uncomfortable wait. The bartender usually has a place setting ready to lay before you, and you can drink in comfort until the food arrives. Drinking alone is not something admonishable—bars are made for that—and if you are in need of conversation, that is a bartender's duty. J.S.

4

BURAN

There is still served throughout the Arab crescent from Spain to India various versions of a dish that originated at a gorgeous wedding more than a thousand years ago and was named for the bride. The wedding was that of the son and successor of Harun al-Rashid, the most famous of the caliphs, immortalized by the *Thousand and One Nights*. Baghdad and the vast Islamic empire were at their zenith. In a special palace built just for the occasion, the bridegroom stood on a gold tray and a waterfall of pearls was poured upon him. There were night-long feasts during the weeks of celebration, and an exotic food from India was the basis of the enduring dish. It was eggplant fried in oil. The bride's nickname was Buran, and the many related dishes still carry some form of it.

5

MAX

JAMES BEARD

1903. James Beard is born in Portland, Oregon, to an English mother who ran a boardinghouse and was an accomplished cook, passionate about food. Beard's own thwarted passion was for the theater. He worked in it and even studied to be a singer. His attempts, in America and Europe, lasted into his thirties, when, to support himself, he became involved in catering, opened a small food shop, and published, in 1940, a first cookbook, focused on hors d'oeuvres. He went on to write eighteen others, as well as to become, over a long career, the country's most visible and authentic culinary figure.

As with Julia Child, it was television that brought him fame. Large, sociable, and a living symbol of his métier, his first show, *I Love to Eat,* was fittingly named for its host. He taught cooking, was a consultant to restaurants, sold wine, and endorsed food products, describing himself once as a great gastronomic whore. His credo, stemming from his youth in a bountiful and unspoiled Oregon, was fresh, wholesome ingredients honestly prepared.

He died in 1985 at the age of eighty-one.

6

M A Y

M U S T A R D

No hot dog or corned beef sandwich is complete without it. In fact, since prehistoric times, mustard has grown so readily in so many places that, next to pepper, it is the condiment most commonly available in the world for adding sharpness and flavor to food. The oil from the black mustard seed is widely used in India in cooking, hair tonic, and as a liniment. It once represented fertility to Hindus. The Chinese are more likely to use the greens as a flavoring vegetable, as did the ancient Romans.

When the tiny seeds are crushed, they release an oil that forms a paste. Brought into contact with water, this results in a volatile, pungent compound that gains strength for about ten minutes and then begins to diminish. The idea is to let the flavor develop and then stop it at the chosen strength by adding an acid, such as vinegar. The result is "made mustard," in a form ready for use. German, French, and American mustards are made this way, with the bright yellow of the American type created by adding the herb turmeric.

In France, Dijon became the center of mustard making in the 14th century, and by the mid-15th century, Louis XI was traveling with his own pot of it. The process and the ingredients have been regulated since that time, and white wine and the juice of unripened grapes are used instead of vinegar. It was here that Antoine Maille developed his mustards and vinegars in the 18th century and where in the next, Maurice Grey invented the Poupon mustard he named for himself.

Across the Channel in England at about the same time, Jeremiah Coleman was popularizing his brand of dry mustard, using an old technique of making a powder of the seeds. The powder was then mixed with water when needed, producing a far stronger mustard than the French and rivaled for bite only by the Chinese.

7

S P O O N S

In prehistoric times, people used shells as spoons, and both the Greek and Latin words for spoon come from *cocklea,* which meant "a kind of shell." The English word—a pleasure to say, making a sound almost like a description of the object itself—is from the word *spon,* meaning "a small piece of wood," which was also used as an early spoon. If the shell or bit of wood was fastened to a stick, it gave a longer reach into hot liquids when cooking or eating. In ancient times there were two forms—an oval, often with a point on the end, and a round bowl, used especially for eating eggs.

Most broths, however, were drunk directly from a bowl, usually shared with others. If the broth contained meat or vegetables, they were pulled out with the fingers. It wasn't until almost the 17th century that the upper classes began to adopt a new approach to complement the latest fashions. High lace collars and long lace cuffs made it nearly impossible to use the old method without the food ending up on the clothes. Spoons were the answer, and it was common to bring your own to a meal.

Owning enough utensils to supply the guests who came to dine became a measure of wealth and social standing. At first they were usually made of valuable materials, and later often of silver. Being "born with a silver spoon in one's mouth" actually reflected family position. It was only after lesser metals began to be used that people of more modest incomes could afford them.

8

M A Y

VICTORY IN EUROPE

Dinners can end abruptly. On VE Day, May 8, 1945, a family named Graham was sitting around their kitchen table in Great Barrington, Massachusetts, celebrating the return home that day of their son, who had been a prisoner of war in Europe. As it grew late, they heard the sound of an airplane passing low overhead in the darkness. It receded, then came back again and again. It seemed, perhaps, a tribute of some sort to their son. On the third approach of the plane, they went out into the street to look.

The AT-6 was piloted by nineteen-year-old James Salter, flying a solo training mission. The winds aloft had pushed him, along with other student pilots, drastically off course, and he was lost late at night, with very little fuel remaining, desperately looking for a place large enough to land. Below him was a black expanse that could have been a lake, or, if he was lucky, a field. He dropped lower, flying just above the ground to try to see. Suddenly, looming ahead of him at the end of what turned out to be a park, were tall trees. He banked to fly through them, but just beyond were even bigger ones. His wing hit one and tore off. Immediately ahead was a house.

The Grahams had just reached the street when the plane slammed nose-first into the kitchen.

Jim lost a tooth and some dignity. The mayor of Great Barrington put him up at his house that night. He wasn't washed out of the training program and went on to become a fighter pilot in the Korean War. Years later, in the Pacific, a postcard was forwarded from Great Barrington. "We are still praying for you here," it read.

9

M A Y

❧———————————☙

SUN KING

Louis XIV, known as the Sun King, whose long reign in France lasted for seventy-two years (1643–1715), was among other things, a great patron of the arts, cordial to Molière, Racine, and La Fontaine, among others. Under him, the immense palace at Versailles was built, and the court inhabiting it, *the* court of Europe, became ceremonial and introverted.

The king's long list of mistresses included Mlle de La Valliere, Mme de Montespan, and Mme de Maintenon, whom he eventually married. He was fond of food as well, and cooking was spectacular at the court. One observer noted that she had frequently seen the king consume at a sitting four different plates of soup, an entire pheasant, a partridge, a large salad, mutton, and two large pieces of ham, followed by a plateful of cakes, fruits, and jams.

He ate in two ways, *au grand couvert,* which was by himself but in public, or at least in courtiers' view, and at the *petit couvert,* private and intimate, where he and the ladies sometimes threw little balls of bread at each other.

10

M A Y

R U M

1655. Admiral William Penn, whose son of the same name became the famed American colonist, seizes Jamaica, a relatively unimportant provisioning base, from Spain. Rum, distilled there and throughout the West Indies, began to replace beer as a British seaman's ration in Caribbean waters. The custom would later spread throughout the fleet and remain in effect until 1970.

Distilled from sugar cane juice or molasses, a process that occurs almost naturally in the hot climate of the islands, rum is essentially colorless. Caramel, added as a matter of style, makes it pale gold, amber, tawny, or dark brown. There is mention of it in Barbados in 1600, and it became the overwhelmingly favorite drink of American colonists, as well as an essential part of the triangular trade that made considerable fortunes for New England ship owners. Their ships sailed to Africa with a cargo of rum, returned to the West Indies with black slaves to work on the plantations, and took molasses from there back to New England to be made into rum. When Paul Revere started out on his famous ride to warn of the coming of the British, he began shouting only after a stop and several drinks of rum at the house of a distiller, Isaac Hall.

Many fine rums have beautiful island names: Rhum Barbancourt from Haiti; Demarara from Guyana; Mount Gay from Barbados, rich and smooth; Rhum St. James and Rhum Clement from Martinique, the latter aged for six years; and Ron Rico and Bacardi from Puerto

Rico. Were it not for rum, who would ever have heard of the tiny West Indies island called Dead Man's Chest?

Cuba was once famous for rum, and, in fact, Bacardi originated there in 1862 but later moved to Bermuda and Puerto Rico. A mass producer, it has come to dominate both the U.S. and world markets.

Legend says that when Horatio Nelson was killed at Trafalgar, his body, in order to be preserved, made the voyage back to England in a cask filled with the spirits of the navy—rum—although, in fact, it was brandy.

11

MAY

VEGETARIANISM

Eating honey for breakfast and barley bread and vegetables for dinner, Pythagoras in the sixth century B.C. developed the theorems that underlie the mathematics of geometry and much of music and astronomy. One of the first vegetarians, he believed that animals have souls as we do and should not be killed. Later, Diogenes, Plato, and Plutarch followed his precepts, if not his exact diet.

Ovid and Seneca were vegetarians, and it was the Romans who gave the practice its name, referring not to vegetables but to the Latin word *vegetus,* meaning "vigorous" or "active." Leonardo da Vinci, Voltaire, Shelley, Tolstoy, and Wagner were all vegetarians. But it was not only a Western idea. Buddha forbade killing any living creature and, by extension, eating meat. Gandhi taught that the protection of the sacred cow was meant to include the entire animal kingdom, but there is no concensus on vegetarianism in Hinduism.

Within vegetarianism, there is a wide spectrum of practice. At one end are those who eliminate only meat, poultry, and fish; at the other are those, vegans, who give up eating not only all animals, but everything that comes from them, including milk, cheese, and eggs, which makes it more complicated, but not impossible, to get all the protein and amino acids needed for good health.

12

MAY

GOSKY PATTIES

On this day in 1812, Edward Lear first looked on a world that, as an illustrator and humorist, he would populate with an owl and a cat setting out to sea:

> *The owl looked up to the stars above,*
> *And sang to a small guitar,*
> *"O lovely Pussy, O Pussy, my love,*
> *What a beautiful Pussy you are."*

A pig later figures in the poem, as one does in Lear's recipe for Gosky Patties:

> Take a pig three or four years of age, and tie him by the off
> hindleg to a post. Place 5 pounds of currants, 3 of sugar, 2
> pecks of peas, 18 roast chestnuts, a candle, and 6 bushels

of turnips, within his reach: if he eats these, constantly provide him with more.

Then procure some cream, some slices of Cheshire cheese, 4 quires of foolscap paper, and a packet of black pins. Work the whole into a paste, and spread it out to dry on a sheet of clean brown waterproof linen.

When the paste is perfectly dry, but not before, proceed to beat the pig violently with the handle of a large broom. If he squeals, beat him again.

Visit the paste and beat the pig alternately for some days, and ascertain if, at the end of that period, the whole is about to turn into Gosky Patties.

If it does not then, it never will; and in that case the pig may be let loose, and the whole process may be considered as finished.

13

MAY

STRANGE KITCHENS

In a rented house, the kitchen is more or less a matter of chance: what is in it, where things can be found, what is missing. It is a good idea to bring along a few essentials. We include:

- A good knife. Usually, there is not a decent one.
- A vegetable peeler
- A corkscrew
- A garlic press. Some of those found are of unimaginable design.
- A good cookbook. We normally take our own, the one we've

compiled, eclectic but proven. Patricia Wells's *Bistro Cooking* is
another favorite and the right size.

- A good wine book. Hugh Johnson's *Pocket Encyclopedia* is small,
succinct, and up to date.

Amend the list to your needs.

14

MAY

CHEESE

Cheese is entirely a milk product. Made from cow, sheep, goat, water
buffalo, or even reindeer milk, it almost certainly originated as a way
to preserve milk and has a relatively long life. It also has a season, a
time when it is at its best, usually depending on the pasturage at the
time of milking. Generally, the finest milk comes with the rich grasses
in late summer and early fall. Cheeses that do not require much
aging, such as goat cheeses—chèvres—are best then. Brie and
Camembert are best in the early fall. Reblochon and tomme de
Savoie are best in early winter. Gruyère is best in the heart of winter,
January and February.

Most of the cheese in supermarkets
and grocery stores is not worth much,
commercially manufactured and bland
or simplified. The good cheeses are
nearly all imported, though some superior cheeses are being made by small

entrepreneurs in the United States. The best are made from raw or unpasteurized milk, but U.S. health regulations bar these unless aged for sixty days or more, which rules out Brie and Camembert, among a number of others.

Regarding cheese:

- Always serve it at room temperature.
- Avoid cheese with a wax or plastic rind.
- In most cases, do not eat the rind, although this can be a matter of preference. The French often eat the rind of Camembert, Roquefort, Muenster, and others.
- Store cheese carefully, with the pieces separately wrapped in aluminum foil and/or plastic wrap and stored near the bottom of the refrigerator. Chèvre, however, seems not to like plastic.
- Think twice about freezing cheese. Some authorities suggest it, but others unequivocally say no, and few things are better for having been frozen.
- If possible, buy from a cheese store where the stock is unpackaged and fresh. A good store will let you sample the cheese.

15

MAY

SALMON

Salmon begin their lives in small rivers and streams, later making their way to the sea, where they spend their adult years and where, for centuries, their whereabouts were unknown. In the end, they almost magically return home to spawn and die. This final act, upstream and against all obstacles, males and females together, can be an epic struggle. Before attempting it, the salmon feed heavily, and once they have begun, they eat nothing more. Their lower jaws are extended and hooked, as if in determination. After spawning, most of them die.

Salmon were once so numerous that they were a common food for the poor. Salmon and poverty went together, Dickens said. The Rhine, the Thames, and even the Seine as far inland as Paris were rich in salmon, but pollution and in certain cases the building of great dams have drastically reduced their breeding grounds. Salmon are still plentiful, but for the most part they are farmed salmon, raised in pens. Their flavor and quality are not as good, though some deny this. Their flesh is fattier, and even its attractive color comes from chemicals added to the food pellets the fish are fed. As Waverly Root noted, salmon are like men, and too soft a life is not good for them.

Smoked salmon almost without exception is farm-raised, though smoked wild salmon from Scotland or Ireland can sometimes be found. Lox, a popular term for smoked salmon along with Nova, really means salmon cured in brine, though real lox, like wild salmon, is hard to find. Gravlax or gravid lax, the Swedish version, is raw salmon pressed and preserved in salt, sugar, vinegar, pepper, and dill. It is especially good with black bread.

A good friend and exceptional cook, Belinda Frishman, makes her gravlax this way:

GRAVLAX

2 *tablespoons coarse salt*	1 *3- to 5-pound whole filleted*
2 *tablespoons brown sugar*	*salmon, cut in half*
2 *teaspoons coarsely ground*	*Fresh dill to taste*
pepper	*Vodka or aquavit to taste*

Mix together the salt, brown sugar, and pepper. Rub the mixture thoroughly into both sides of the salmon. In a Pyrex dish, lay one half of the salmon skin-side down on a layer of fresh dill, place additional dill on top, and then lay the second half of the salmon flesh-side down, on top, adding more dill to the top. Moisten with vodka or aquavit. Cover with another glass or Pyrex dish in which you can set bricks or canned foods to press the salmon. Refrigerate overnight or up to a maximum of about twelve hours. Wipe off the dill, salt, sugar, and pepper with the aid of a little more vodka. To serve, chill briefly in the freezer to make it firm enough to slice thinly. It is even better after it has been frozen. It can be cut into smaller pieces before freezing for easier handling. Serves at least twenty-four.

16

MAY

BOSWELL MEETS JOHNSON

On this spring evening in 1763, James Boswell had just finished tea at a bookshop near Covent Garden when Samuel Johnson, the most famous literary figure of London, whom Boswell had been eager to meet, arrived unexpectedly. Boswell, nervously remembering Johnson's reputed prejudice against the Scots and hoping to deflect it, lightly apologized, "Mr. Johnson, I do indeed come from Scotland, but I cannot help it."

"That, Sir," replied Johnson, "I find, is what a great many of your countrymen cannot help."

Others might have been flattened, but Boswell persevered, and on that day and many that followed, they took meals, tea, and stronger drink together. As different temperamentally as men could be and despite more than thirty years' difference in age, they nevertheless forged a friendship that carried them both into immortality.

Over the next two decades they walked, talked, and often raised a glass together. Johnson held forth on the subject of drink, saying of claret that it was so weak "a man would be drowned by it before it made him drunk. . . . Claret is the liquor for boys, port for men, but he who aspires to be a hero must drink brandy."

Boswell reminded him of their early drinking days together, saying that he used to have a headache afterward.

"Nay, Sir," replied Johnson. "It was not the wine that made your head ache, but the *sense* I put into it."

"What, Sir! Will sense make the head ache?"

"Yes, Sir," answered Johnson with a smile, "when it is not used to it."

Johnson occasionally gave up liquor altogether, explaining, "Abstinence is as easy to me as temperance would be difficult." At other times he indulged himself, saying, "Wine makes a man better pleased with himself. I do not say that it makes him more pleasing to others."

Seven years after Johnson's death in 1784, Boswell published his *Life of Johnson*, still considered perhaps the greatest biography ever written, the perfect match of subject and author.

17

M A Y

SALAD

Lettuce has been around so long that it is hard to say just when it began to be eaten raw with a dressing. It may have been as early as the 14th century. By the 17th, salads were elaborate and often included fruits, meats, and flowers, along with what we'd recognize as something similar to a vinaigrette.

The Chevalier D'Albignac, a French nobleman who had fallen on hard times, made his fortune when, by chance, he exported the salad craze to London in the early 1800s. He was asked one day at a tavern to demonstrate the reputed French skill at making salads. He

gave such an impressive performance that he was soon being summoned to fashionable restaurants and private dining rooms to dress the greens. Before long, he was arriving in his own carriage with a servant carrying a special case for his tools and exotic ingredients. He described the performance: "Finally, I put the salad back into the salad bowl and let my servant toss it. And I let fall on it, from a height, a pinch of paprika."

Should one serve salad before or after the meal? Originally it was served as a first course to encourage the appetite. Today, certain salads always come before, especially those with a variety of ingredients, such as the Caesar or Waldorf. In Europe, a simple green salad is often served after the meal, sometimes with a cheese course.

Peggy O'Shea, a friend who lived in Paris for a number of years and studied the ways of the French, says that it is customary there for the host to toss the salad and take the first portion to spare the other guests the danger of being spattered by dressing from a full serving bowl.

What to drink with green salad is simpler. Neither red nor white wine, but rather a glass of chilled Vichy—sparkling—water.

18

MAY

CIGARS

The aroma of fine cigars at the end of a meal was for a long time not unusual. At a London dinner once we were offered genuine Havanas afterward, and as Jim admired the elegant shape he was holding, he began to recite, "There's peace in a Larranaga, there's calm in a Henry Clay . . ."

It had become quiet. He went on: "But the best cigar in an hour is finished and thrown away, thrown away for another as perfect and ripe and brown . . ."

There was dead silence. They were staring at him.

"Kipling, right?" he said.

The brilliant woman who was the ballet critic of the *London Times* had been watching Jim as if transfixed. She breathed a sigh of relief.

"Thank God," she said. "I was mad with envy. I thought you were making it up."

19

MAY

NELLIE MELBA

When she performed at London's Covent Garden as the reigning operatic soprano of her day, the royal laryngologist declared her vocal cords "the most perfect I have ever seen." But as Nellie Melba said of herself, "It's no use having a perfect voice unless you have brains, personality, magnetism, great willpower, health, strength, and determination." She had them all in spades and was so famous that her name became attached to toast, wafers, and a dessert made of peaches and ice cream created by the great 19th-century French chef Escoffier.

She was born near Melbourne, Australia, on this day in 1861. For her operatic debut in *Rigoletto,* she changed her name from Helen Mitchell to Nellie Melba, in honor of her birthplace. "See to everything yourself" was her motto, and at Covent Garden she negotiated a singing fee one pound higher than Caruso's at the height of his career. She dazzled audiences and critics at the Metropolitan Opera House in New York and others across Europe and, using the media to her own ends, welcomed publicity no matter how unfavorable. Adored in Australia as a local girl who made good, she returned for seven triumphal tours and, finally, for her death at age sixty-nine from blood poisoning after a botched face-lift. Today, her face looks out from the Australian hundred-dollar bill. She probably would have preferred the thousand-dollar.

Peach Melba made its own debut at a dinner given in honor of Nellie Melba by the Duke of Orleans at the Savoy Hotel in London when she stayed there in 1893 while performing in *Lohengrin.* Escoffier's first version featured a swan made of ice that held peaches on vanilla ice cream, garnished with spun sugar. Seven years later, when he served it at the world famous Carlton Hotel, he abandoned the swan, and the spun sugar was replaced by a raspberry purée.

Today it rarely appears on a menu but can be made with pitted peaches, peeled and poached in sugar and water with a vanilla pod. They're served over vanilla ice cream and topped with a purée of raspberries and sometimes a scattering of slivered almonds.

MAY

BALZAC

1799. Honoré Balzac is born in Tours—the "de" that was added in late life was an invention of his own. Trained as a lawyer, he turned to writing, achieving his first success at the age of thirty. During the next twenty years, he created the stupendous edifice called *La comédie humaine,* a vast series of novels depicting French society in intense detail.

He regularly wrote feverishly from midnight until noon or even afternoon of the following day, subsisting on only black coffee, eggs, and fruit, but when periods of work were over, he dined lavishly. At one notable sitting, he feasted on a hundred oysters, a dozen cutlets, a couple of partridges, a duck, and a Normandy sole, as well as dessert and fruit.

During the marzipan craze, he owned a confectionary shop in Paris, and his novels contain a number of gourmets, one of whom, Père Rouget, was so discriminating that he believed an omelet was superior when the whites and yolks of eggs were beaten separately.

CHEF UNIFORMS

The uniform of a traditional chef is as recognizable as that of a military officer or a priest. The white jacket and the tall toque separate those who create the meals from those who do lesser cooking, serve, or clean up afterward. Toques were once made of fabric so heavy that it intensified the heat of the kitchen, with each of the many pleats representing one of the ways a chef can cook an egg. Complicated to launder, they're now often made of viscose that can be thrown away.

Worn in one form or another for over four hundred years, the jacket and hat only became white about 150 years ago at the urging of the great chef Carême, who wanted the color to signify cleanliness. He also redesigned the jacket to be double-breasted so it could be buttoned either way to hide stains.

21

M A Y

SECOND WINES

The immense care taken in choosing the best of the grapes and blending the best batches of each vintage makes wine from the great châteaus of Bordeaux expensive. Wine, however, that for one reason or another falls slightly below the highest standard may be sold under a different name and called a second wine.

Some of the seconds are of very good quality and can closely resemble the *grands vins* they are related to. They are also more attractively priced.

The best seconds, as might be expected, are those of the outstanding firsts. Among them:

Carruades de Lafite (from Château Lafite-Rothschild)

Les Forts de Latour (from Château Latour)

Pavillon Rouge (from Château Margaux)

Bahans-Haut-Brion (from Château Haut-Brion)

Réserve de la Comtesse (from Château Pichon-Laland)

Clos de Marquis (from Château Leoville-Las Cases)

Les Fiefs de Lagrange (from Château Lagrange)

Hauts-Bages-Averous (from Château Lynch-Bages)

Le Petit Cheval (from Château Cheval Blanc)

It rarely makes sense to buy the seconds of lesser, little-known vineyards.

22

MAY

SWANS

Edmund Spenser wrote:

> *. . . I saw two Swans of goodly hue,*
> *Come softly swimming down along the Lee;*
> *Two fairer birds I yet did never see;*
> *The snow which doth the top of Pindus strew,*
> *Did never whiter show,*
> *Nor Jove himself when he a Swan would be*
> *For love of Leda, whiter did appear . . .*

Graceful and long-necked, though mean-spirited and even dangerous, swans are admired for their beauty as well as for their monogamous behavior. They are, of course, a supreme ornament to rivers and ponds, but for almost a thousand years, from the 8th century to the early 18th, they were, like the peacock, a sumptuous roast at banquets. Raised in great quantities for consumption, they were the most expensive birds in the old London poultry market for a very long time.

For a splendid meal, the swans were plucked and roasted on a spit. Afterward, they were often redressed in skin and feathers, sometimes gilded, and brought ceremoniously to the table.

Young swans—cygnets—especially when fattened on oats, were the most delicious, and it was in large part the arrival of the turkey, less difficult to raise, that brought a gradual end to the eating of swans.

23

MAY

MICHELIN GUIDE

Thick, red, and intimidating, written in French, with indecipherable symbols and abbreviations, the Michelin guide on first viewing seemed hardly comprehensible, let alone helpful, but over the years, in successive versions, it has been a constant companion. Our old editions include notes on favorite rooms in hotels, beautiful roads, places where we didn't have time to stop but wanted to come back to.

We open it a dozen times a day on the road, and the late afternoon ritual—having checked into a hotel—is to examine the restaurant possibilities for that evening. Simply reading the names can produce anticipation: Auberge du Quai, Au Plaisir Gourmand, Le Vivier.

The Michelin guide was first published as a twenty-page volume in 1900 by the Michelin Tire Company in the early days of auto travel and was intended to help the motorist by identifying gas stations, repair shops, and hotels along the route. Eventually, restaurants were added. In 1931 its cover changed permanently from blue to red, and a rating system of stars, initiated in 1923 to refer to comfort and price levels, was evolved to designate the best restaurants. There are approximately thirty inspectors—all men and specially trained—who work full time to update the listings every year. To make sure they're not recognized, they're never assigned to go back to the same place within an eight-year period. They identify themselves as Michelin inspectors only after their meal or hotel stay, when they ask questions and examine kitchens.

Of the stars—one, two, or three—that Michelin awards outstanding restaurants, it is said that one will provide the owner with a good living and three will make him rich. They are coveted, and chefs have been known to commit suicide upon losing a star. One named Alain Zick shot himself in 1966, and Bernard Loiseau, who had had three stars for twelve years, shot himself upon hearing the rumor—which turned out to be false—that he would be losing one in 2003.

But there's more than just where to eat and sleep; the guide also features the number of inhabitants of the city; its distance from Paris and closer cities; the most important sights; and for the five hundred largest towns, a map that locates not only the hotels and restaurants but also the post office, hospital, train station, airport, and even museums, sports facilities, and noteworthy views. There's a section on regional wines and even a listing of French school holidays so you can avoid traveling at that time. And with the advent of the euro and a more cohesive continent, there are major road maps, international phone codes, and even a chart identifying regional and foreign license plates.

There are red Michelin guides for other countries, including one for New York City, but it seems the information tends to be not quite as reliable and perhaps the standards not quite as high as in the guide for France.

24
MAY

PEPYS

Strange to see how a good dinner and feasting reconciles everybody.
— S A M U E L   P E P Y S , *The Diary of Samuel Pepys*

25
MAY

MONTAIGNE

At table, I prefer the witty to the grave; in bed, beauty before goodness; and in common discourse, eloquence, whether or no there be sincerity.
— M O N T A I G N E , *Essays*

There were magnificent gourmets in ancient Rome, where feasts and extravagance were famous—Lucullus, Cicero, and Pompey among them. The Emperor Vitellius (15–69 A.D.) spent more than the equivalent of ten million dollars on his table during his brief reign of less than a year and is said to have habitually eaten a hundred dozen oysters at a sitting.

Apicius, who also lived in the first century A.D. and is responsible for the oldest Roman cookbook that still exists, had a vast fortune, almost all of which he spent on eating. When there was only a fraction left, he committed suicide rather than being forced to live a meager life.

26

MAY

FIGS

"Virtue! A fig!" Iago exclaimed.

He didn't have much regard for a fig. The ancients did. Cultivation of figs began in Egypt or Arabia at least five thousand years ago. They were grown in the Hanging Gardens of Babylon, one of the vanished seven wonders of the ancient world, and are mentioned in Homer and repeatedly in the Bible. There were more than two dozen types known to the Romans of this sweetest of all fruits— according to Pliny, the best came from Ibiza.

What we think of as a fig is actually the fleshy container of innumerable tiny seeds—these can be spread, even when figs are eaten by birds, since the seeds pass through them unharmed.

Figs can be eaten fresh—purple, green, or deep amber and best of all, Smyrna figs— or dried. Oddly enough, they are more nutritious when dried, which is done by putting them out in the sun or even burying them in hot desert sand.

The Buddha, it is somehow consoling to know, in the search for perfect understanding, sat in meditation beneath a fig—a *bo*—tree.

RESTAURANT SEATING

Restaurants, like houses, have places where it is agreeable to sit and others where it is not. Every restaurant is different, and sometimes the best tables are not where you might expect, but there are some general rules:

- Sit near the bar in most cases, if it is not too noisy. A restaurant may not have a bar, but it has a kitchen and washrooms. Don't sit near either.
- The second floor is almost always undesirable, in some cases unacceptable. It is removed from the drama. The same goes for adjoining rooms.
- Oddly, the personality of many restaurants is altered when they are enlarged or a room is added. Little can be done about this, but the old section is usually the best.
- Don't be afraid to decline a table. In a good restaurant, they will try to find you another.

27
MAY

DUMAS' FAVORITE DRESSING

Alexandre Dumas, a renowned patron of Parisian restaurants, in at least one of which he had his own private room, had a favorite salad dressing that he always prepared himself, not infrequently at after-theater suppers in the apartment of his mistress, the actress Mlle George. These repasts might be small or well-attended. The pleasures of dining, as Brillat-Savarin wrote, can mingle with all the other pleasures.

In a large salad bowl, Dumas mashed the yolks of hard-boiled eggs in olive oil—one for every two persons—added chervil, crushed thyme, crushed anchovies, chopped gherkins, chopped egg whites, salt, pepper, and at the last some good vinegar.

The greens were then put in, all was tossed, and a pinch of paprika added.

28

MAG

GARUM

The condiment of ancient Greece and Rome, fundamental to their cooking and dominating recipes, was called garum, derived from fermented fish. The innards or pieces of fish were salted and layered. Some months later, a liquid was drawn off. This was garum, often mixed with olive oil, vinegar, or wine.

"Delenda est Carthago!" was Cato's repeated demand to the Roman senate—Carthage must be destroyed. Its greatest general, Hannibal, had triumphed everywhere. The best garum, as it happened, came from Carthage, made from mackerel. Carthage was leveled and disappeared from history, though garum continued to be used until medieval times.

It happens that the defining seasoning in Vietnamese cooking, *nuoc mam,* is also a fish sauce and is to the Vietnamese what salt is to Westerners and soy sauce is to the Chinese. It is made in almost exactly the way that the ancients made garum. Small, silvery anchovies are layered, salted, and fermented for months in wooden barrels. The first liquid is drawn off after three months and poured back. After another six months the extraction, more or less like the first pressing of olive oil, yields the finest sauce. There are further pressings of lesser quality.

Nuoc mam mixed with lime juice, white rice vinegar, sugar, garlic, shallots, and fresh chilies is *nuoc cham,* the wonderful dipping sauce. Squid Brand Fish Sauce is the name of probably the best *nuoc mam* marketed widely and can be found in Asian food stores. It should read *ca com,* made only with anchovies.

29

M A Y

E D W A R D   R O B E R T   B U L W E R - L Y T T O N

It was after his success as a poet and playwright, using the pen name Owen Meredith, that Edward Robert Bulwer-Lytton, 1st Earl of Lytton, served Queen Victoria as viceroy of India and, later, ambassador in Paris. His father was Edward George Bulwer-Lytton, who coined the phrase "The pen is mightier than the sword" and wrote the novel *Paul Clifford,* famous only for its opening "It was a dark and stormy night . . ."

The son's long verse-romance, *Lucile,* includes this tribute:

> *He may live without books,—what is knowledge but grieving?*
> *He may live without hope,—what is hope but deceiving?*
> *He may live without love,—what is passion but pining?*
> *But where is the man that can live without dining?*

THE SIX SENSES

One cannot think well, love well, sleep well, if one has not dined well.
—VIRGINIA WOOLF

Brillat-Savarin recognized the five basic senses—taste, touch, hearing, sight, and smell—but he also believed there was a sixth: physical desire, a unique and distinctly French idea.

Everything subtle and ingenious about the first five senses, he wrote, was due to this sixth, "to the desire, the hope, the gratitude that spring from sexual union."

30
MAY

PRETZEL

The pretzel is said to have been invented almost fourteen hundred years ago in a monastery in southern France where a monk frugally twisted leftover scraps of dough into a shape like that of arms folded in prayer, with the three openings representing the Trinity. They were called *pretiola,* meaning "little reward" in Latin, and were given to children who learned their prayers. The name evolved into *brachiola,* which means "little arms," and then to *bretzel* or *pretzel* when they became popular in Germany and Austria.

Sold by street vendors as early as the 15th century, pretzels were associated with good luck and even became part of wedding ceremonies, used in "tying the knot." Pilgrims brought them to the New World and found the Indians eager customers, and a century later the Pennsylvania Dutch created the first commercial pretzel bakery in America.

From the beginning, pretzels were made, as the best still are today, of the simplest ingredients, the same as those for bread: wheat flour, water, yeast, and salt. At first they were baked like bread, too, to be soft. The story is that a baker fell asleep and overcooked a batch, resulting in the perfect, crisp, golden-colored pretzel. No sugar, no fat, and no cholesterol.

31

MAY

PEPYS'S DIARY

1669. Deteriorating eyesight forces Samuel Pepys, an official in the British admiralty, to make the last entry in the diary he has been keeping since New Year's Day of 1660, encoded because of its candor. The diary, the greatest in the English language, was finally deciphered and published more than 150 years later. It was filled with gossip, description, confession, and many references to what was drunk, including Rhine, Canary, and English wine, as well as something quite new called champagne, introduced to London society in 1662 by a French nobleman, the Marquis de St-Évremond.

Pepys had seen grass growing in the streets of London, the Great Fire, and Cromwell's head on a pike, and somewhere there is a first mention of a French wine called Ho Bryan—Haut Brion, surely—reminiscent of the much later Irish poet and writer, Harry Craig, returning to New York from abroad and calling out for bottles of "Chateau O'Brian" to celebrate. He had just been awarded the title of Pen of Islam for his work writing a film of the life of the Prophet Muhammad, a task made challenging because the Prophet's likeness could not in any way be shown.

J U N E

1

FRUITS THAT RIPEN OR DON'T

The slightly hard peach or melon that you buy in the supermarket and hope will ripen in a few days never will. It will soften, but that's all. Peaches and melons do not ripen after they are picked. Other fruits in this category are:

ALL BERRIES • CHERRIES • GRAPES
ALL CITRUS FRUITS • PINEAPPLES
APPLES (EXCEPT FOR GOLDEN DELICIOUS)

Some fruits do ripen further at room temperature:

PEARS • PAPAYA • APRICOTS
PLUMS • BANANAS • MANGOES

The avocado will ripen *only* after being picked.

HIVES

If you're susceptible to hives from eating too many strawberries or other acidic foods, there's a way to cure them without an expensive doctor's visit and prescription:

1 teaspoon cream of tartar
2 tablespoons lemon juice
Half a glass or more of water

Combine all ingredients. Drink the mixture and expect a cure within about half an hour.

ASPARAGUS

Asparagus should be cooked until just barely tender, so it still has a slight bite to it when eaten. Emperor Caesar Augustus knew this to be true when he coined the phrase *velocius quam asparagi coquantor,* or "faster than you can cook asparagus."

Julius Caesar liked his with melted butter, while French encyclopedist Bernard le Bovier de Fontenelle was partial to oil on this favorite dish. His cook was preparing some in just that way when the Abbé Terrasson arrived unexpectedly and asked to stay to dinner. Dismayed that he would be deprived of half his asparagus, Fontenelle nevertheless ordered that the Abbé's be served with the white sauce he preferred. As dinner was about to be served, the Abbé suddenly toppled to the floor, felled by a stroke. Fontenelle immediately took action, calling out to the kitchen, "All the asparagus with oil!"

3

JUNE

BREAD

Man may not live by bread alone, but it has been a staple of the human diet for ten thousand years. It was unleavened until the time of the Egyptians, who added the yeast that made it ferment and then expand when baked. While flatbreads can be made from many kinds of ground grains, wheat flour, by itself or mixed with rye or corn flour, is the only choice for leavened breads because it alone has enough gluten to rise without ending up either too moist or too dry.

The basic ingredients in a classic loaf are flour, water, salt, and yeast, but there are endless variations in terms of proportions and treatment. The spectrum runs from the thick, chewy, heavy-crusted loaves made by hand to the limp, presliced, sugar-added types made commercially and found in supermarkets. The baguette, almost a symbol of France, is bought fresh each day and is worthless by the next, though it doesn't usually last that long. A good, handmade loaf will have a hard, golden crust and the inside will be slightly chewy, with large, irregular holes created by the expanding gas. Mass-produced loaves are pallid in color and uniform inside, with small, if any, air holes. They are often made of frozen dough and can also be identified by the tiny dots on the bottom that come from industrial ovens. According to the GaultMillau, rival to the Michelin guide, the quality of the bread is one of the most reliable ways to judge the quality of a restaurant. The other is the coffee.

In every village in France and Italy, local bakers have their follow-ings. One summer when we were in the Dordogne, the longest line in the market square every day led to the back of a small truck where the baker, who arrived late morning, sold out his entire supply in a mat-ter of minutes. After learning that he lived across several fields from our house, we began walking over early in the morning when, cov-ered with a dusting of flour, he was just pulling the last of his loaves out of a wood-burning oven. He was happy to let a couple of them go while they were still warm.

4

J U N E

CHOISISSEZ-VOUS

In France—in the old France, that is, the France of the '40s and '50s—there was often a printed sign behind the bar that read:

La vie moyenne d'un buveur d'eau: cinquante-six annees.
La vie moyenne d'un buveur de vin: soixante-dix-sept annees.
Choisissez-vous.

(Average life of a water drinker, fifty-six years. Average life of a wine drinker, seventy-seven years. You choose.)

1898. The Hôtel Ritz opened in Paris this day on the Place Vendôme. The lavish dinner and reception had drawn the richest and most socially prominent people in Europe, though rain prevented admiration of the gardens. Every last detail of construction and decor had been overseen by César Ritz, for whom the hotel and its perfection had been a cherished dream.

Born in a small village of wooden houses in Switzerland in 1850, Ritz began his career at the age of seventeen as an apprentice wine waiter at the Hôtel des Trois-Couronnes in Brig. He was finally advised by the owner to try something else, as it was clear he was not cut out for hotel work. In ten years he rose to manage large hotels and over the next twenty made his name known throughout the world and synonymous with service, elegance, and style. Also central to his success was the idea of having his hotels serve outstanding food. A loyal clientele followed him from city to city, and the Prince of Wales, who especially favored him, is reported to have said, "Where Ritz goes, I go."

6

JUNE

SOLE

James Beard observed that nearly every fillet of whitefish was called "sole" in American restaurants, and consequently, his countrymen had little idea at the time what they were eating, which was usually some form of flounder.

Real sole, *Solea solea*, in its ichthyologic Latin name, is a superb fish found only in European waters, from the Mediterranean up to the North Sea. Nearly oval in shape and, like other flatfish, white on its underside and gray to brown on the upper, it has been a favorite since Roman times. There are more recipes for sole than for any other fish.

Dover sole is actually found in all the seas around England, including the Atlantic. Its name comes not from where it is caught but for the town once famous for supplying fresh sole to London.

The best sole comes from the deepest and coldest waters. Properly refrigerated or iced, its flavor is usually better a day or two after it is caught, a quality it shares with flounder that applies to almost no other fish.

SUSHI AND SASHIMI

Sushi originated as a way of preserving fish by fermenting it, packed in unboiled rice, but in the early 19th century in Edo (now Tokyo), it assumed its modern form: raw, fresh seafood, sometimes raw vegetables, rolled in lightly vinegared rice and usually with an outer layer of pressed seaweed. The vinegared rice, which has a pleasant tartness, is the distinguishing element.

Sashimi refers to cuts of the finest raw fish. There are four principal cuts, depending on the particular fish, one of them, *uzu zukuri,* of slices so thin that the plate can be seen through them. The skill, or better, art, of making sushi or sashimi used to call for ten years of training, and the practitioners were heirs to hundreds of years of history and even the samurai tradition. High standards of cleanliness and pride still prevail, although the years of training have been shortened. Sushi chefs wear spotless *ghis* (uniforms) and a knotted headband. The carbon steel knives they use are sharpened to the point that they can literally slice a human hair lengthwise. They are cleaned after every few strokes.

Sushi can be eaten with the fingers, but sashimi should not be, and any piece of sushi is meant to be eaten in one bite. Sake is usually not drunk with sushi—rice wine with rice is disfavored.

C A R Ê M E

The founder of French grande cuisine, Marie-Antoine Carême, is born on this day in Paris in 1783. The sixteenth child of a desperately poor family, he was abandoned to the streets at the age of ten and ended up with the owner of a low-class restaurant, where he discovered an interest in cooking.

By the time he was sixteen, he was apprenticed to a famed pastry chef, Sylvain Bailly, who permitted him to pursue unusual passions at the National Library—copying architectural drawings and learning to read. The drawings would later form the basis of his own incredible confectionary creations. This was at a time when pastry chefs had tremendous prestige and were responsible for the huge decorative centerpieces, *pièces montées,* that were the glory of formal dinners.

Carême attracted the attention of Talleyrand, who conducted diplomacy at his famous table and spent an hour each morning going over the day's menu. The employment with Talleyrand lasted twelve years and was followed—Carême was himself now a celebrity—by work in England for the future George IV, in Russia for Czar Alexander I, and back in Paris for the Baron James de Rothschild. He had, in the end, created hundred of menus and dishes in the most exalted houses in Europe.

His definitive cookbook, *L'art de la cuisine française aux XIX-e siècle,* was published in 1833, two years before his death. He had risen before dawn for years to begin work and choose ingredients in the markets and had labored intensely in hot kitchens where the windows, half an hour before serving, were even shut to keep the dishes warm. He died at fifty, burnt out, it was said, "by the flame of his genius and the charcoal of the roasting spit." Many of his recipes are still used today, especially those for sauces, of which 289 are described in his five-volume book. To read him is to sit at the tables of emperors and kings. Alexander I said, "What we did not know was that he taught us to eat."

THARID

On this day in 632 A.D., the prophet Muhammad, founder of Islam, died in the arms of his favorite wife, A'isha. He had once said that as A'isha surpassed other women, so did *tharíd* surpass other dishes. *Tharíd,* an ancient Arabian stew, was made of meat mixed or layered with bread. The Prophet's praise made it popular throughout the Muslim world, where variations are still eaten from the Middle to the Far East.

9

JUNE

AUTOMAT

1902. The first Automat, a marvel of its time, opens its doors on Chestnut Street in Philadelphia, an outgrowth of a café started fifteen years earlier by Joseph Horn and Frank Hardart, who divided the duties of cooking and serving. The success of Horn & Hardart was based at first on the quality of the coffee, made every twenty minutes from freshly ground beans using the new drip method, an enormous improvement over boiling coffee grounds for hours with eggshells to make it less muddy.

People came for the coffee and stayed for the food. Horn and Hardart were the precursors of both fast-food restaurants and coffeehouse chains, eventually serving over a quarter of a million customers a day in New York, New Jersey, and Pennsylvania. Waiters and cashiers were replaced by self-service—a cafeteria with a vast array of small windows, each displaying one dish and its price. Customers dropped in coins and opened the window.

With growing competition, the Automats waned, and the last one, at 42nd Street and Third Avenue in New York City, closed on April 8, 1991. But over its nearly ninety-year history, the Automat became an American institution. A section of the very first one is preserved at the Smithsonian.

10

JUNE

POILÂNE

1945. Lionel Poilâne, who would bridge the gap between the quality and quantity in the production of bread, is born in Paris. At fourteen he began work in his father's bakery and soon came to scorn mechanical production. He revived traditional methods, making his signature loaf a large, round country *boule,* kneaded by hand and baked in wood-burning ovens. After inheriting his father's bakery, he spent the next thirty years turning it into a ten-million-dollar business that produced fifteen thousand loaves a day by hand for Parisian shops, restaurants, and customers in twenty countries around the world. His success helped encourage French legislation that bans the use of the word *boulangerie* unless the bread is made by hand entirely on the premises, and caused as many as five thousand shops in France to change their signs.

11
JUNE

NOT COMPLICATED DINNER

1977. June 11. Dinners need not be complicated to make. Gordon and Greta Forbes, Thorny and Liz Penfield, and P. C. Harper, who had a wonderful forehand and loved to dance, come.

Brie; a caviar pie; Caesar salad dressed at the table as in showy restaurants; eggplant parmigiana; fresh strawberries and peaches in rum; and coffee, tea, cognac, chocolates, cigars. The wine (unidentified) was in a carafe and was "drunk fiercely," according to our dinner book. Huge helpings, it was noted. "They simply wouldn't go home."

CAVIAR PIE (AS AN HORS D'OEUVRE)

½ *white onion, finely chopped*
2 *hard-boiled eggs, chopped*
  Sour cream
  Black lumpfish caviar (available in supermarkets)

In a rather small, shallow serving dish, layer the ingredients: first the onion, then the egg, then the sour cream (put dollops on top of the egg and smooth the dollops together), then the caviar in a thin layer. Serve with crackers to spread it on. Serves about six.

12

J U N E

STRAWBERRIES

Strawberries, though not depicted in the art of ancient Egypt or Greece, were familiar to the Romans and thought to have healing powers. The French philosopher Bernard le Bovier de Fontenelle (1657–1757) attributed his exceptionally long life to them and ate them every day they were in season.

A symbol of the delights of summer—highly perishable—strawberries are low in calories and rich in vitamin C and potassium. The cream—either fresh or, as preferred in some parts of Europe, sour—that so naturally goes with them is probably less beneficial.

Strawberries grew wild in both the Old and New Worlds. They have been cultivated since about the 13th century. Wild strawberries are smaller and darker with greater flavor and fragrance. Called *fraises des bois,* they can sometimes be found in shops.

Thérèse Cabarrus was the stylish ex-wife of a marquis and a prisoner under the charge of Jean Tallien, an organizer of the dreaded Reign of Terror after the French Revolution. He saved her from execution when she had become his mistress. Later he married her. Her salon became famous, as did her habit of adding the juice from twenty-two pounds of crushed strawberries to her bath to keep her skin smooth and silky. She divorced Tallien in 1802 and married a banker.

13

JUNE

FRUITS WITH LIQUEURS

Fresh fruit in season, cut up and with an appropriate liqueur poured over it makes one of the best desserts. The choice of liqueur is important, and the best is often an echo of the fruit itself.

These suit one another:

ORANGES	*Orange liqueur (such as Grand Marnier)*
APPLES	*Calvados*
PEARS	*Pear brandy*
PEACHES	*Orange liqueur*
PINEAPPLE	*Rum*
RASPBERRIES	*Framboise*
STRAWBERRIES	*Orange liqueur or kirsch*
ITALIAN PLUMS	*Slivovitz*

14

JUNE

CHICKEN MARENGO

Chicken Marengo is one of the few, if not only, dishes named for a battle. It was created during one of Napoleon's by his steward, from limited ingredients he had at hand, notably using olive oil instead of butter.

Napoleon was a man who ate merely as a matter of necessity. The outcome at Marengo, one of those battles when his destiny flickered and nearly went out, was in grave doubt on this day in 1800 when he told one of his generals, Desaix—who was killed that evening—to do as he pleased, but that he, Napoleon, was going to eat. Desaix's charge saved the day.

The dish is easy and is even better made in advance and reheated.

CHICKEN MARENGO

1 onion, thinly sliced	2 cups Italian plum tomatoes,
Olive oil	fresh or canned
1 chicken, cut into pieces	Salt
½ cup dry white wine	Pepper
1 garlic clove, crushed	Small white onions
1 bay leaf	Mushrooms, sliced
1 sprig parsley, plus more	Juice of 1 lemon
for garnish	1 cup chicken broth
¾ cup pitted black olives	Cognac or Madeira
½ teaspoon thyme	

Sauté the onion in the olive oil. Remove the onion and brown the pieces of chicken in the oil. Add the wine, garlic, bay leaf, parsley, chicken broth, thyme, tomatoes, salt, and pepper. Cover and simmer for an hour. Meanwhile, separately sauté the small white onions and sliced mushrooms in olive oil with the lemon juice. Remove the now-tender chicken. Strain and reduce the sauce by about half. Place the olives in a deep casserole and arrange the chicken, mushrooms, and onions on top. Sprinkle with some cognac or Madeira. Add the sauce. Heat in a 350 degree F oven until thoroughly warm.

Garnish with parsley. Serves four. It can be refrigerated for a day before reheating.

15

JUNE

STEINBERG

On this day in 1914, the artist and cartoonist Saul Steinberg, who has been compared to Daumier, Picasso, and Samuel Beckett, was born in a small town near Bucharest in Romania. His father owned a factory that made boxes, and two of his uncles were sign painters. Trained in Milan as an architect, he never practiced. He might have become a writer, he once said, if he had been born into "a good language."

Immigrating to the United States, Steinberg became a citizen and a naval officer on the same day and served during World War II. He always maintained a jaundiced view of the state of gastronomy in his adopted country, however. In America, he observed, you don't ask someone to point out a good restaurant—they don't understand what a good restaurant is. The food in America was governed by the tastes of children—spaghetti and hamburgers. The only good meal nationwide, he felt, was breakfast, with its ham, bacon, eggs, home fries, thick pancakes, and waffles. The nicest waitresses were in the Midwest. When he traveled, Steinberg usually ate breakfast three times a day.

He was also fond of diners, with their evocation of railroad luxury and style. The booths were comfortable, he liked the jukeboxes, and the service was informal and fast. He compared them—he was always imaginative—to French brasseries, even the Brasserie Lipp, though usually having inferior views.

16

JUNE

SINGING

After lunch, nap, the Romans said; after dinner, walk. This does not seem to apply to after a dinner party. Poker is a possibility, or watching a film, or even dancing. There is also singing, right there at the table, provided the mood is right and there are a few people capable of carrying a tune. Irishmen like to sing, and at the writer Dennis Smith's one night after dinner, he, Bill Kennedy, and Frank McCourt sang on and on. McCourt's rendition of "The Rose of Tralee," as it might be sung by John McCormack, the famed tenor, or one of his lessers, is memorable. He does not do it at the drop of a hat, but he can be persuaded.

Persuasion and coaxing finally made Salman Rushdie perform. He was still under the notorious fatwah at the time, and his movements were secret. He came unheralded to a dinner party, partially disguised by a big straw hat. The hostess, Barbara Thomas, who had gone to school in India as a girl, wanted him to join her in singing the Indian national anthem. Rushdie declined, he could not sing, he said, he did not know the words. She, meanwhile, was on her feet, beginning to sing and urging him to join her. After a few lines, he stood, too, and they finished the song spiritedly. It made him the hero of the party.

17

JUNE

MARQUIS DE CUSSY

The Marquis de Cussy (1766–1837), a witty and famed gastronome who had been born into wealth, was the chief steward of Napoleon's household, with authority that covered everything: clothes, furniture, food (though Napoleon ate hurriedly and preferably alone), and even, it was said, young women who were admitted to the emperor's apartments at night. De Cussy was said to have examined "all aspects" of them.

After Napoleon, de Cussy served Louis XVIII, the last king of France, who initially wanted nothing to do with him but changed his mind based on his appreciation of *fraises à la Cussy,* one of the countless dishes credited to the Marquis.

FRAISES À LA CUSSY

1 quart strawberries (in season)
½ bottle sec or demi-sec champagne (need not be of high quality)
½ cup sugar (approximately)
1 pint heavy cream (or better, double cream, if you can find it)

Hull the strawberries, slice in half lengthwise unless very small, and soak for an hour in a mixture of the sugar dissolved in half the champagne. Mix the cream with some of the remaining champagne, not making it too thin, and pour over the drained strawberries arranged in serving dishes. Serves four.

18

HOSPITALITY

During a holiday in France, Alice Waters, Anne Isaak, I, and our three children, on the way back to the house after a day at the beach, stopped for an early dinner. We waited in the garden of the restaurant—it was in the country—for twenty minutes, until the official opening time. Yes, they had room, but the owner made his distaste clear for this casually dressed group without a man.

There were flowers and white linen on the tables, but though the dining room was empty, the service was slow. Anne, who owns two New York restaurants, ordered wine but sent it back for an unspoiled bottle. We had appetizers, then the regional specialties, and finally dessert. Gradually, it became clear that we would be the only customers that night, and as a result, the service warmed and finally fawned.

When we got home, Alice sat at a desk for a couple of hours, composing a letter in French to the owner of the restaurant. She said that she, too, owned a restaurant, adding modestly that she didn't expect he had heard of it. She said that being in the business herself, she had been somewhat disappointed in the evening despite the pleasant surroundings and good food. She had, she wrote, felt that his establishment had displayed little of what she considered the most important quality of any restaurant, great or small, which was the friendly and generous welcoming of those who came there. In a word: hospitality.

K.S.

_____

PLACES NOT TO EAT

Avoid, if possible, any restaurant that:
- Has glass atop the table
- Has waiters who tell you their names (nearly unavoidable in certain locales)
- Offers coffee when the menu is presented, except at breakfast
- Serves baked potatoes and/or butter wrapped in foil
- Allows any dishes to be cleared before everyone at the table has finished eating
- Makes you wait more than twenty minutes when you're on time for a reservation.

It used to be that Chinese food was largely represented by chop suey and chow mein. Mexican food is engaged in the same uphill battle to establish itself as something more than fast food or a plateful of indistinguishable beans, rice, and something hidden under sauce. Second only to Chinese cuisine in variety, Mexican food relies on the combination of relatively few essential ingredients, including corn, beans, chili peppers, and tomatoes.

When the Spanish invaded Mexico and conquered the Aztecs in the early 1500s, they discovered an already ancient tradition of agriculture and cooking. One of the conquistadors, Bernal Díaz del Castillo, wrote in detail of lavish banquets in Montezuma's palace. The Spanish brought with them the animals that added meat to the diet. Centuries later, another amalgamation took place between Texas and New Mexico cowboy cooking and that of northern Mexico. The resulting Tex-Mex cuisine improved both.

Corn plays the central role in Mexican cooking, as it has for millennia. It was once considered sacred in its cycle of planting, harvesting, grinding, cooking, and eating. It is used in many ways, but the basic one is the tortilla, Spanish for the Aztec *tlaxcalli*. Tortillas are often eaten fresh and warm as bread, and when eaten by hand, they are used almost as a plate and spoon—folded, rolled, or stuffed with other ingredients, often including *frijoles refritos*. Mistranslated as "refried beans," the beans, in fact, are first cooked in water and then fried—once only—until nearly dry. Tomatoes—along with chili peppers that are roasted, fried, stewed, or used fresh—create the sauces whose hotness varies according to the peppers, of which there are some two thousand varieties.

20

JUNE

BUTTERMILK

Buttermilk, for centuries a drink of shepherds and milkmaids, is a byproduct of the churning of butter. Slightly sour-tasting and thicker than ordinary milk, it also, contrary to its name, contains less fat. Real buttermilk is not so easy to find. The product that is labeled "cultured buttermilk" is a manufactured replica, but not as good.

21

JUNE

LEARNED HAND

Learned Hand, known as the greatest American judge never to serve on the Supreme Court and admired for his many, often-cited decisions, once gave a description of what would be, for him, a perfect day:

A soft, summer day in June would begin with a walk in the garden with his wife and, much later, after a number of other events, a nap

with her, then cocktails with all the friends they had valued throughout life. Crowning it all would be a magnificent dinner and afterward, conversation with the most brilliant and glorious figures in
history, the climax of which would be Marcus Aurelius turning to
Voltaire and saying, "Oh, shut up. I want to hear what Learned Hand
has to say."

JUNE

BLUEBERRIES

According to Waverly Root, certain Alaskan voles are so fond of
blueberries that they have blue teeth during the season. These are
wild blueberries, of course, smaller and less sweet than the cultivated
variety found in stores and widely agreed to be better in pies.

Barbara Stone, who ran a modeling agency in New York and is an
expert cook, has the following recipe for an open blueberry pie that
takes no more than twenty minutes to prepare, with superior results.

BLUEBERRY PIE

1 cup blueberries, mashed
¾ cup sugar
½ cup water
2 tablespoons cornstarch
3 cups whole blueberries

In a saucepan, cook the first four ingredients over high heat, stirring into a thick sauce (it thickens suddenly). Remove from the stove and immediately mix in the three cups of whole blueberries. Put into a baked pie shell—the best quality frozen pie shell available. Serve with whipped or ice cream.

23

JUNE

DINNER COMPANIONS

Epicurus, Montaigne, and many others offer the same advice: choose the companions first. Certain people will be better with certain others. A few will go well with anybody.

Once in London, Robert Ginna, at the time a film producer and afterward editor in chief of Little, Brown and Company, was invited with his wife to dinner at the Savoy. The host was a wealthy man who had racehorses and also a stunning French mistress who was present, along with the host's son and daughter-in-law. Ginna sat next to the mistress, who was wearing emeralds and who, throughout the meal, ignored him until the very end, when for a few dizzying minutes she directed her full powers at him. He imagined he behaved normally.

Afterward they all walked to the bar. Margaret, Ginna's wife, was walking beside him. "That's all right, darling," she consoled him in a low voice. "When you get to be his age, you can have one, too. Every boy should."

24
JUNE

FETA

In an ordinary small grocery store in Greece there will often be three or four containers of differing qualities of feta, white and crumbly, the signature cheese of Greece. Feta, like the French Roquefort, is made from sheep's milk. At a certain point, its ripening is arrested with brine, and the cheese stays in brine to keep its freshness and flavor. It is sold in bulk, the amount you desire being cut off and weighed. *Feta,* in Greek, means "slice."

Excellent when accompanied by nothing more than country bread, Greek olives, and wine, it is also good in salad. If it is rinsed in cool water before use, some of the saltiness can be eliminated, and it keeps well refrigerated, in a shallow bath of plain milk.

25
JUNE

WEDDING CAKE

In Roman times, wedding cake was worn instead of eaten. Grains of wheat represented fertility and were thrown at the newly married to ensure fruitfulness. Later, wheat was baked into small cakes, which were crumbled over the bride's head. She and the groom were supposed to eat them—a tradition called *confarreatio,* or "eating together," and the origin of "confetti." The "bride's ale" that was used to wash down the crumbs evolved into "bridal."

As a sign of prosperity, wealthy families began to stack the wheat cakes into piles, which over the centuries became the formal tiered wedding cake, but it took some doing. Bakers had to solve the structural engineering problems so that the upper layer of cake could be supported. In 1840 when Queen Victoria married her beloved Albert, the cake at the wedding breakfast weighed three hundred pounds, with a circumference of nine feet at the base. On the second tier were three figures, each nearly a foot high, of Britannia blessing the bride and groom, wearing ancient Roman dress.

As always, the French differ from the English in their approach. We were married in Paris, and it seemed only fitting that we have a *croquembouche,* which means "crunch in the mouth," a traditional type of French wedding cake made of frosted macaroons applied with icing to a tall cone. There is no ceremony of cutting the cake. The construction is dismantled, and the macaroons are distributed, often with a fruit compote alongside.

26
JUNE

THE GOLD RUSH

1925. This day was the Hollywood premiere of *The Gold Rush,* considered the best comedy of Charlie Chaplin, who wrote, directed, produced, scored, and starred in it. Set in the snow-swept Klondike of the Alaskan gold rush, Chaplin plays his classic character in Fatty Arbuckle's pants, oversized shoes, an undersized bowler hat, a tight cutaway coat, and toothbrush mustache. Though only five feet, five inches tall, he was larger than life. His first performance in a movie had been in 1914, quickly followed by thirty-four more that year. A master of physical comedy and of heart-tugging pathos, he successfully crossed from silent films to talkies. Hitler was such a fan that he gave up his handlebar mustache to grow one like Chaplin's.

In a remote cabin, Thanksgiving dawns on the Little Tramp and a Lone Prospector, another in a long series of difficult days in which they have nothing to eat. Undaunted, Charlie is preparing a memorable meal, stirring something in a pot on the wood-burning stove. He forks it onto a plate—voila!—his own boiled shoe. He adds ladles of "gravy" from the pot, brings it to the table with a flourish. The burly Prospector takes the upper part. Chaplin bites delicately into the leather sole, nibbling around the nails as if around the small bones of a turkey. "Not at all bad," his expression says, and he twirls the shoelace around his fork like pasta, then chews it with satisfaction.

FRUIT WITH CHEESE

In the same way that fresh fruits and certain liqueurs go together, fresh fruits and certain cheeses go well with one another:

APPLES	*Camembert*
	Cheddar
	Blue cheeses
	Parmigiano-Reggiano
	Brie
BANANAS	*Chèvre*
CHERRIES	*Crema Danica*
FIGS	*Stilton*
GRAPES	*Camembert*
	Provolone
	Pont l'Évêque
	Appenzeller
NECTARINES	*Brie*
ORANGES	*Gorgonzola*
PEACHES	*Triple crèmes*
	Gorgonzola
PINEAPPLE	*Camembert*
PLUMS (RED)	*Appenzeller*
PLUMS (PURPLE)	*Stilton*
STRAWBERRIES	*Triple crèmes*

TWO RULES FOR TRAVEL

For years we followed two rules when traveling:

- Never stay in at night. It will only lead to depression. Go out, have a meal, wander the streets, breathe in the life of the place.
- Never eat in a museum restaurant.

This second rule was abandoned after a lunch—recommended by friends—at Le Grand Louvre in the Paris museum. The quality of the food, supervised by Andre Daguin, and the elegance of the room encouraged us to try another in Paris—the Restaurant du Musée d'Orsay—on the second floor of the old train station converted into a museum of modern art in 1986. Originally the drawing room of a palace overlooking the Seine, its ceilings are frescoed, gilded, and hung with chandeliers.

29

JUNE

BLOODY MARY

It was probably in Harry's New York Bar in Paris, legendary and dingy, that the Bloody Mary was first served in the early 1920s and named either for Mary, Queen of Scots, or a girl in Chicago who worked at a bar called Bucket of Blood. The formula was inspired and simple: tomato juice and vodka in a two-to-one ratio, some lemon juice, Worcestershire sauce, Tabasco, salt, and pepper. It may even have been thought to be health-giving.

Exact proportions are to taste, but with six ounces of tomato juice there should be three ounces of vodka, the juice of half a lemon, five or six dashes of Worcestershire sauce, and a couple dashes of Tabasco.

Over the years, there have been many enhancements and variations: celery salt, fresh horseradish, sweet and sour mixer, beef bouillon, and even ketchup have been added in various quantities.

The original will still satisfy. It can be drunk at any hour, but it is somehow especially good at a late breakfast.

PICNIC

The word "picnic" first appeared in English in the mid-18th century, from the French *piquer,* meaning "to pick," combined with *nique,* an outdated word that meant "trifle." Today, it covers everything from a sandwich in the park to an outdoor barbeque, to Manet's sophisticated painting *Le déjeuner sur l'herbe,* showing two men dressed in jackets and ties sitting on the ground beside a naked woman and a toppled basket of bread and fruit. But it is always a shared meal outdoors.

A wonderful and comprehensive picnic menu appears in Kenneth Grahame's *The Wind in the Willows,* originally a series of stories he told his young son, Alistair. In the book, the water Rat introduces his friend Mole to the pleasures of a day boating on the river:

[He] reappeared staggering under a fat, wicker luncheon basket.

"Shove that under your feet," he observed to Mole, as he passed it down into the boat. Then he untied the painter and took the skulls again.

"What's inside it?" asked the Mole, wriggling with curiosity.

"There's cold chicken inside it," replied the Rat briefly: "coldtonguecoldhamcoldbeefpickledgherkinssaladfrenchrolls-cressandwidgepottedmeat-gingerbeerlemonadesodawater—"

You can say, "Don't feed him," but people sometimes think, "Oh, just this little bit." Too many good-hearted people, especially at a big party, can make a dog happy, but then pretty sick.

A remedy that usually works is to feed your dog the following for two or three days:

> 1 or ½ tablet Pepto-Bismol twice a day
> Boiled white rice
> Boiled skinless chicken or lean meat

It may be a little difficult getting the Pepto-Bismol down. You have to be smarter than he is.

JULY

MELONS • CHOPSTICKS
M. F. K. FISHER • THOMAS JEFFERSON
SYLVESTER GRAHAM • CRABS • MAYONNAISE
YEAR OF EATING • GARLIC • JULIETTE RÉCAMIER
NAXOS LUNCH • WEDGWOOD • ICE CREAM
TOUR D'ARGENT • GAZPACHO • ADDERS
GLASSWARE • LOBSTER • DRESS • LANG RULES
DAIQUIRI • BARBECUE • MARTINI
GREEK BOYFRIEND • ICE-CREAM TYPES
SHAW • FRANCILLON SALAD • BEER
THE HEDGES • DISASTER
TASTING THE FOOD
SUGAR

1

M E L O N S

"There are only two good things in the world, women and roses," said French poet François de Malherbe, whose nickname was Father Lust, "and two choice tidbits, women and melons." He was a man of his time, the late 16th century, when melons were enormously popular, not least with his king, Henry IV, and the one who followed, Louis XIII, for whom Malherbe was also the court poet. In 1583, a scholarly document listed fifty ways to eat melons. Nearly one hundred years later, they were still the rage, and an anonymous writer noted that there was not a single meal that did not include them, "served in pyramids and mountains, as if it were necessary to eat it to the point of suffocation."

These early melons were cantaloupes, first grown in Europe from seeds brought from Persia and planted in a town named Cantalupo outside Rome. They belong to the most perishable group, called muskmelons. There are also winter melons, including honeydew and casaba. The best we've ever eaten are called Cavaillons for the town in Provence where they're grown. Small, very sweet, and immensely fragrant, they were the favorite of Alexandre Dumas, who gave Cavaillon a complete set of his works—over three hundred volumes—in exchange for a lifetime supply.

When fully ripe, all melons fall away from the stem or can be removed with the slightest pressure. Nevertheless, some are cut or pulled away prematurely, and although they may become softer and juicier, they will not ripen further. To find a ripe cantaloupe—American cantaloupes are actually muskmelons—check for deep ridges on the surface, for the sweet smell of melon, and for a fruit with a slight softening at the stem end. For the best flavor, they should be cool but not chilled.

2

JULY

CHOPSTICKS

Chopsticks were invented in China over four thousand years ago, probably evolving from twigs used to spear food from a cooking pot. Knives took over this function in the West, but Confucius, who considered knives instruments of aggression, encouraged the use of chopsticks as part of his teaching of nonviolence. The name in Chinese is *kuai zi,* which means "quick little fellows." "Chop" came from the pidgin English for *kuai.*

Chopsticks spread throughout the Orient, those belonging to the rich made of gold, silver, ivory, or jade. Most, however, were—and are—made of bamboo, which was plentiful and cheap, with no taste or smell that could affect the food. The Japanese made them from a variety of woods and lacquered them for durability. It was not until the late 19th century that the disposable bamboo variety became popular.

Traditionally, Chinese and Japanese chopsticks differ in length and shape. The Chinese are ten inches long, square, and blunt at the tip, while the Japanese are rounded, come to a point, and are a couple of inches shorter. They are efficient enough to pick up a single grain of rice, but the accepted way to eat rice is to use the chopsticks almost like a scoop, moving the grains from a small bowl held close to the mouth.

Chopstick etiquette says you should not gesture with them as you talk, nor should you use them to pass food. And you're inviting misfortune if you drop them or place them crossed on your plate, unless you do it in a restaurant to show the waiter you're finished and ready for the check.

3

J U L Y

M . F . K . F I S H E R

On this day in 1908, Mary Frances Kennedy was born in Albion, Michigan. As M. F. K. Fisher, a name more masculine than feminine—Fisher was the name of her first husband—she was to become the foremost American writer on gastronomy, author of more than twenty books and onetime columnist on the subject for *The New Yorker*. The purity and toughness of her prose made her greatly admired, and her extolling of life as it should be lived, as well as her demonstration of it, distinguished her from others.

Her father was editor and part-owner of a newspaper in Whittier, California, and by the age of fifteen or sixteen, M. F. K. was a part-time journalist. She learned to write by more or less breathing it in. As a newlywed in 1929, she made the first of many trips to France, and as she later wrote: "It was there, I now understand, that I started to grow up, to study, to make love, to eat and drink, to be me and not what I was expected to be."

She married three times, two of them ending in fond divorce and the fated middle one, the most passionate of them, with the suicide of her husband, who was weary and ill. *The Gastronomical Me,* a memoir and probably the finest of her books, describes part of this and stands with the work of A. J. Liebling and Ernest Hemingway about some of the same places and times. She once said that she always had to write toward someone she loved, to make it seem real, and that someone turns out to be the reader, with whom she is oddly intimate.

About eating her first oyster at the age of sixteen and being scared pale at the prospect, she wrote: "I remembered hearing Mother say that it was vulgar as well as extremely unpleasant to do anything with an oyster but swallow it as quickly as possible, without *thinking,* but that the after-taste was rather nice."

A friend of, among many others, Julia Child and Janet Flanner, she died in California in 1992.

4

JULY

THOMAS JEFFERSON

At Monticello, on July 4, 1826, Thomas Jefferson died at the age of eighty-three. It was the fiftieth anniversary of the signing of the Declaration of Independence, which he had written. Having served first as vice president and then as president, he retired from the "hated occupations of politics" in 1809 and spent the last seventeen years of his life contentedly at his Virginia farm. He grew more than 250 kinds of vegetables, including thirty varieties of the one he liked best—peas. They were imported from all over the country and the world, along with berries, fruit trees, and grape vines for wine production. He kept an extensive garden book, noting his successes, failures, and favorites, including the Carnation cherry, rare if even existing today, described as "so superior to all others that no other deserves the name of cherry." But he saved his greatest praise for the olive tree, "the richest gift of Heaven."

5

J U L Y

SYLVESTER GRAHAM

On this day in 1794, Sylvester Graham was born. Two years later, he was orphaned, along with his sixteen brothers and sisters. A man of fervent convictions, he became a minister like his father and used his pulpit to advocate health-promoting fresh air and exercise. His rigorous program included giving up meat and alcohol, not to mention sex. He urged young men to practice chastity, telling them that intercourse caused cholera, or worse, insanity, and that with each ejaculation, their lives were shortened.

In some other ways, he was merely ahead of his time. He believed that much of the indigestion suffered by Americans in the mid-1800s was caused by refined white flour and urged a diet of bran and coarsely ground wheat. The flour itself wasn't new, but his intense belief in its power brought it to public attention. Graham invented a cracker made of it, combined with molasses, that is essentially the same recipe used today.

6

C R A B S

John Hay, who was secretary of state under Presidents William McKinley and Theodore Roosevelt, as well as ambassador to Great Britain, wrote that there were three types of creatures that seemed to be coming when they were going and going when they were coming: diplomats, crabs, and women.

Actually, crabs move sideways. There are well over four thousand species of them, of which the largest is the Japanese giant crab, with a span of up to twelve and a half feet. And all crabs, even land crabs, are born in the sea.

Crabs, like lobsters, are exoskele-tal—their skeletons are their external shells, and from time to time, they struggle through the impressive act of somehow freeing themselves from the outgrown shell and hiding while they grow a new one. Soft-shell crabs are those harvested in this interval.

On the West Coast, the most popular crabs are the Dungeness and the Alaskan king crab. In Florida and on the Gulf, it is the stone crab, and along the East Coast, the blue crab, *Callenectus sapidus,* which means, in part, "beautiful swimmer," the title of William Warner's wonderful book about them. A shame they are so delicious.

7

J U L Y

M A Y O N N A I S E

The first summer we lived together, in a borrowed house near the beach north of Los Angeles, we made a lot of homemade mayonnaise. This was in the days before the use of raw eggs could be dangerous, and in a house with a minimal kitchen. At the time it seemed more authentic somehow—not to mention a lot more exercise—to blend the oil, egg yolks, and lemon juice by hand instead of simply buying an electric mixer. Drop by drop, we would drizzle the oil into the other ingredients until the mixture was smooth and, eventually, thickened. We used it to bind the ingredients in Russian salad, with its cooked and diced carrots, beets, potatoes, peas, and green beans. What with the ocean and a tennis court that came with the house, our place was very popular for lunch and spending the afternoon.

The writer Ambrose Bierce called mayonnaise "one of the sauces which serve the French in place of a state religion." The origin of the name is murky, though certainly French. The straightforward explanation is that it is derived from *moyeunaise,* with *moyeu* being the old

French word for "egg yolk." Or perhaps from *manier,* which means "to handle."

Other theories have to do with military triumphs, one as early as 1589. Another says it wasn't named or even created until almost two hundred years later, during the Seven Years War, in honor of Colonel Rochambeau's victory at Port Maho in the western Mediterranean. His commander, the Duc de Richelieu, ordered a celebratory dinner, and the chef invented a new sauce for the occasion, *mahonnaise,* named for the conquered city. Alexandre Dumas, imaginative if not always accurate, also ties mayonnaise to Richelieu, writing in his dictionary of food that the sauce was named *momonnaise* in honor of the Duc's capture of General Mamon.

The secret, then as now, is first to have all the ingredients at room temperature.

MAYONNAISE

2 *eggs*	2 *cups olive oil*
1 *teaspoon salt*	¼ *cup lemon juice or*
½ *teaspoon dry mustard*	*wine vinegar*

With a fork or whisk (or an electric mixer), beat the egg yolks until they're thick, then add the salt and dry mustard. Beat in, a few drops at a time, the olive oil, blending completely with each addition. Adding too much oil at a time will make the mayonnaise curdle. When it's thick, stir in lemon juice or wine vinegar to thin it to the desired consistency. Makes about two cups.

8

YEAR OF EATING

Following a wedding in ancient Egypt, there was a kind of trial period for the marriage that took place not only in the sleeping quarters but also at the table. It was called "a year of eating," after which the bride and groom either parted or continued as a couple. Presumably, this took into account that a married couple would spend many more of their waking hours at the table than in bed, and this was where true compatibility lay.

9
J U L Y

GARLIC

When Amelia Simmons wrote the first American cookbook in 1796, she said that "Garlicks, tho' used by the French, are better adapted to the uses of medicine than cookery."

She was only echoing something that had been common knowledge for several thousand years, though there is still no clear understanding of just what makes garlic effective against leprosy, heart problems, the common cold, headaches, and even certain cancers. In ancient Greece, it was also thought to give strength; soldiers ate it before battle, and athletes before competition.

The most potent member of the onion family, garlic has not only been eaten since antiquity but has been used for everything from mummification to fending off vampires. Also known as the "stinking rose," garlic in cooking has at times been considered the height of sophistication and at others, a mark of the lower classes.

Harvested only once a year, in late spring or early summer, garlic is so mild when it is new that you can eat it raw; it grows stronger as it ages and dries. The white varieties found in most supermarkets last for about six months, but once the cloves grow soft or develop spots, they can't be used, and even before that, the green sprout in the center should be removed to keep it from giving off a bitter taste.

10

JULY

JULIETTE RÉCAMIER

In 1792, at the age of fifteen, Juliette Bernard married a wealthy French banker named Récamier, almost three times her age. It was an arranged marriage, and the young wife devoted herself not to her husband, but to a fashionable salon she later established, attracting important literary and political figures. Many of them fell in love with her, and she was painted by both David and Gérard as seductive and beautiful, though she had little interest in physical pleasures.

When she was forty, she herself fell in love for the first time, with Vicomte François René de Chateaubriand, the founder of Romanticism in French literature. Her husband had recently gone bankrupt—again—and she took up residence in a convent in the Faubourg Saint-Germain, where Chateaubriand visited her every day to read to her from the memoirs he was writing. At one point, she became so ill that it seemed the end was near. She refused to eat but was finally enticed into keeping up her strength with a bowl of fresh peaches in cream. That was the beginning of her recovery, and she lived to be seventy-two.

11

JULY

NAXOS LUNCH

We had lunch in a small mountain village named Kata Potamia in a café overlooking parched brown hillsides. The tables were beneath trees with whitewashed trunks. We had been walking since eight in the morning along steep paths bordered by stone walls, through other villages, past fields with olive trees and a few goats, encountering only a couple of old men leading donkeys and no other walkers. It was as if we had the country to ourselves. The waiter brought omelets, Greek salad, and fried potatoes almost too hot to bite.

There was the sound of cicadas, sometimes a great noise that rose with a rush and then fell, like a passing train. We were just below the church, old and white like every other building, and at noon its bell rang. It sounded like a hammer on an iron stove, without reverberation. You could hear the waiter and cook talking in the kitchen. The sun was ferocious, though not beneath the trees. The bill for the three of us was 4,600 drachmas, about eleven dollars. The lunch was worth far more.

12
JULY

WEDGWOOD

Josiah Wedgwood was born this day in 1730 in Staffordshire, England, in the town of Burslem, where his family made pottery. At nine, he began work in his brother's plant, and before he was thirty, he started his own, eventually building a village nearby for his workmen that he named Etruria, which included schools, reflecting his concern for the quality of their lives.

Wedgwood's distinctive pale blue ceramics, embossed with Greek figures in white, were a leap forward from the merely practical pottery produced until that time. Along with his other innovations and designs, Josiah Wedgwood turned what had been a backwater trade into a prominent industry, setting the highest standards in craftsmanship. His partner, Thomas Bentley, was expert at promotion, and they marketed the elegant new dishes and decorative items to the upper classes, renaming one collection Queen's Ware when Queen Charlotte made a purchase. He also created a dinner service for Catherine the Great.

His patterns are still produced by his descendants, but Wedgwood left behind more than a thriving business and a new elegance in the dining room. One of his grandsons was Charles Darwin, who had some original ideas of his own.

13

JULY

ICE CREAM

The emperor Nero, accustomed to getting what he wanted, ordered runners from the Alps to carry snow to Rome, which his cooks flavored with fruit purées into a kind of sorbet. When the Roman Empire collapsed, the recipe was forgotten until Marco Polo rediscovered something much like it in China in the 13th century and brought it back to Italy. With this double legacy, Italian *sorbetto* could easily be called the best in the world, if it weren't for France. Catherine de' Medici, who brought the seeds and recipes for her favorite foods, as well as her cooks, when she went to France to marry Henry II, also carried with her the idea of iced desserts.

They have their fullest realization in the *glaces* and *sorbets* made by Bertillon in seventy flavors and sold at various outlets around Paris, but most famously on the Ile Saint-Louis at a little window identified by the line in front of it. When our son was less than a month old, he had his first taste of their *poire,* which seems the absolute essence of the fruit, and pears have been a favorite ever since.

Or perhaps it's in his genes. Kay's grandfather owned a creamery until World War II and—long before there was an understanding of cholesterol—prided himself on the high butterfat content of his ice creams. Kay's father worked for him as a teenager and was, as a result, an indispensable member of refreshment committees. He courted her mother by always showing up with ice cream.

14

JULY

TOUR D'ARGENT

The oldest restaurant in Paris, the Tour d'Argent, can be traced back to the 16th century, when it existed as an inn where the king, Henry IV, known as the Evergreen Lover, came to dine on heron pâté. Later, Cardinal Richelieu and Mme de Pompadour ate there.

The real origin of the Tour d'Argent as a restaurant, however, was in 1780. Crowned heads of Europe and celebrated people of all sorts have since frequented it. The view from the great windows high above the Seine is staggering. The most renowned cathedral in France, Notre Dame, lies beneath you. The bill can be staggering, as well.

Like a famed vineyard, the restaurant has long been in the same hands. Its specialty, pressed duck, has been served for more than a century. Another specialty is *quenelles de brochet,* a delicious kind of log-shaped dumpling made of minced pike, flour, butter, and eggs. The wines include every great label of France.

15

J U L Y

GAZPACHO

Gazpacho was once a food of the poor, who took it with them to eat when they worked in the fields of Andalusia in southern Spain. At first it was simply water, bread, and olive oil mashed together to form a paste. Later vegetables were added to make a soup, which is now always served cold, as if to counter the soaring temperatures of Spanish summers.

There are as many varieties as there are regions of Spain, but the classic gazpacho comes from the area around Seville and Córdoba. As early as the Middle Ages, cucumber and garlic were diced and added, with some vinegar, to the bread, water, and oil mixture, along with tomatoes. After Columbus brought green pepper to Spain from the New World, it was added to the mix. The soup didn't migrate into the rest of Europe and the United States until the 19th century.

Recipes from parts of Spain may now include mayonnaise, almonds, grapes, anchovies, green beans, and egg whites. The ingredients of some gazpachos are puréed. In others, they remain distinct, floating in the broth. Sometimes it's a combination of both, as in the recipe of a Spanish friend, Corina Arranz, who has perfected her version over twenty years. Her sister serves it every summer at her restaurant in the village of Vallelado, near Segovia.

GAZPACHO

4 pounds ripe tomatoes	For the garnish:
1 small cucumber	1 small cucumber, peeled,
1 small green pepper	seeded, and finely diced
⅓ medium onion	2 small tomatoes, peeled,
½ clove garlic	seeded, and finely diced
1 cup virgin olive oil	1 green pepper, finely diced
2 tablespoons red wine vinegar	1 small onion, finely diced
1 4 x 4-inch piece of day-old	Dice-sized pieces of
French bread or baguette	fresh bread, lightly
Salt to taste	toasted in oven

Peel and slice the tomatoes and cucumber. Cut the tomatoes, cucumber, green pepper, onion, and garlic into pieces and put them in a blender, along with the olive oil, vinegar, and salt. Blend them to smoothness, and taste to see if extra oil, vinegar, or salt is needed.

Place the bread in a shallow bowl of cold water. When it has softened, squeeze the water from the bread by hand, and add the bread to the blender and mix to smoothness.

Refrigerate the soup for at least two hours before serving. To serve, you can add some cubes of ice to the mixture to chill it further, but don't serve the ice. Place the diced toppings on the table in separate small bowls. People can add a tablespoon of each to the puréed soup, if desired. Serves six to eight.

16

JULY

ADDERS

Born without arms or legs, moving only by the graceful action of a supple body, snakes generally have been feared and detested by humans. They have also, poisonous and otherwise, been eaten by humans everywhere that they exist. It is said by some that the venomous species are tastier.

As long as two thousand years ago, the Chinese were eating them dried. Boa constrictors, cobras, pythons, and rattlesnakes—all are eaten. Rattlesnake meat, not uncommon in the southwest United States, is described as similar to chicken. Pythons are said to taste like a cross between chicken and tuna fish.

In England, there has been a long tradition of adder soup, and adder diets were fashionable in France until the 18th century. They were thought to be healthful and to enhance beauty. Mme de Sévigné, famous in French literature for letters to her daughter, urged her daughter to go on a month-long adder diet annually.

We had a large house near Chinon one summer, and the gardener warned us to watch out for vipers on the extensive grounds. There were many, he said, but they could be frightened away if they heard you coming. The best thing to do, he said, was to wear a bell around your ankle. That seemed a little too prudent. We were also afraid he was trying to make fools of us, ignorant foreigners. We went without the bells, and no one was bitten.

17

J U L Y

G L A S S W A R E

Glass in 18th-century England was a sign of wealth, and windows were taxed so heavily that people bricked them up. In the case of table glasses, the result was more positive. Glasses were taxed by weight, so there was every incentive to produce the lightest possible designs, often with delicate stems.

For economic reasons, Ireland was exempt from the tax. There the leaded glass invented by Englishman George Ravenscroft in about 1675 flourished in coastal towns like Waterford and Cork, where fuel, in the form of coal, was available and cheap. Using Ravenscroft's techniques, George and William Penrose founded the Waterford Glass House in 1783, which prospered for over sixty-five years before falling beneath the weight of a tax law that extended to Ireland, along with the potato famine that forced many skilled workers to leave. Waterford Glass—crystal—wasn't revived for another one hundred years.

18

LOBSTER

The lobster begins life as one of ten thousand to twenty thousand fertilized eggs that the female slowly releases into the sea. She has carried them for nine months or more. The eggs hatch into larvae about one-third of an inch long, and these swim in the water for several weeks within a few feet of the surface, where they are helpless prey to seabirds and fish. Those that survive become good swimmers and descend in the water, searching for a suitable place on the bottom to hide.

For several years, the young lobsters live thus, in small tunnels, crevices, or concealed beneath seaweed, rarely venturing forth. They molt—shed their shell and form a new one—many times as they grow, and as adults continue to do so about once a year, lying on their sides and flexing their bodies to work out of the old shell, which they then eat to help make the replacement.

Lobsters grow more quickly in warm water than in cold. In the icy North Atlantic, it may take six or seven years before a lobster weighs one pound and reaches market size. Males grow faster than females and have larger claws; the females have larger tails (abdomens, actually).

The grown lobster is a marvelous, formidable creature, dark blue or greenish in color. It is nocturnal, solitary, and territorial. The males, like many mammals and birds, will fight to establish dominance, and females seek out the largest, strongest males.

Mating occurs just after the female has molted, and the act is surprisingly gentle, the male turning the female's unprotected body over with great care. European and American lobsters are virtually the same species, though the American type grows slightly larger. The various species from tropical waters, lacking claws, are not true lobsters, though they are commonly called that. Codfish and flounder will eat small lobsters, but their one great enemy is humans.

The only lobsters you are likely to see are the unlucky ones, caught and destined to be eaten.

In selecting lobsters:

- Look for the liveliest ones, those that thrash their tails and move their claws.
- Among those that are about the same size, the heaviest will have more meat.
- Be sure the shell is hard—the hardest shells come from the coldest water, and this usually means the firmest and most flavorful meat. Avoid lobsters with soft shells—this indicates molting, and the meat will be watery and poor.

19
JULY

DRESS

The Romans not only changed their shoes before entering the dining room, as the Greeks did, but changed their clothes as well, putting on a tunic for the occasion. Dishes were brought in accompanied by music.

In France before the 17th century, it was customary to wear a hat while eating. Even today, in the Western world, ladies who wear hats to lunch keep them on. The French, incidentally, are taught to keep their hands in sight during a meal, while the English rest theirs in their laps.

Napkins are a relatively recent development. In the Middle Ages, people wiped their mouths on the tablecloth. Tying a napkin around one's neck is practical but inelegant, except when eating seafood such as lobster. It is a mark, however, of a serious, usually older, and somewhat overweight diner, as in a Daumier drawing.

Dinner dress means black and white—tuxedo and black tie for men, and evening gowns, not necessarily black and white, for women. You can see it in the movies of the 1920s and '30s. In New York years ago, cops in the silk-stocking district of the Upper East Side knew how to tie a bow tie for a young man without the experience to do it himself.

JULY

LANG RULES

George Lang, the restaurateur and author of *Nobody Knows the Truffles I've Seen,* had a number of infallible rules for giving a successful dinner party. Among them were:

- Try to give the impression that the party is the first and last you will ever give and not just another in a long series.

- Serve familiar but not ordinary food.
- Seat the guests so that their neighbor is interesting for some reason, be it an occupation or a low-cut dress.
- Invite beautiful women.
- Choose the wine with care, as it is a clear indication of the importance the host gives the occasion.

21

J U L Y

D A I Q U I R I

Ernest Hemingway was born on this day in 1899. Paris, bullfighting, Africa, Key West, and Spain were all glorified in his writing, as was Cuba and its classic rum drink, the daiquiri. The best Cuban rums are light and come from the area around Santiago de Cuba. It appears the daiquiri also originated there around 1900, when American mining engineers cooled off in the bar of the Venus Hotel after a sweltering day. They drank a mixture of rum, lime, ice, and sugar that came to be named for the mines, daiquiri.

Here is the version from the Floridita bar in Havana where Hemingway reigned.

Juice of half a lime   *Dash of maraschino*

1 teaspoon sugar   *1 cup crushed ice*

1 ½ ounces light rum

Shake together all ingredients except the rum. Add rum.
Shake until frost appears on the outside. Strain and
serve. Makes one daiquiri.

22

J U L Y

BARBECUE

When meat was blackened from cooking too close to the coals on the
grill, we used to joke that the charred parts were good roughage. It
turns out, however, that among the dangers in barbecuing is eating
the burned and fatty parts of the meat or chicken. This is where the
compounds—HCAs—are formed that cause cancer in laboratory
animals. The longer and hotter the meat is cooked and the more fat
it contains, the more concentrated the carcinogens. Cutting the fat
from the meat before cooking and then eating it rare (except for
chicken) or medium is safer than making it well-done.

One of the most effective ways to minimize HCAs—for reasons
still unknown—is to marinate meat, chicken, or fish for as little as
fifteen minutes to an hour. Bottled marinades, however, often contain sugar or corn syrup, which, over a flame, carbonizes and pro-

motes charring. A marinade light on oil and heavy on vinegar, lemon juice, or teriyaki works best. Don't baste with the same liquid in which the meat was marinated. Instead, keep some aside to use during the actual cooking.

23

J U L Y

M A R T I N I

Bernard DeVoto, the critic and editor, called them the supreme American gift to world culture. E. B. White admitted he drank them the way other people took aspirin. All in all, a well-made dry martini served icy cold and straight up in a traditional martini glass with a narrow stem is a turning point in the evening or day. The origin of the drink's name is not known for certain; devotees have affectionate names for it, including see-through, silver bullet, and, as the painter Sheridan Lord, who had one every night, called them, a straight right to the heart.

This refers to gin martinis, of course. There are other kinds, some very creative, but all lesser. It cannot be said that the following instructions produce the greatest martini of all time, but you may very well come to believe they do.

First, use a good English gin—Beefeater or Tanqueray, both ninety-four proof, are preferred. The dry vermouth should be Noilly Prat or Martini & Rossi, although you can have decent results with Tribuno or Stock. Vermouth is a fortified white wine that is about eighteen percent alcohol and once opened will go bad unless refrigerated. Even then it does not last indefinitely, so it is best to buy small bottles.

In a pitcher or shaker put about six or eight cubes of hard ice cracked by hand (place the cube in the palm of your hand and hit it smartly with a heavy spoon). It is important that the ice be cracked so as to present the maximum cold surface to the gin and vermouth—a martini is and should be a slightly diluted drink.

Pour one or one and a half small capfuls of vermouth over the ice. Add enough gin to fill, or nearly fill, the martini glass. Experience will teach the amount, but about five ounces. Stir or shake until the contents are very cold. A martini that is not absolutely icy is a failure. (The glasses can be placed in the freezer beforehand, but this is not essential.)

Pour the drink, without any ice, into the glasses. It should fill it almost to the brim. Add an olive—single, green, unflavored, and pitted—or a twist of lemon peel—about an inch and a half long, deftly pinched with the fingers to spray a bit of oily essence—or a single cocktail onion (making the drink technically a Gibson). The matter of the olive or onion is important since the flavor is imparted to the drink. I prefer B&G cocktail onions and add a few drops of their liquid to the unstirred drink.

A martini is a made-by-hand creation, and it is best to make no more than two at a time. It's also best to drink only one, or things become blurred. As James Thurber commented, "One is all right, two is too many, and three is not enough." With the first sip, the drink's perfume and strong, clean taste give an extraordinary sense of well-being that lasts for an hour or more.

Do not make martinis ahead of time. The remarkable freshness will not be there. In DeVoto's words, "You can no more keep a martini in the refrigerator than you can keep a kiss there."

There is a final, unconventional secret. Shake a Lea & Perrins Worcestershire sauce bottle, then quickly remove the cap and with it dash a faint smudge of the contents—far less than a drop—into the bottom of the shaker before beginning. It adds the faint, unidentifiable touch of greatness.   J.S.

24

JULY

GREEK BOYFRIEND

Summer night. Cold tomato soup, fresh corn, and steak salad. Talking about a good-looking woman we know who had more or less broken up with a Greek boyfriend but still visits him in the little Peloponnese town where he has a house and invites her, saying there will be wonderful days and no sex: "Only if absolutely necessary."

25

I C E - C R E A M   T Y P E S

Ice cream is made of milk, cream, egg yolks, and flavoring. Its high fat content is what makes it smooth and rich-tasting. The incorporation of air as it is churned is what keeps it from turning into a frozen block, but the amount of air is limited by law. Italian ice cream— gelato—has less air and so is a bit denser than either American ice cream or French *glace.* It is smooth and not oversweet.

Iced milk is essentially a sorbet to which milk has been added. It has less fat and more air, which gives it a lighter texture than ice cream, and it often has more sugar. It was first made in Arabia, where it was called *sharbah,* the origin of "sherbet" and "sorbet."

Frozen yogurt is made primarily with yogurt instead of milk or cream. It is thought to be more healthful and have the benefit of the bacteria in yogurt, but most of these are destroyed by the cold.

Sherbet (sorbet) is also called an ice or fruit ice. It is made of puréed fruit, juice, and sugar syrup. French sorbets have less sugar and a more intense fruit flavor, while Italian *sorbettos* are sweeter. Also Italian is the *granita,* which is less sweet and more granular.

26

J U L Y

S H A W

1885. On this day George Bernard Shaw celebrated his twenty-ninth birthday by losing his virginity to a widow fifteen years older. Some time later, at a formal dinner party in London at which, according to custom, the host invited guests to make a toast on particular topics, Shaw was asked for one on sex. He stood, raised his glass, and began, "It gives me great pleasure . . . ," and took his seat.

27

J U L Y

F R A N C I L L O N   S A L A D

1824. Alexandre Dumas *fils,* illegitimate son of the writer and Marie-Catherine Labay, a dressmaker, is born in Paris. Dumas *fils,* as he was called, was a writer himself, famous for his hugely successful play *La Dame aux Camelias,* partly autobiographical and taken from his youthful love affair with Marie Duplessis, a young courtesan. Known in English as *Camille,* a great favorite of actresses, it was the basis of Verdi's *La traviata.* Marie Duplessis died of tuberculosis in 1847, though the works she inspired continue to live.

In another of his plays, *Francillon,* Dumas *fils* had a character give the recipe for a salad that was guaranteed to please. Hurriedly copied down by members of the audience, it quickly became popular on restaurant menus in Paris as *salade francillon*. The original recipe included fresh truffle slices which are omitted here.

FRANCILLON SALAD

5–6 medium-sized red potatoes	*Pepper to taste*
Beef bouillon cube	*Chives to taste*
Extra virgin olive oil	*Parsley to taste*
Wine vinegar	*Rosemary to taste*
1 ½ cups Chablis	*3–4 tablespoons butter*
(approximately)	*1 celery stalk*
Salt to taste	*1 pound live mussels*

Begin preparation about an hour and a half before serving. Cook the potatoes in diluted beef bouillon. Allow to cool, then peel, slice about ¼ inch thick, season with a vinaigrette (3:1) of the olive oil and vinegar. Add ½ cup or less of the Chablis and the salt, pepper, and chopped herbs. Mix gently, and allow to marinate.

Put the butter, celery stalk, 1 cup of the Chablis, and the scrubbed mussels in a large pot.

Cover and steam for about ten minutes or until the mussels open, but no longer. Remove the mussels from their shells—throw away those that did not open—drain thoroughly, and mix gently into the potatoes.

Cover with aluminum foil, chill for thirty or forty minutes in the refrigerator, pour off any excess liquid, add salt if necessary, and serve cold. Serves five or six.

28

BEER

Beer has been made nearly as long as—and almost wherever—there have been people to drink it. The ingredients are often readily available: grain, water, hops, and yeast. Usually the grain is barley, though in Japan beer is made from rice and in Africa from millet. Worldwide, more than 35 billion gallons of beer are made each year. Though the ingredients are simple, the brewing process is carefully controlled. Barley is roasted, which stops its germination and turns it into malt. The longer the barley is roasted, the darker it becomes, and it is the proportion of lighter and darker barley chosen for the final mix that determines the color of the beer.

The malt is ground and hot water added to turn it into a porridge-like mixture called wort, which is then boiled to purify it. The extreme sweetness of the wort is countered by adding hops. The choice of the hops—the female seeds from one of a large variety of vinelike plants—determines the flavor of the beer.

The mixture then goes to a fermenter, where yeast is waiting to convert the natural sugars into alcohol. In general, the range is between 3.2 percent to 7 percent alcohol, though it can be as high as 12 percent. The fermentation produces carbon dioxide—a natural carbonation. Today it is vented off, and the carbonation is later added artificially when the beer is canned, bottled, or transferred into kegs.

The two basic kinds of beer—lagers and ales—differ partly because of their finish and partly due to the yeasts that are used.

Lagers ferment for a longer period of time at cooler temperatures, producing a lighter-tasting beer, while ales take less time at higher temperatures. Ales tend to be darker and to taste heavier, though they contain about the same number of calories as lagers.

In England and Ireland, where beer drinking is elevated to a social ritual in local pubs where regulars gather, the indigenous yeast produces ales, including stout, bitter, and porter. The quintessential ale is Guinness Stout from Dublin. In Germany and the Czech Republic, the local yeasts produce lagers, with the most famous being Pilsner.

The Czech Republic holds the title for per-capita consumption at over 160 liters per year, followed by Ireland and Germany. The United States, where beer first arrived with the Pilgrims, now produces more than any other country, though it ranks only twelfth in consumption at about eighty-five liters per person.

Most American beers are lagers and are served at 39 degrees F to satisfy American tastes, though the cold tends to diminish the taste somewhat. Ales are not served warm even in England but at about 55 degrees F, or about the same temperature as red wine. Once chilled, beer should not be removed from the refrigerator to be rechilled later, since fluctuating temperatures affect the taste, as does light, which is why beer is canned or bottled in colored glass. The best-quality beer is usually on tap, since the temperature has been properly maintained from the time it was made.

Like wine, there is a special vocabulary to describe the qualities of beer: fruity, dry, hoppy, sweet, toasty, etc. And like wine, the price is usually an accurate reflection of the quality of the beer. Unlike wine, beer does not improve with age.

29

JULY

THE HEDGES

1954. On this day in East Hampton, Long Island, in an old white house near the entrance to town, Henri Soulé opened The Hedges with table linen and wine from Le Pavillon, his restaurant in New York. The walk to the ocean down a beautiful street of large summer houses made him feel he was in paradise.

The Hedges, no longer in existence, was small and simple but elegant. Two wealthy women who were visiting the area arrived for lunch one day. Soulé, who knew them, came out from the kitchen in an apron, apologizing for his appearance. He seated them and asked what they would like. The restaurant was empty; to the women, things seemed ominously slow. But the meal was memorable. After the lunch and excellent wine, they asked for the check. There was no check. No check? Well, The Hedges was not open for lunch, Soulé gracefully explained.

30

JULY

DISASTER

2002. Dinner party was a complete disaster. Everything, from beginning to end—the food was bad, there were too many people, the presentation was chaotic. We broke two fundamental rules: (1) serving two things we'd never made before and (2) having too much that had to be prepared at the last minute. The carrots in ginger were burned. The gratin of potatoes had too much cream and was undercooked. The elaborate baked meat turned out to be crumbly, more like a shepherd's pie. On and on . . .

We sat on the couch together after everyone had gone, reflecting on what had gone wrong rather than facing the piles of dishes and debris. The only good thing was that there had been a lot of drinking. They might not remember clearly.

Everyone called the next day: fabulous party.

TASTING THE FOOD

The most important secret in cooking is to taste the food, in some cases before, but always during and especially after cooking. No recipe, however exact, is to be trusted without tasting, and no previous success guarantees another.

31

JULY

SUGAR

The Peace of Breda, concluded on this day in 1667, settled the three-year war between the Netherlands and England. The Netherlands retained Surinam, and the English the New Netherlands, which would become New York. The sugar plantations of Surinam were considered so valuable that the Dutch were thought to have gotten the better of the deal.

In the 17th century, only the rich could afford sugar, which was brought to Venice from India and sold as a luxury item or sometimes as a medicine. The slave trade was essentially created to support its production, especially in the Caribbean and Brazil, where on large plantations with cost-free labor it could be produced much less expensively than with sugar beets grown in Europe.

Today, available and cheap, sugar, along with corn syrup, is the number one food additive in the United States. Made from sugar cane or sugar beets, it takes a number of forms: white or refined sugar; brown sugar, which is incompletely refined and retains some molasses that gives it color; confectioners' sugar; and molasses itself, produced during refining. For white sugar, the refining process involves half a dozen steps, starting with the crushing of the cane. The resulting liquid is filtered to remove impurities and the color of the molasses that coated the sucrose crystals of the raw sugar; then the liquid is evaporated and dries into granulated white sugar.

Sugar provides quick energy, but its nutritional value is essentially nil. Yet Americans now consume, on average, about 150 pounds of it a year per person in food or drinks, the equivalent of about 32 teaspoons per day. A single teaspoon doesn't have many calories—only about fifteen, compared to about two for artificial sweetners.

AUGUST

1

VICHYSSOISE

It is hard to resist a dish with a wonderful name. Eggplant—which is actually a fruit—as a name is nothing, and even eggplant parmigiana is not much better, but *imam bayıldı,* which means "the priest fainted," is another matter. The eggplant is stuffed with a mixture of chopped onion, tomato, and parsley, all browned with garlic and currants and baked slowly. It was the aroma of this dish that made the legendary priest faint from sheer joy.

Then there is vichyssoise, cold, smooth leek and potato soup, now a classic. Julia Child dismissed it as an American invention based on the genuine leek and potato soup ("smells good, tastes good, and is simplicity itself to make"), and Richard Olney, an equally great authority, cast only a brief glance at it while extolling *potage aux poireaux et pommes de terre,* as it is prepared night after night in French working-class homes, which carries, Olney said, a message of well-being that he would be happy to receive every evening of his life.

Vichyssoise, in a sense, is American. It was created by a French chef, Louis Diat, in New York, in the first part of the 20th century. Diat came from the region around Vichy, and the soup was based on the memory of one of his mother's. Oddly enough, he didn't call it vichyssoise in his own cookbook, but the name was attractive, and it stuck.

The recipe for vichyssoise is, in fact, simple:

VICHYSSOISE

3 cups sliced white leeks
1 medium onion, sliced
    (optional)
    Butter
3 cups potatoes, peeled and
    thinly sliced

1 ½ quarts chicken broth or
    bouillon
1 cup heavy cream or mixed
    heavy cream and milk
Salt to taste
Chives, minced

Soften the leeks and onion in butter in a covered pan.
Add the potatoes and chicken broth or bouillon, and
cook for thirty minutes or so, until all are tender. Purée
in a blender or force through a fine sieve. Return this to
the pot and add the cream. Stir. Bring nearly to a boil,
then season with salt. Cool, then chill.

Julia Child added the useful advice to oversalt slightly,
as salt loses its strength in a cold dish. The soup should
be moderately thick.

Serve chilled with fresh minced chives sprinkled on
top. Serves five or six.

2

AUGUST

OUZO, RAKI, ARAK

Ouzo, the traditional liquor of Greece, is clear in color, flavored
with anise, and often diluted with water, which turns it a cloudy
white and somewhat lessens its considerable wallop. The equivalent
in Turkey is raki, and in Indonesia arak, both distilled liquors made

from fermented fruit, with or without the addition of anise. Both raki and arak are fiery and rather harsh and come from the Arabic word meaning "sweat," which may refer to its effects, depending on the quantity.

But it is not just about the alcohol. It's about a way of life, a state of mind. To sit in a taverna at the end of the day, perhaps in the old Plaka neighborhood in Athens at the foot of the Acropolis without the summer crowds, sipping ouzo, this is pleasure. At hand are the traditional hors d'oeuvres called *meze* and usually included in the price of the drink. They might be a small plate of meatballs, fried fish, a salad of tomatoes and cucumbers, or cheese, especially feta.

If you are sitting alone, it tends to be a contented solitude. Wafting over you is conversation from other tables. Passersby drift past through the narrow street. Life seems coherent and to be proceeding at the right pace for a change. Or with friends, an evening of the kind in Kazantzakis's *Zorba the Greek* or Henry Miller's *The Colossus of Maroussi,* when talk is animated and passionate, touching on all matters, into the night.

3

AUGUST

COLUMBUS

Eighty-eight men under Christopher Columbus set sail this day in 1492 from Spain aboard the *Niña,* the *Pinta,* and the flagship *Santa María* on a voyage intended to prove a radical notion, that the earth is round. They sailed with enough food on board to last for a year. The wooden casks that held it, however, expanded and contracted in the sea air, allowing the brine that preserved the meats to leak out and dampness to invade and mold the dry supplies, including rice, beans, flour, and hard biscuits. The spoiling meat and any fish that were caught were cooked on deck over a fire built on a bed of sand, then served in a communal bowl. There was also salt cod, anchovies, almonds, raisins, molasses, honey, olives, and olive oil on board, along with strong red wine.

It had been thirty-four days since they had stopped at the Canary Islands for fresh water, and the men were close to mutiny, fearing their captain was mistaken—that the world was, indeed, flat and that they were nearing the edge. Columbus persuaded them to persevere for three more days, and on the very next, October 11, they spotted land.

4

AUGUST

WATERMELON

The best watermelon ever was on the island of Naxos in the Aegean, when, after hiking for hours, we collapsed into café chairs under the trees to cool off on an intensely hot August day. We were served large chunks of exceptionally juicy fruit, and you could understand why in ancient times watermelons were carried as a source of liquid when water was scarce or undrinkable.

Originating in Africa and well-known in ancient Egypt, watermelons came to America with the slave trade. It wasn't long ago that they weighed twenty pounds or more, enough to serve everyone at a large picnic. Today, with smaller families and less patience with the seeds, the most popular varieties are closer to ten pounds and can fit into a refrigerator without cutting. They're also seedless, based on research with sterile hybrids done half a century ago by a Japanese scientist.

The rind is actually more fragile than it seems, and watermelons are picked by hand in the fields and passed hand to hand to the truck. It is a myth that you can judge a good one by thumping it. Instead, look for a dull, rather than shiny, rind and a yellow underside where it rested on the ground. If the underside is white or pale green, it was picked before it was ready, after which it will ripen no further.

5

AUGUST

SOYER

Alexis Benoît Soyer died on this day in 1858 in London at the age of fifty-eight. One of the most famous names of his time, he'd been born outside of Paris at Meaux-en-Brie, the town for which the cheese was named. His family had envisioned a career in the church. Instead, he apprenticed as a cook and seven years later joined his older brother, who was a chef in London for the Duke of Cambridge.

His connection with the noble families of England led him to the famously liberal Reform Club, where he was chef for fifteen years while also writing books on cooking and nutrition, including *The Gastronomic Regenerator*, with its two thousand recipes divided into "Kitchens of the Wealthy" and "Kitchens at Home." Its great popularity was rivaled only by *Soyer's Shilling Cookery*, with inexpensive, appetizing recipes for ordinary households. In addition, he invented ingenious clocks, egg cookers, coffeepots, and baking dishes for kitchens, as well as sauces and relishes that were marketed by his friends, Mr. Crosse and Mr. Blackwell. Flamboyant in dress, he also designed his own clothes, hats, and even visiting cards.

Simultaneous with his success in the chic, upper-class milieu, Soyer was asked by the British government to organize soup kitchens in Ireland during the potato famine of 1847, and he was soon feeding eight thousand starving people a day in Dublin. Six years later, during the Crimean War, he volunteered to design a mobile field kitchen, which was so efficient that it was still in use during World War II. Setting new standards, he transformed what had been nearly inedible rations into nutritious meals. Serving alongside Florence Nightingale, he caught a fever and returned to England, but he never fully recovered and died three years later.

6

AUGUST

YOGURT

"Yogurt" is a Turkish word, and the product itself—essentially fermented milk—probably originated in Turkey, though it also has a long history in India, parts of Asia, and Arab countries. During fermentation, the lactose in milk becomes lactic acid, which gives the slightly sour taste and also makes yogurt digestible by people who cannot tolerate lactose. In France, its first appearance occurred during the reign of François I, whose digestive ills were treated with yogurt by a doctor from Constantinople who went home without divulging the secret of its preparation.

Yogurt is slightly laxative, and some types are a little alcoholic. It is thought to contribute to health and long life, but the famous Bulgarian farmhouse yogurt upon which many longevity claims are based can be found only there. The bacteria responsible for its formation are strictly regional.

A simple and irresistible form of the Indian dish *raita* can be quickly made from yogurt and cucumbers:

RAITA

Large peeled cucumber	*Pepper to taste*
1 cup or less plain yogurt	*1 teaspoon lemon juice*
Paprika to taste	*Chervil and chives, chopped*
Salt to taste	

Split the cucumber lengthwise. Remove the seeds and slice thin. Sprinkle with a teaspoon of salt and let drain for half an hour in a colander. Mix the yogurt, paprika, salt, pepper, lemon juice, chervil, and chives. Rinse the cucumber with cold water, pat the slices dry, and combine with the yogurt mix. Serves two.

F I R S T   H O M E - C O O K E D   M E A L

In 1973 the Atlanta Braves won their first no-hitter game, with Phil Niekro pitching. Just three weeks earlier, the Senate Select Committee on Presidential Campaign Activities, investigating a break-in at The Watergate, had been electrified by the testimony of Alexander Butterfield, who reported that there was a taping system in place in Nixon's Oval Office. And on this day, in a breakthrough of my own, I was cooking my first meal for Jim.

I'd like to say I'd been inspired by the introduction to what Julia Child calls open-faced tarts in her *Mastering the Art of French Cooking*: "It is practically foolproof. . . . Serve it with a salad, hot French bread, and a cold white wine; follow it with fruit, and you have a perfect lunch or supper menu." However, I don't think I was familiar with Julia Child at that point. *Joy of Cooking* was more like it and probably where I found my recipe for quiche lorraine, that combination of eggs, bacon, and cream, baked in a pie crust and described elsewhere as a classic, perfect for breakfast, brunch, lunch, dinner, or a snack.

Jim made a vinaigrette dressing for the green salad. He praised the quiche. There were fresh peaches for dessert. In a nod to Italy, chilled Soave on the hot August day. It was in my new apartment on the top floor of an old house, looking out on the dense green of elms. We sat at a square, heavy-legged cherry table, the first piece of furniture I'd bought for myself. Was it a perfect lunch or a perfect dinner? Whichever, it was only the first. K.S.

8

AUGUST

DOG LIFE

"Oh, my God! Get him out of here!"

A great, if infrequent, crisis occurs in the country when the dog comes in from a healthy outing—for some reason it always seems to happen just before dinner—and the house is filled with the unmistakable odor of skunk.

The old wives' remedy was tomato juice. Of course, someone had to go to the store to get it while the dog, unashamed, even somewhat bewildered, was made to stay outside.

A more effective method, credited to an engineer named Paul Krebaum, is to mix, in a large, open container—the "open" is important:

1 quart 3 percent hydrogen peroxide
1 cup baking soda (bicarbonate of soda)
1 teaspoon mild liquid soap

Work this strong oxidizing mixture into the coat, avoiding the eyes, and allow it to remain for some minutes until the odor is noticeably diminished. Rinse thoroughly and apply again if needed or after a day or two if the odor persists.

The dog can relax after this exhausting episode in an unused guest bedroom, at least until dinner is over.

TOMATOES

Thomas Jefferson kept gardening records and even, when he was president, a record of when various vegetables appeared in Washington markets. Tomatoes are among these, along with note of one long season, July 16 to November 17. It is not certain how Jefferson ate tomatoes, since it was an early theory that they should be well cooked.

Over the years, the popularity of the tomato has worked against it. To make them available year-round, tomatoes that are relatively tasteless and tough-skinned to withstand mechanical picking have been developed, the botanical advancement being entirely in favor of the seller. Many tomatoes are harvested while still green and reddened with ethylene gas.

The best tomatoes are those that are locally grown and vine-ripened. They are seasonal, like peaches and corn. In season, one should look for tomatoes that are firm but not hard, with uniform good color and aroma. They should stand for a day or two at room temperature, stem side up, to make them perfect. Though while growing they love it, do not let them stand in sunlight.

Do not refrigerate tomatoes; it ruins their taste.

Canned tomatoes are a completely acceptable cooking alternative. Marcella Hazan and other authorities recommend the Italian-packed, whole plum San Marzano variety that are grown in the Naples area, hand-picked when they are fully ripe. Other types are suitable as well. If slightly acidic in taste, they can be improved by adding a small quantity of salt. Tomatoes themselves are low in sodium and calories, rich in vitamins C, A, and B, and, like all fruit, have no cholesterol. They are also mildly laxative.

10

AUGUST

CLOS MONTMARTRE

There's a vineyard that still exists in the middle of Paris, in Montmartre, the last survivor of the many, mostly abbey-owned, that were in the city when it had walls, few bridges, and a great iron cauldron near the river in which counterfeiters were boiled alive in oil.

The vineyard is at the corner of rue des Saules and rue Saint-Vincent, a few streets from Sacré-Coeur. It is small, producing only five hundred bottles of wine a year that are sold in the *mairie* of the 18th arrondissement and also at auction. It's called Clos Montmartre, not expensive and not great, but from the heart of the heart of France.

11

PEACHES

The peach has been celebrated for more than four thousand years for its erotic qualities: its shape, the delicate down of its surface, as well as its flesh-like tones. It came originally from China, where it was considered both a symbol of immortality and of female genitalia. A bride was called a peach, and even today the expression "She's a peach" isn't entirely out of fashion.

Our son Theo worked for three summers at a local peach stand, sorting and selling. He learned:

- To reach maximum sweetness, peaches must ripen on the tree. Those sold at supermarkets have often been picked too early and then shipped.
- A ripe peach will yield slightly to finger pressure. Those much softer will spoil quickly.
- Size doesn't matter.
- Both yellow and white peaches are good for eating fresh. Yellow are better in pies and can be bought a bit harder for easier slicing since they'll soften during baking. White are better in Bellinis (in the opinion of his more knowledgeable customers).

Bellinis might taste best in Venice overlooking the Grand Canal, where they were invented at Harry's Bar in the 1930s, but nevertheless:

BELLINI

2 ounces fresh white peach purée
  Dash of lemon juice
6 ounces chilled champagne

Stir the lemon juice into the purée, place in a champagne glass, and add the champagne. Makes one Bellini.

12

AUGUST

DIAMOND JIM BRADY

1856. James Buchanan Brady, later to be celebrated as "Diamond Jim" and a legendary eater, is born in New York. The son of a saloon keeper, he became a wealthy, though not upper-class, figure in the city, with diamonds on his tiepin, cuff links, and canes, the result of advice he had been given as a youth that to make money you had to look like money, and nothing looked more like it than diamonds.

Large and convivial, Brady had a famous friendship with Lillian Russell, a singer and actress with a notable figure and appetite. Meals were more copious in those days. At dinner, Diamond Jim Brady would eat several dozen oysters, some crabs, turtle soup, two entire ducks, half a dozen lobsters, a sirloin steak, some terrapin, and for dessert, a platter of pastries and candy. The owner of his favorite restaurant, Rector's, called him "my best twenty-five customers." He died at the age of sixty-one.

13

AUGUST

GUACAMOLE

Known to the early Aztecs, guacamole is one of the few genuine Mexican foods found north of the border. A favorite for its luxurious taste, it is a more or less perfect harmony of avocado, tomato, salt, and onion or chili. It's good anytime and before any meal—perhaps excluding breakfast—as an hors d'oeuvre or even appetizer, but seems especially good in summer.

There are endless variations, depending on the proportions, the consistency, and the tastes of the cook. Bill Benton, a poet who grew up in Galveston and lived for a time in Santa Fe and who is our guide in these matters, introduced us to the recipe from Ronald Johnson's *Southwestern Cooking: New and Old,* on which we base our own. We make it spicier.

GUACAMOLE

2 ripe avocados, peeled and
pitted (save the pits)

1 tablespoon lemon juice

½ cup scallions, minced,
including part of the green

1 tomato, peeled and diced small

1 small clove minced garlic

1 teaspoon salt

1 teaspoon chili powder

8 or more drops Tabasco
sauce

Cut the avocados in half lengthwise, twist the halves apart, remove (and keep) the pit, scoop out the flesh, and mash until slightly chunky. Sprinkle with lemon juice. Add all the other ingredients and mix to the consistency you prefer. Taste seasoning.

Place the pits into a bowl with the guacamole and cover with plastic wrap laid directly on the surface. Allow to stand for ten to fifteen minutes to blend. The pits and lemon juice help to keep the avocado from darkening—it's the air that causes this—but guacamole should be served within an hour of being made. Serves about four.

14

AUGUST

BLACKOUT

2003. At 4:11 p.m., the kitchen lights slowly dim and then go out, one small failure in the enormous power blackout that sweeps across the Northeast from Ohio to New York. At first it seems just a local outage, since losing power on eastern Long Island isn't unusual. It almost happens during many wind and rain storms, often involving just a few streets where a line has been knocked down. It always happens during the hurricanes that move north from the Caribbean, when you chart each day's progress so there's plenty of time to buy duct tape for the windows, along with extra flashlight batteries and candles.

In the fall of 1985, we were living in a borrowed house while construction was being completed on ours, far behind schedule. Hurricane Gloria, making its way up the coast, now looked as though it would pass directly over our part of Long Island. We reinforced our windows and those of friends who used their houses only on weekends, and ate as much of the ice cream in their freezers as we could, to limit any loss. When Gloria was within striking distance, since our water was pumped electrically, we filled buckets, pots and pans, and the bathtub with water to use for what we assumed would be several days without power. That first night we were invited to dinner at a friend's who had a gas stove. For the next few meals, we used bread, peanut butter, and a can opener.

In 2003, at four in the afternoon, there had been no warning and no time to prepare, except for the hours before it got dark. We gathered every candle we had in the house, along with a couple of flashlights and a battery-powered radio to follow developments, especially in the city, where mass transit was at a standstill as rush hour approached and people were being rescued from elevators and subway trains in pitch-black tunnels.

By comparison, we were lucky. We had already finished making the first course and the dessert for a dinner party. The main course was to be *polpettonne alla toscana* (page 125), along with braised endive and glazed carrots. Instead, we got out the grill and charcoal and turned the elegant meatloaf into six hamburgers. There were only a few ice cubes for drinks, but on the other hand, as one guest commented, "Doesn't everyone look wonderful by candlelight?"

15

AUGUST

JULIA CHILD

On this day in 1912, Julia McWilliams, who under her married name of Julia Child would become a major figure in American cooking, was born in Pasadena, California. Her father was well-to-do. The family always had a cook, and Julia did not begin cooking until she was thirty-two. Before that, she said, "I just ate."

She graduated from Smith College in 1934—tall, animated, and at ease with herself—worked as a copywriter in New York for a while, but then returned home. When the country entered World War II, she signed up with the glamorous OSS—Office of Strategic Services—hoping to become a spy, all six feet two inches of her. She was sent instead to be a file clerk in Ceylon, where, as it turned out, she met her husband.

She and Paul Child were married in 1946 and soon moved to Paris, where, trying to learn to cook, she attended the Cordon Bleu, the only woman in the class. She met Louisette Bertholle and Simone Beck, and the three of them started a cooking school of their own and collaborated on what was to become her influential work, *Mastering the Art of French Cooking*, which took ten years to write. It was dedicated to France and its people, who, through generations of invention and concentration, had created "one of the world's great arts."

Her true popularity came through television. She whisked up an omelet on her first appearance, and viewers loved her from the start, her manner and high, enthusiastic voice. She established herself as a personality, lively and imperturbable. "I fell in love with the public," she said, "the public fell in love with me, and I tried to keep it that way."

Fervent, dedicated to instructing, she was always so relaxed that it was often thought she had been drinking. She became a national figure and remained true to her principles, as well as to public television, where she had the freedom to cook tripe, kidneys, and other things unthinkable on commercial TV.

During her career she wrote ten cookbooks, all of them noted for their clarity. She once said that her ideal house would have just two rooms, a bedroom and a kitchen, and when she was asked what her guilty pleasures were, replied, "I don't have any guilt."

She died in California two days before she would have been ninety-two.

16

AUGUST

CORKAGE

Many restaurants—though not all—let customers bring their own bottle of wine and then charge to open and serve it. This fee, called a corkage fee, can range from ten to fifty dollars a bottle, but may be waived for certain clients or occasions, depending on the restaurant. The fee presumably is meant to cover the service of opening and pouring, along with washing the glasses afterward, costs normally included in the price of a wine on the restaurant's own list.

Obviously, a restaurant would rather sell wine, which contributes to its profits. Hence, the fee. And, as some restaurateurs point out, they are in the business of selling food and drink and don't allow clients to bring their own food.

Customers, on the other hand, wary of high markups on wine lists, sometimes find it less expensive to bring their own, even with a corkage fee. However, the client should keep in mind a certain etiquette:

- Call ahead to check on the restaurant's policies.
- Don't bring a wine that's on the restaurant's list.
- Don't take advantage of a generous policy by bringing several bottles of wine that require fresh glasses, and don't bring multiple bottles for large parties.
- Try to order a wine from the wine list to supplement your own.
- Tip as though the cost of your own wine were part of the bill.

17

AUGUST

VAUX-LE-VICOMTE

On this evening in 1661, the young French king, Louis XIV, attended a magnificent feast at a château—a palace, really, that had just been built by his chief of finances, Nicolas Fouquet. The six thousand guests had passed by *tableaux vivants* of satyrs and nymphs in the woods leading to the château. Fountains were playing in the vast gardens, and bejeweled elephants stood among the trees. The guests were served food prepared by the famed Vatel on plates of solid silver or gold. There was music especially written for the occasion by Jean-Baptiste Lully, fireworks, and a comedy by Molière.

The château, Vaux-le-Vicomte, had risen in only four or five years, and at times more than eighteen thousand men were working on the construction. The architect was Le Vau, who later designed Versailles; the gardens were done by Le Notre and the frescoes and decoration by Lebrun, the latter two also contributing to Versailles. Fouquet had found them first and introduced them to his monarch, as it were. Vaux-le-Vicomte had a huge collection of paintings and sculpture, as well as a library of 27,000 volumes.

The incredible display of wealth and perhaps the possibility that one of the paintings by Lebrun contained what seemed to be a portrait of Mlle de la Vallière, already a royal mistress, aroused the king's deep suspicion and envy. He was of a mind to leave abruptly, but his mother persuaded him not to spoil the grand evening. He did not, however, spend the night in the royal suite that had been designed especially for him, and Fouquet may have realized the seriousness of this.

Fouquet was a capable minister and had acquired his immense wealth in what was then a recognized manner, but the king angrily felt he was stealing "beyond his station." Fouquet was arrested, and his three-year trial was the most famous of its time, rigged to a certain extent. Despite the intervention and pleading of loyal friends, including Mme de Sévigné and the poet La Fontaine, he was convicted and sentenced to exile, which the king changed to imprisonment.

Fouquet's property and fortune were confiscated, and he died in prison, nineteen years after the fatal evening.

Vaux-le-Vicomte, only slightly diminished, still exists. Less than forty miles from Paris, it can be reached by train or car and is open to the public, though privately owned.

18

AUGUST

WINE STAINS

Someone always spills red wine, either on the carpet, the tablecloth, or themselves. Unless you take immediate steps, the stain is almost impossible to get out. Don't wait: cover the stain with a layer of table salt and let it stand, leaching the wine out of the fabric, until it can be washed later. An alternative is soda water—a diluted form of salt—especially for clothing, where you can't leave the salt itself in place.

19

OLIVES

Olives come in many sizes and shapes, but are essentially the same fruit. When you see a vast, varied selection, the differences are largely a matter of when they were harvested—some are picked green—and how they were treated afterward.

Some of the most widely known types include:

• From Greece, not only the large, popular Kalamata, but also the Naphlion olive, dark green and cracked with a mallet to allow the brine to penetrate during curing.

• From Italy, the mild, black Gaeta, dried or brine-cured.

• From Spain, among many varieties, the green Manzanilla.

• From France, the small, dark Niçoise; the green Provençal, often marinated in herbs; and the Picholine (also grown in California), which is green and good for curing.

• From Morocco, dark, dried, and oil-cured olives.

• From California, the large Barouni, originally from Tunisia; the purple-black Mission and Sevillano; and the green Ascolano, all used mainly for pickling.

Except for those that are dried, you can pit them yourself. Smack the olive with the broad side of a large knife blade, and it will usually loosen the flesh enough to squeeze out the pit without cutting open the olive.

The olive tree itself is venerated and extremely long-lived. Its slender silver-gray leaves seem to reflect the spare land where it thrives, though in spring, vast hillsides of trees turn white with blossoms that will mature into the fruit. An olive branch in the beak of a dove was God's sign to Noah that the flood was abating and is a sign of peace even today. The immense, gnarled olive tree growing in the Garden of Gethsemane, under which Jesus was said to have prayed the night before his crucifixion, looks as though it could be two thousand years old even if, in reality, it isn't.

20

AUGUST

ARTICHOKES

Artichokes are flowers—buds, actually—and members of the thistle family, with stiff, pointed petals. When cooked, the base of each artichoke leaf, pulled off between the teeth, is edible, the basis for the Italian expression *la politica del carciofo,* which means "dealing with opponents one at a time." Once the leaves are gone, the inedible choke is revealed, and when this is cut away, there is the most desirable part, the heart.

Boiling or steaming are the easiest methods of preparation, but there are many recipes for stuffed artichokes or for artichoke hearts. Hot or cold, the leaves are best when dipped in melted butter or vinaigrette. Mayonnaise, hollandaise, mousseline, and tartar sauce can also be used.

In selecting artichokes, choose these are are firm and heavy, with closed leaves and no discoloration at the tips. They can be kept for several days uncooked with the stem in water like flowers. After cooking they will keep for not much more than a day in the refrigerator.

21

AUGUST

CRU DES PTOLÉMÉES

The great vineyards of ancient Egypt—from which came the wine that Cleopatra served to Caesar—disappeared beneath the wave of Islam and its prohibition of alcohol until early in the 20th century, when, in the area where Alexandria once existed, they were revived. Two wines they produce today, Cru des Ptolémées and Queen Cleopatra—both whites—though perhaps not quite equal to what used to be laid down in the tombs of the pharaohs, nevertheless transport you back through the ages.

22

AUGUST

DENIS PAPIN

One day, wandering the streets of Blois, city of the great feudal lords of France in the Middle Ages, we came upon the prominent statue of a man and the inscription: Denis Papin, August 22, 1647, inventor in

1679 of the *marmite à pression*. We had to look it up in a French dictionary: "pressure cooker."

Three hundred years ago? It was only during World War II that the
pressure cooker became widely used because it saved fuel and was able
to cook food in a far shorter time while preserving its flavor and moisture, the same qualities that make the microwave so popular today.
From the first, Papin had imagined it in the kitchen and was disappointed when it was used instead as an industrial sterilizer. Far ahead
of his time, he was also working on designs for a submarine and a
grenade launcher, as well as a steam engine, as was James Watt at about
the same time. Watt based his early versions on Papin's pressure cooker
and eventually laid the groundwork for what became the Industrial
Revolution. Papin himself died in poverty in London in 1712.

23

AUGUST

APRICOTS

Apricots first grew wild in the mountains of China and have been
cultivated there for over four thousand years. They migrated west
and were called "eggs of the sun" in Persia and *praecocium*—meaning
"precocious" and the origin of the word "apricot"—by the Romans
because they ripened so early in the spring. They actually turn orange
before they are fully ripe and may be mistakenly picked too early,
before their flavor has completely matured. They also come in white,
pink, gray, and even black, and vary in size from that of a cranberry to
that of a softball.

Less than five percent of apricots are eaten fresh. The others are canned or, more popularly, dried. Turkey and California, where they were introduced by the Spanish explorers and planted by the missionaries, produce the most. California apricots are cut in half before drying, while the Turkish are dried whole after the pit has been removed. Sun-drying on trays for about three days is the best way to preserve both color and taste. They are loaded with vitamin A and provide as much roughage as their cousin, the prune.

24

AUGUST

POMPEII

Until Vesuvius erupted on this day in 79 A.D., Pompeii, a resort town on the coast near Naples, was known for its fish sauces, its cabbage, and its luxurious villas. There were forty bakeries, many producing the traditional round loaves still made in the area. Nearby were cultivated oyster beds and shellfish that produced the deep purple dye used for royal togas. There were elaborate wineries with machinery to press and strain grapes and shops to sell what was made.

When the volcano began to erupt, many of the twenty thousand inhabitants of Pompeii fled immediately. Those who lingered—some two thousand of them—were asphyxiated by sulfurous fumes or buried in the spewing pumice, ash, and lava. Among them was Pliny, commander of Roman ships based nearby in the Bay of Naples, who sailed across to Pompeii to rescue friends. They tied pillows on top of their heads to protect themselves from the rain of rock, but as they made their way to the ship, Pliny was overcome by fumes, collapsed, and died in the street.

Pompeii's great gladiatorial arena, its two theaters, taverns, public baths, and brothels all became tombs. When excavation began almost seventeen hundred years later, everything uncovered was just as it had been during those last minutes before the devastation: bottles of wine, a kind of pizza, fruit and nuts on the tables, toilet articles, kitchen utensils. There were more than three thousand frescoes, many of the most decorative in the dining rooms, depicting scenes from the lives of gods and goddesses. The entryways of houses had mosaics of pets, with the words *cave canem,* "beware of dog," but the danger came from elsewhere.

25

FIGS IN WHISKEY

There was a one-star restaurant in Plaisance in southwest France where we had dinner with a descendant of the man on whom Dumas based his fictional d'Artagnan. Dessert was delicious, plump figs in a syrupy alcoholic liquid. The chef, Maurice Coscuella, appeared in the dining room to make a round of the tables and greet the customers. We asked about the fig recipe. It was his own, he said. He admired the glasses, a ten-dollar pair from an American drugstore, that Jim had put on to read the bill. Just what he needed, Coscuella said. Where could he find them? We'd send him a pair, we said. In the meantime, he gave us his recipe, which we've often served:

FIGS IN WHISKEY

1 *package dried figs*

2 *cups sugar*

1 ½ *cups Scotch whiskey*

Boil the figs in about one quart of water with the sugar for twenty minutes. Allow to cool until tepid, drain off about half the remaining water, and add the whiskey. Set aside in a covered bowl to steep before serving. Serves four or five.

POISONOUS MUSHROOMS

It is difficult to tell by looking whether a mushroom is poisonous. You have to be able to accurately identify them. There are over two thousand species around the world that are perfectly good to eat and only about thirty that are dangerous. Of the latter, one—the *Amanita phalloides* or "death cap"—accounts for almost all deaths. A white mushroom with a delicate stem and a swollen sac at the base, it is found widely.

In 54 A.D., Roman Emperor Claudius fell victim to this variety, added to his food by his fourth wife, Agrippina II, so that Nero, her son by a former husband, could ascend the throne. Claudius's symptoms—a cold sweat, a raging thirst, abdominal pain, diarrhea, and vomiting—were the classic ones, which tend to appear about ten hours or so after eating.

In Sacha Guitry's 1936 film *The Story of a Cheat,* a twelve-year-old boy, by way of poisonous mushrooms, learns a lifelong lesson in the consequences of bad behavior. Late for a family dinner because he was out stealing, he's sent to his room. In the morning, he discovers that his entire family is dead, having mistakenly eaten *Amanita phalloides* at the meal he missed.

Even after centuries, the precise formulas for the liqueurs Benedictine and Chartreuse—both brandy-based and originated by monks, Benedictine around 1510 and Chartreuse some one hundred years later—remain secret. It is said that only three living people know the formula for Benedictine at any one time.

The composition of Angostura bitters, created by a surgeon in Simón Bolívar's army in Venezuela in the early 1800s and intended to reduce fever and act as a tonic, is also still a secret.

27

AUGUST

CHERRIES

A member of the rose family, the cherry is a drupe—that is, it has a pit, like plums, peaches, and apricots. That of the cherry is a perfect projectile for spitting competitions, with the current Guinness world record of ninety-five feet, one inch set on this day in 1994, in Langenthal, Germany.

It is the fruit most frequently represented by poets and painters. There are nearly one thousand varieties, sweet and sour, with the most popular in the United States being

the Bing, first grown in the 1870s in Oregon by Henderson Lewelling, who named it for one of his Chinese workmen.

The blossoming cherry trees associated with Japan bear no fruit. Their name, *Sakura,* is a favorite for Japanese girls, though the tree symbolizes not long life but its fleeting quality. But then, what's in a name? A week after the Japanese attack on Pearl Harbor, probably as retaliation, someone cut down four of the cherry trees in Washington, D.C. They were among the three thousand that had been given to the city by Tokyo forty years earlier. To prevent more vandalism during the war, from then on they were called oriental cherry trees.

The maraschino cherry started in Yugoslavia as a variety called Marasca that was preserved in liqueur. Once in the United States, the Royal Anne cherry was substituted, the alcohol eliminated, and it ended up on top of children's ice cream sundaes.

And of course, George Washington, as a boy, never did cut down a cherry tree.

28

AUGUST

ARMAGNAC

Gascony, in southwestern France, is the home of *The Three Muske-teers,* foie gras, and Armagnac, the earthy, intense cousin of Cognac, loved by Henry IV, who in the 16th century wrote to his mistress, Gabrielle d'Estrées, "As God lives, dearest, nothing is comparable to Armagnac."

During August, when the French take their holiday, a group of boyhood friends who grew up in Gascony—the *departments* of Gers and Landes east of Biarritz—return to their châteaus there and host dinners for one another at which each man in turn offers a toast to his host, his friends, and their wives at the end of the meal. Armagnac is invariably served. Several of the men even make and bottle their own, but as with much Armagnac, it is so popular locally that little is exported, and consequently, in the United States, more than one hundred bottles of Cognac are sold for every one of Armagnac. Both are distilled wines, but while Cognac is distilled twice and then aged in white oak, Armagnac is distilled only once and aged in black, giving it what the French call *goût de terroir,* a greater essence of the land in which it is grown. The best Armagnac is aged for a quarter of a century before being bottled, after which it improves no further.

We were spending the month in a large farmhouse near Lectoure and were invited to several of the dinners through friends. At one for forty people on a hot summer night, the host was raising his glass and proposing, in the famously robust, life-loving fashion of the region, that after the meal everyone adjourn to the drawing room for a singing contest. Suddenly, at another table, a man shrieked and leapt to his feet, and moments later, a woman did the same. It took a few minutes to realize that, eighteen feet up on the molding, wasps were being overcome by the rising heat of the many candles and were dropping like shot to the tables, stinging wherever they landed.

The singing competition was postponed, but Armagnac was passed around again as an antidote and consolation.

29

CHINESE CUISINE

It is difficult to speak of a Chinese cuisine, since the country is so vast that it includes significantly different styles. They are:

- Northern, or Beijing: garlic and sesame, little rice
- Central and Western, or Szechuan: sweet-sour and spicy or hot
- Southeastern, or Shanghai: soy sauce
- Southern, or Cantonese: seafood, black bean, and garlic

The essence of Chinese cooking is the art of mixing, both ingredients and basic flavors, of which there are five: sweet, bitter, salt, sour, and hot. Sweet and sour, for example, make an interesting mix, while sour and salt tend to negate each other.

A meal has two main elements, the "necessary," or *fan,* and the "pleasure-giving," or *ts'ai.* Rice or other grains are *fan.* Meat, fish, and vegetable dishes are *ts'ai.*

Customarily, the bowl of rice is refilled at the end of the meal but is left untouched to indicate that hunger has disappeared.

Men traditionally sit on one side of the table and women on the other, which turns out to be not a bad arrangement, at least for talking.

DONALD SULTAN DINNER

The dining room in Donald Sultan's small country house is longer than it is wide, with a worn floor painted in a brilliant black-and-white diamond design. It adjoins a square, far-from-modern kitchen. A painter, one imagines, possesses a sense of style. Maybe not Francis Bacon or Jackson Pollock, but definitely Donald Sultan, who has, among other things, designed the decor for a hotel named for him in Budapest and who is a remarkably good cook. He gave an impromptu dinner one August night that involved, however, not more than ten minutes of cooking.

With drinks there were two cheeses. One, he seemed to remember, was yak cheese, though this seemed unlikely, and the other a Fribourg. There was also a hard Italian salami on a board with a sharp knife and crackers. The dining table was covered with a beautiful cloth, and plates and silverware had been set out. There were many candles, including some in wall sconces.

On a large platter were sliced red and green tomatoes with fresh mozzarella and basil, and on another, quartered store-roasted capons. First, however, came soft-boiled eggs, decapitated in their shells, with a dollop of caviar on top. A bit later, a plate of steaming corn-on-the-cob was brought in.

There were five of us. After the egg, one ate as one pleased. As always, there was good wine, and for dessert, thin handmade cookies from the best local source.

Pleasurable in every way—the food, intimacy, ease, and presentation. The reaction was predictable: we ought to do this ourselves.

31

AUGUST

CORN

"People have tried and they have tried," Garrison Keillor wrote, "but sex is not better than sweet corn."

Sweet country corn, freshly picked, is seasonal, and the sugar in many varieties begins to turn into starch as soon as the ears are picked. The kernels can be eaten raw like other vegetables but, in any case, should be cooked for only a short time, thirty seconds according to some experts and certainly no longer than three or four minutes in boiling water. The longer corn is cooked, the tougher it becomes. No salt should be added to the water, as this also toughens the kernels.

The sweet corn found year-round in supermarkets is usually a supersweet variety that converts into starch much more slowly. It is all right, but nothing like the corn that comes from a local field.

You needn't strip back the husk to inspect an ear as the suspicious city dwellers do. You can feel from the outside if it is a healthy, full ear, and the rare little worm is not dangerous. Corn can even be cooked with most of the husk on and only the tough outer leaves removed. The flavor is even enhanced this way, and after being removed from the water, the ears will stay warm longer.

Corn can also be steamed or roasted, and in the latter case, with the husk off, the kernels tend to caramelize, which is a triumph.

We usually serve summer corn as a separate, complete course with a stick of butter on a plate for everyone to roll it in and nothing else besides salt and pepper. James Beard liked to put butter and bacon crumbs on his corn. Others use olive oil, herbs, and even chili.

SEPTEMBER

1

SEPTEMBER

DINNER TABLES

Small rooms or dwellings discipline the mind, Leonardo da Vinci said, and large ones weaken it. Something similar might be said of dinner tables. The smaller the size, the greater the intimacy; big ones are for castles.

If a table is too wide, it is awkward to talk across it; you can speak only to those on either side. If it is too narrow, the opposite is true, and you talk more easily to those across. The ideal is a width of about thirty-two inches. The length varies according to the size of the room.

2

SEPTEMBER

PEANUT BUTTER

Two tablespoons is about the usual serving—of peanut butter, that is—when making a sandwich. Popular lore is that the average fifteen hundred peanut-butter sandwiches consumed by the time a child is in high school are responsible for the greatly increased height of Americans over the past decades.

Peanut butter is a good source of protein and even fiber, with around 550 peanuts in a twelve-ounce jar. It has no cholesterol, though it is relatively fattening at almost one hundred calories per tablespoon and is required by law to be ninety percent peanuts. The extra bits of nut are added afterward for crunchy style. Hydrogenated vegetable oil, discredited now, maintains the consistency and gives it a shelf life of a year. In natural peanut butter, with nothing added, the oil from the peanuts soon separates from the nuts, and it grows rancid unless refrigerated.

South American Indians and African tribes had eaten a form of mashed peanuts for centuries, but peanut butter was invented in 1890 by Ambrose Straub, a St. Louis doctor looking for a source of protein for elderly patients whose teeth made it hard to chew. He patented his "mill for grinding peanuts for butter" in 1903 and introduced it at the St. Louis World's Fair the next year. It was an immediate hit, and on average, Americans today eat over three pounds per person per year.

At a lunch in France one day, we remarked that it was hard to find certain things in the local grocery store.

"What can you not find?" asked the hostess.

"Well, baking soda, for one thing. Peanut butter."

"I *het* it," she said simply.

Tea is not made by filling a cup with warm or hot water and dropping in a tea bag. This only resembles tea.

The usual proportion for brewing real tea is one teaspoon of black or green leaves for every six ounces—not quite a cup—of water. The water should be cold and fresh to begin—soft water, preferably, since it improves the final quality. The pot should be preheated by filling it for a few minutes with hot water, emptying it, then adding tea leaves. When the tea water reaches a rolling boil, it is immediately poured over the leaves. The famous English dictum is: Always bring the pot to the kettle, never bring the kettle to the pot.

Allow the tea to steep for three to five minutes while the leaves open and release their full flavor. Stir and serve, pouring through a small strainer specially made for the purpose. (Under field conditions, as they say, the leaves will remain for the most part in the bottom of the pot if about an inch of boiling water is poured in first, allowing them to expand and settle.)

Cover the pot with a tea cozy, if you can ever find one to buy.

Italians, French, and Americans drink coffee. Turks and Germans also. The Chinese, Japanese, and English drink tea. Tea, Russian-style, is served in a glass with lemon. English-style is often with milk. The five o'clock English tea with small sandwiches, scones, cakes, and so forth is said to have been created by the Duchess of Bedford in the early 1800s, when dinners were very late.

Most Indian teas are black, with Assam and Darjeeling among the best known.

CHATEAUBRIAND

In a house built into the ramparts of Saint-Malo on the Brittany coast, François René de Chateaubriand was born on this day in 1768. The last of ten children and son of a prosperous ship owner and captain, he was buried here, too, in 1848, on a small rocky outcropping called Grand Be Island, which can be reached on foot only at low tide. According to his wishes, there is no name or date on the grave, only a cross large enough to be seen from shore.

Chateaubriand, whose rich, romantic prose and tragic love stories made him the most important French writer of the time, served in Napoleon's government but eventually became disillusioned and anti-Bonapartist. Later, he was ambassador to London for the Bourbons and then minister of foreign affairs. Famous for his books and his love affairs, his name is now best known for the steak created in his honor by Montmireil, his chef at the embassy in London. Cut a couple of inches thick from the tenderloin, the beef is slathered with butter, seasoned with pepper, and grilled or broiled. It is usually considered a dish for two and is often cut into thin slices, topped with a mixture of butter and parsley, and served with a béarnaise sauce.

5
SEPTEMBER

FALERNIAN

In Caesar's time, there were already Roman vineyards in the Rhône Valley and around Bordeaux that laid the foundation for the great modern wines that were to come.

The most famed Roman wine, Falernian, "the wine of the emperors," not in existence today, was of three types: a dry white, a sweetish yellow presumably like a Sauternes, and a red. It was extremely long-lived, and the great vintage of 121 B.C. was still being drunk, it was said, a century later. The poet Horace praised Falernian, though it was too expensive for him to drink, he complained, the Château Pétrus of its day.

6
SEPTEMBER

SALSA

You can assess the quality of any Mexican restaurant by one of the first things brought to the table: the salsa. The word itself is Spanish for "sauce" or "gravy" and appears as early as 1571 in accounts of conquistadors in the New World.

The best is made fresh, and every restaurant—and Mexican home—has its own favored recipe, varying in consistency and hotness of ingredients, which include approximately equal amounts of chopped tomatoes—fresh or canned—and onions. Scallions are usually preferred, but regular onions—red, yellow, or white—are fine. Added to these and determining the degree of hotness are chopped green chili peppers and jalapeño peppers, again either fresh or canned. Chopped parsley, a bit of lime juice or vinegar, and salt also appear in most recipes, along with coriander. Many recipes add garlic, oregano, some oil, and even a little sugar.

Salsa was originally made by the ancient Aztecs, Mayans, and Incas from tomatoes, native to the region, along with onions and spices. It was served as a condiment by Aztecs rich enough to have meat and fish on their tables, while the poor used it on tortillas. Today salsa means the Mexican dip used with chips that in the United States is even more popular than ketchup.

SEPTEMBER

APPLES

Although the apple has them—and there is the legendary figure named Johnny Appleseed who is usually pictured inaccurately as spreading them from a bag over his shoulder—seeds do not produce a consistent variety of apple. The long history of the apple has been one of cultivation and grafting—cuttings from a good tree grafted onto another where they bear the desired fruit. The result of planting apple seeds is a series of trees whose fruit is unpredictable.

The apple that Eve is holding in many paintings is not mentioned in the Bible—the fruit there is unnamed, merely from the tree of knowledge. Probably its depiction results from the value it had in ancient times—to the Romans it was a luxury. In ancient Greece, cultivated apples were also rare and expensive, so much so that there was a decree that a bridal couple might share only one apple before proceeding to the marriage bed. In Sicily today, tradition has it that a girl who tosses an apple into the street beneath her window will marry the boy who picks it up. If a priest picks it up, she will die a virgin.

Apples—and there are more than ten thousand named varieties—are available year-round, though more plentiful and of higher quality in the summer and fall, the time of their natural harvest. Markets carry the most profitable, not necessarily the best, apples, and it is usually blandness that results in popularity.

Of those that appear in most supermarkets, some are good for almost every use: Jonathans, McIntosh, Gala, Courtland, Granny Smith. Some varieties tend to be better for one purpose than another:

- Applesauce: McIntosh, Cortland, Fuji, Gala
- Pies and tarts: Granny Smith, Rome Beauty, Cortland, Pippin
- Cider: Winesap

An apple has only about ninety calories, abundant vitamin C, no fat, and aids digestion. Three medium apples equal about a pound, and two pounds, or six medium apples, are about the right amount for a pie.

SEPTEMBER

BISTROS AND BRASSERIES

Bistros are small bars or restaurants, and brasseries were originally breweries but are now restaurants. It can be difficult to tell them apart—the definitions are somewhat elastic.

A bistro is really a place where one can have something to eat and drink in relative informality. The idea of simple food served in a warm atmosphere has appeal. The origin of the word itself is the subject of debate. One school believes it is from the Russian word for "quick" and came into use after Russian troops occupied Paris in 1815. Another theory is that it comes from the French word *bistrouille,* which is a mixture of coffee and brandy.

The word "brasserie," on the other hand, has meant brewery from the beginning, and brasseries have evolved from places where beer was made to those where it was sold, along with food and other drinks. Brasseries serve a basic menu all day and often until quite late at night. They have traditionally been favored by artists, writers, journalists, and politicians.

In Paris there is the haughty Brasserie Lipp, celebrated by Hemingway and later the choice of Herman Goering. Also Bofinger, a

Belle Époque treasure from the 19th century, along with one of our favorites, Flo, on a narrow alley in the tenth arrondissement. At Lipp, unknowns are sent up to exile on the second floor, but Flo has only one floor.

9

SEPTEMBER

PARMESAN CHEESE

During the Great Fire that destroyed London in 1666, Samuel Pepys took measures to protect certain valuables from the almost total destruction. "[I]n the evening Sir W. Penn and I did dig another [pit in the garden] and put our wine in it, and I my parmazan cheese."

Parmesan cheese—Parmigiano-Reggiano—is technically a *grana,* a somewhat hard and grainy cheese bearing little resemblance to the packaged, grated product in supermarkets. Genuine Parmigiano-Reggiano is handmade in five northern Italian provinces from partly skimmed, raw milk that is produced only between April and mid-November. It comes in huge wheels weighing more than sixty pounds, with the name etched in small dots all around the rim. It is aged from eighteen months up to several years—the older the cheese, the greater the flavor. Straw-colored, moist, and crumbly, it should properly not be cut from the wheel with a knife, but scored and then pried off in chunks as if being quarried.

One of the world's great cheeses, it has a tremendous, irresistible, and slightly salty flavor either eaten whole or grated. It should never be bought already grated, however, as the flavor dissipates rapidly. For pasta it is best coarsely grated and finely grated for soups and other dishes. The fat content, because of the skimmed milk, is unexpectedly low, about thirty percent.

Parmesan should be stored, wrapped tightly in several thicknesses of aluminum foil and/or plastic, in the lower part of the refrigerator and be brought, still wrapped, to room temperature before serving. Afterward, it should be freshly rewrapped. If the cheese becomes dry or begins to whiten, wrap it in moistened cheesecloth first and put it away for a day in the refrigerator. Clean off any mold.

10

SEPTEMBER

CAHORS

Cahors is a beautiful town, a provincial capital, surrounded on three sides by a river. Like much of southern France, it was famous in Roman times, and boasts a remarkable seven-hundred-year-old bridge, with the stone piers of its arches pointed into the flow of the river like prows.

A lesser-known but distinctive wine is produced here, one we often buy, unmistakable because of its dark color and pronounced tannic properties. Cahors wine, if drunk early, within five years or so after it is bottled, tends to be harsh, but when mature is well-balanced, rich, and has an elegant fragrance. The vineyards of Bordeaux are not that far off, along with greatness, perhaps, but this is a very good wine.

11

SIMPLE DINNER IDEAS

A good recipe is one thing, but a complete dinner is another. When there is no time and nothing has been prepared ahead, it can be worthwhile to have a few full menus, easy to prepare, listed in the back of your cookbook—guests can sit around and drink while you're doing dinner.

Among ours is:

BRUSCHETTA (TOASTED ITALIAN BREAD RUBBED WHILE STILL
WARM WITH GARLIC AND SOME OLIVE OIL)
CAESAR SALAD WITHOUT EGG
FILET MIGNONS ENCIRCLED WITH BACON STRIPS
AND THEN SKILLET-BROWNED
BAKED POTATOES
SORBET
COFFEE

12

MUSHROOMS

In 1959, Jacques Pépin, well-known chef and writer on food, moved from France to the United States, having apprenticed first in his parents' restaurant near Lyon and then in Paris before serving as personal chef to three French heads of state, including de Gaulle. When he arrived in New York, he was amazed to find that there were no mushrooms for sale in American supermarkets. Twenty-five years later, there were little white ones in boxes, but unfortunately they had no flavor. Now another twenty years have passed, and a food revolution has taken place. Mushrooms are plentiful.

The familiar white ones are cultivated, of course, but the same is true of most varieties of mushrooms that once grew only in the wild. This makes them available year-round, either fresh or dried. The most abundant among them are members of the boletus family, including the Italian porcini, the Japanese shiitake, and the French cèpes. Used in dishes such as soups, stews, stir-fries, and even as a meat substitute in sandwiches, they're also delicious sautéed on their own.

Chanterelles are large with a vivid orange color and are most often stewed. Another showy variety is the bright red lobster mushroom, which is best when sautéed.

The tiny enoki mushrooms of Japan are used in salads and stir-fries, more for their texture than their flavor, which tends to be bland.

Oyster mushrooms, pale gray and with an oyster-like shape, are firm and go especially well with meat and game.

The rarest of the wild mushrooms, because they cannot be cultivated and grow only in the wild, are morels. Identified by their conical caps, they are hard to find in stores except in early May. In dried form, reconstituted in cream, they still have an intense, earthy taste.

Any fresh mushrooms can be refrigerated for a day or two, loosely wrapped to help hold in moisture. They shouldn't be washed, and never soaked, because they will absorb the water instead of the intended liquids or fats when cooking. Instead, they should be wiped clean with a damp paper towel or soft brush.

13

SEPTEMBER

EN-CAS

In France, an *en-cas* is a snack or light meal. The word means, literally, "in case," and in the châteaus of the ancien régime, some cold food was usually laid out on a small table for those returning late. King Louis XIV's *en-cas* at Versailles was bread, two bottles of wine, and a carafe of water for the night.

14

B L I N I

The word "buckwheat" sounds American, though the plant originated in Asia in the remote past and still grows wild there. The name actually comes from the Dutch *boeke,* "beech," and *weite,* "wheat," probably because the seeds look like small beechnuts. Buckwheat is not really wheat, but is of the same family as rhubarb. It grows faster in colder climates and poorer soil and is said to be good for high blood pressure and is not good for making bread. The famed Japanese noodles, soba, are made from it, as are the small pancakes—delicious with sour cream and caviar or smoked salmon—called blini.

"Blini" is Russian, the plural of blin, which is "a small pancake." In Russia in the old days, blini and vodka were served at funerals, and some of both were cast into the grave, as a farewell to the things of this earth or perhaps as provisions for the voyage ahead.

Blini are perfect for a late breakfast or for lunch or, made smaller, as hors d'oeuvres, adapted from the recipe used by the Russian Tea Room restaurant before it closed.

BLINI

1 cup warm water	*1 teaspoon salt*
1 (¼ ounce) package active dry	*1 cup whole milk, heated to*
yeast	*warm*
Pinch of sugar	*1 stick unsalted butter, melted*
1 cup all-purpose flour, sifted	*and cooled*
before measuring	*2 large eggs, lightly beaten*
1 cup buckwheat flour, sifted	*Sour cream to taste*
before measuring	*Caviar to taste*

Stir together warm water, yeast, and sugar in a bowl and let stand for about five minutes until foamy. If it doesn't foam, start over with fresh yeast.

Add the all-purpose and buckwheat flours and salt, then stir in the milk, three tablespoons of the butter, and the eggs. Cover the bowl with plastic wrap and set in a pan filled with an inch of warm water. Let the mixture rise in a warm place for about one to two hours until it increases in volume, has bubbles breaking the surface, and is stringy when scooped.

The batter can be made up to three days in advance and chilled, covered, at this point. If necessary, thin the batter with a few teaspoons of milk before using.

Preheat the oven to 250 degrees F. Heat a large non-stick frying pan over moderately high heat until hot and brush with some of the remaining melted butter. Don't let the butter brown. Stir the batter. Spoon a heaping teaspoon of batter into the skillet for each blin, or a tablespoon for larger blini. Cook, turning once, until both sides are golden brown, about two minutes. Keep warm in the oven until all are made.

Serve topped with a little sour cream and caviar.
Makes two or three dozen blini.

A salmon filling can be rolled up in larger blini:

SALMON FILLING

2 minced onions
3 tablespoons butter
1 cup white wine
1 pound smoked salmon, cut into irregular pieces
  Melted butter

Lightly brown the onions in the butter. Add the wine
and smoked salmon, and simmer lightly for about an
hour. Put about two tablespoons of this mixture onto
one edge of the warm blini, roll up, set in a shallow
baking dish, cover with aluminum foil, and warm for a
few minutes in a 300 degree F oven. Serve with melted
butter. Fills about a dozen blini.

15

SEPTEMBER

DATES

Dates—sweet and with color like amber—most probably originated in
the Middle East, where Iraq has been the largest producer and exporter.
    In Arabic, the date palm is called *nakhla,* "the tree of life." Muham-
mad instructed his followers to cherish it, and dates are still tradi-

tionally the first food eaten at the end of each day of Ramadan. The fruit itself is so nutritious that even today, desert nomads can exist for a long time on only dates and milk from their goats.

Over millennia, date palms have provided not only fruit, but also stalks for rope and roofing, leaves for baskets, and juice for the distilled alcoholic drink called *arak*. The trees have been around since before recorded history and appear in the earliest Egyptian carvings. Dates are also perhaps the oldest intentionally cultivated crop. The palms are either female or male, the first needing pollination by the second in order to bear fruit. Insects won't do the job—they're not attracted to the flowers of the tree. The wind can do it in a haphazard sort of way, but far more effective is deliberately bringing the pollen of the male blossom to that of the female. One male tree can provide enough pollen for fifty or more females.

The trees are mature at about thirty years, and once fertilized, are prolific, with a single female tree usually producing more than one hundred pounds of dates a year for decades. Those usually found in the supermarket are the "soft" variety, with "semi-dry" and "hard" dates being less popular. Sweet, almost sticky in consistency, and relatively high in calories, they're eaten fresh or dried or used in baking, and provide fiber and iron.

In the ancient world, the best dates were said to come from Jericho, which still produces them due to ideal conditions, since date palms, according to Waverly Root, like to have "their heads in the sun and their feet in the water"—which is to say, a desert oasis. During the ripening period from April to September, even dew will spoil the crop.

16

MENUS

The job of a restaurant menu is to list what's available and its price, and it usually reflects a collaboration between chef and owner. The owner wants it to represent the personality of the place, and the chef wants the freedom to develop his own interests and style. The latter often shows up in the form of specials that are announced by the waiter, a list that sometimes seems longer than the menu itself.

The earliest menus were used only by cooks and staff, and were posted in the kitchen as a reminder of the dishes to be served and in what order. The first offered to diners were many pages long and listed the dozen or so dishes that were actually available, along with the hundred the chef might make if he happened to have the ingredients and the inclination.

It used to be in the United States that you had to go into a restaurant to have a look at the menu, but more are now posting them in the window, as in Europe. In Japan, this often takes the form of a display of realistic plastic replicas of dishes, and if your Japanese is weak, the waiter will step outside with you, so you can point to your choice.

17

SEPTEMBER

SEEDLESS

"Seedless," in the citrus trade, doesn't mean there are no seeds, but that there are five seeds or fewer per lemon, orange, or grapefruit.

18

SEPTEMBER

SAMUEL JOHNSON

Some people have a foolish way of not minding, or pretending not to mind, what they eat. . . . I look upon it, that he who does not mind his belly will hardly mind anything else.

— SAMUEL JOHNSON

A man who possessed neither wealth nor power but for whom an age is named, Samuel Johnson was born this day in Lichfield, England, in 1709. His greatness lay in his powerful intellect, his wit, and his influential essays, biography, and criticism. And he wrote, almost single-handedly, the first *Dictionary of the English Language*.

His biographer, James Boswell, said of Johnson, "I never knew any man who relished good eating more than he did. When at table he was totally absorbed in the business of the moment." He ate with a gusto that could disgust onlookers, but he was nevertheless much sought after as a dinner guest for his incomparable conversation. Of the food he was wolfing down, he said, "I, who dine at a variety of good tables, am a much better judge of cooking than a person who has a very good cook but dines mostly at home. His taste is gradually adapted to the taste of his cook, but by trying a wider range, I can more accurately judge."

MICROWAVE

On this day in 1999, Dr. Percy Spencer, an electronics expert, was inducted posthumously into the National Inventors Hall of Fame, whose previous honorees included the Wright brothers and Thomas Edison. His reputation rested mainly on his invention of the microwave oven, which grew out of research on radar after World War II. Standing near a magnetron, Spencer realized that chocolate candy in his pocket was melting. To confirm the magnetron's heating ability, he placed popcorn kernels nearby and watched them explode.

The first microwave oven in 1947 weighed 750 pounds, was as big as a refrigerator, and was used only in restaurants, but over the following decades it was made much smaller and more versatile.

19

M U S S E L S

This day in 1902 was the birthday of American tin tycoon William B. Leeds, a regular at Maxim's in Paris, who was so fond of the rich mussel soup served there that it was renamed for him: billi-bi.

Called "the poor man's oyster" because of their abundance and reasonable price, mussels have been cultivated for more than eight centuries and eaten for thousands of years before that. They are more popular in Europe than in the United States.

BILLI-BI

6 or so quarts unshelled
  mussels
12 tablespoons chopped onions
  and shallots
4 tablespoons chopped parsley,
  plus more for garnish
4 tablespoons butter

1 cup white wine
1 bay leaf
1 teaspoon dried thyme
Salt
Pepper
½ cup cream

Steam the mussels in a deep pot with all the other ingredients. Discard shells that don't open after about ten minutes of steaming. Remove the mussels from the opened shells and keep warm. Meanwhile, strain and reduce the broth, then thicken it with the cream. Add the mussels to the broth and heat just through. Serve topped with more parsley. Serves six to eight.

SEPTEMBER

E PLURIBUS UNUM

History says that Benjamin Franklin, John Adams, and Thomas Jefferson together proposed *E pluribus unum,* "out of many, one," as the official motto of the newly formed United States. It is thought by some, however, that Franklin, with characteristic whimsy, had borrowed the phrase from a traditional recipe for salad dressing.

SEPTEMBER

CHÂTEAU

"Château" in the name of a French wine usually means it is a Bordeaux. The image of a large estate with a great house or castle is sometimes correct, but there are important wine-growing estates without a fine house.

There are often grand names attached to mediocre wines and simple names for great ones. Among the latter are wines like Château Ausone, Château Latour, Château Lafite, and Château Pétrus.

A small number of Burgundies and other wines also have a "Château" in their names, such as Château de Beaucastel (Rhône), Château Fortia (Rhône), Château Fuisse (Burgundy), Château du Nozet (Loire), and Château Vignelaure (Provence), as well as Châteauneuf-du-Pape, the famous, huge denomination near Avignon covering more than eight thousand acres with many growers, the best of whom produce very fine wine—dark, powerful, and long-lived.

22

SEPTEMBER

HOW TO BECOME A REGULAR

It's pleasant being a regular at a restaurant—recognized at the door, greeted, and treated with obvious consideration. How do you qualify? Owners and waiters say there are ways of going about it:

- You don't have to show up every week. Three or four reasonably close visits are usually enough.
- Loyalty is more important than frequency. If you travel to other cities and go to the same restaurant at least once each time, even if it is only twice a year, you often make the grade.
- Spending money is infallible, either on the quantity and quality of what you order, how you tip, or, better, both.
- Attitude can be even more important than money. Customers who are polite and patient, especially when something goes wrong, are held in high regard.
- Owners, chefs, and waiters are devoted to clients who are enthusiasts, who love the food, the service, the ambience—the whole experience—and don't hesitate to say so.

23

SEPTEMBER

CHAMBERTIN

Picasso said a picture lives by its legend, and food and drink do also. Caviar has its aristocratic aura. So do certain wines. The English writer Hilaire Belloc wrote, regarding his youth, that he had forgotten the town, forgotten the girl, but the wine was Chambertin.

In *Out of Africa,* Isak Dinesen serves a bottle of very good wine to Emmanuelson, the disgraced maître d'hôtel who stops, unshaven and in worn-out shoes, at her farm and is given dinner, very likely his last, since he is intending to walk ninety miles through the Masai country along bad roads with savage animals all around. When Emmanuelson's glass is filled, he drinks from it and then holds it toward the light for a long while, finally saying, "Fameaux. Fameaux," and identifying the wine simply by its taste and body, a 1906 Chambertin. That moment fills Dinesen, who had had but slight regard for him, with respect.

Chambertin, however, is not what it once was. The vineyards that had produced extraordinary wine for more than one thousand years were consolidated in 1702 under a single owner named Jobert, who succeeded in giving the name its great cachet and became rich in doing so. The thirty-two acres that comprised his holding have gradually been divided among many owners, now more than two dozen, and not all the wine they produce is great or even good, though it is all Chambertin or Chambertin-Close de Bèze. Today, you need a wine guide or reliable merchant to lead you through the thicket.

24

SEPTEMBER

BROCCOLI

The origins of broccoli are obscure, although it was known to the ancient Romans—the Emperor Tiberius's son was said to be inordinately fond of it. It traveled from Italy to France with Catherine de' Medici in 1533, but then took many years more to make it across the Channel to England. It came to America about the time of the Revolution—John Randolph of Virginia mentions it in his 1775 treatise on gardening.

A member of the cabbage family and extremely rich in vitamins, broccoli should not be overcooked and allowed to become soggy. It is excellent with lemon butter or hollandaise sauce. Its literary fame seems to rest largely on a caption written by E. B. White for a *New Yorker* cartoon. A despairing mother is trying to make a stubborn child eat dinner.

"It's broccoli, dear," she explains.

"I say it's spinach, and I say the hell with it."

25

SEPTEMBER

ROMANÉE-CONTI

Sometime around 1960, I read Alexis Lichine's *The Wines of France* and soon after, inspired, I bought the first great bottle of my life in a wine shop that was a few doors from the St. Regis. The wine was Romanée-Conti—I'm not sure of the vintage, but I think 1956. I remember the price, however: sixteen dollars. Today a bottle can cost more than a thousand.

Romanée-Conti is probably the greatest of all Burgundies. It comes from a small vineyard of some four and a half acres that was already a jewel when Mme de Pompadour coveted it. It went up for auction after the Revolution and was last sold in 1868. It produces between three hundred and five hundred cases in an abundant year. So limited an output, combined with its legend, makes it expensive.

In comparison, a fine Bordeaux like Lynch-Bages will ship some 35,000 to 45,000 cases.

Burgundies—great ones—are known for their aromatic quality and are generally, unlike Bordeaux, not decanted, since their bouquet is diminished in the open air. I didn't know that when I drank the only bottles of Romanée-Conti I am likely to have in this life, but luckily both times it was served directly from the bottle. I trust it was, as red Burgundies should be, a few degrees cooler than a comparable Bordeaux. J.S.

C O L O N E L   J O H N S O N

On this day in 1820, Colonel Robert Gibbon Johnson, nearly fifty and dressed in a black suit, ruffled shirt, and three-cornered hat, mounted the steps of the Salem County courthouse in New Jersey and before a crowd of some two thousand fascinated spectators, proceeded to eat raw tomatoes. Though many believed this would turn out to be an act of public suicide, Johnson showed no ill effects, proving once and for all that tomatoes were not poisonous nor the cause of either stomach cancer or appendicitis.

He had started growing tomatoes on his own farm a dozen years earlier from seeds he brought back from South America, but had never been able to convince his neighbors that tomatoes were good for anything but decoration. New Jersey is now famous for the quality of its tomatoes, and even a hundred years ago there were more than two dozen canning plants in the area, including the Heinz ketchup plant in Salem City itself.

27

SEPTEMBER

RAISINS AND PRUNES

Sometimes a rose by any other name sells better. When a California drought in 1873 shriveled grapes on the vine, an imaginative retailer called them "Peruvian Delicacies" and created the raisin market. More recently, in an effort to improve the image of prunes, millions have been spent to rename them "dried plums."

28

SEPTEMBER

BUYING BEEF

Man has been eating red meat since about 10,000 B.C. and learned early on that it tasted better and was easier to chew and digest if it was cooked. Until recent times, dining on beef was a sign of wealth and position because of the relative scarcity of meat. Even with revolutionary mobs pursuing him, Louis XVI managed to carry a supply of short ribs in his coach to comfort him as he fled.

The Department of Agriculture ranks beef in five grades of quality, though only three are normally found in grocery stores: prime, choice, and good. Good actually refers to meat with less fat, while prime beef—the top classification—is expected to have the marbling of fat that adds to tenderness and flavor.

In addition, there are a few useful guidelines for buying beef:

- It should be a bright to medium red, though meat darkens the longer it's aged.
- It should be firm enough to the touch to spring back when pressed with a finger.
- For maximum flavor and tenderness, it should have white or pale yellow flecks or streaks of fat between the muscle fibers.
- Tenderness is determined by a number of factors, including the age and breed of the cow and what it has been fed. The famous Kobe beef of Japan, probably the most expensive in the world, is given rice, beans, and beer, along with a daily massage. The muscles that have gotten the least exercise during the life of the animal make the most tender cuts, especially those past the shoulder along the back called the rib and the loin that include rib roasts and steaks. The least tender are those containing not only muscle but connective tissue, such as those in the shoulder, the front leg, the haunch, and the underbelly. These provide ground meat, stew meat, briskets, and pot roasts.

Ways to make tougher cuts more tender include grinding the meat; cutting it against the grain, which makes the muscle fibers shorter and therefore easier to chew; or cooking it for a long time in liquid. Dry methods of cooking—roasting, grilling, and frying—are best for more tender cuts. It's not true that meat will retain more juiciness if it's seared or browned as the first step in cooking.

Even those limiting their consumption of red meat admit to its pleasures. As the great chef Carême said, "Beef is the soul of cooking."

29

SEPTEMBER

WORCESTERSHIRE

Worcestershire sauce was already such a standard at meals by 1938 that it was on the dining table in Munich on this day when Adolf Hitler forced Mussolini, Chamberlain, and French premier Daladier to accept disastrous terms. By then, its formula was one hundred years old, created for an English lord who missed the sauce he'd enjoyed as a governor in Bengal, India.

Back home in England, he asked his local pharmacists, John Lea and William Perrins, to try to reproduce the recipe that included anchovies, tamarinds, chilis, and molasses, all marinated in vinegar. The result was so unpalatable that they put it in the basement and forgot it. When they rediscovered it a couple of years later, it had mellowed so successfully that they started to bottle and sell it, claiming, among other things, that it promoted the growth of beautiful hair. The recipe and the aging process have never been changed.

30
SEPTEMBER

AU GRAND COUVERT

You can eat alone, which is a little depressing; in private with others; publicly in a restaurant; or *au grand couvert* as the kings of France from Louis XIV to XVI did, alone but in full view of the court, which stood watching the king eat. Marie Antoinette, married to Louis XVI, was not fond of the ceremony, appearing only once a week and pretending to eat.

MARGARINE

In 1869, a Frenchman, Hippolyte Mège-Mouriés, searching for a cheap substitute for butter, mixed suet, skimmed milk, and a strip of udder together and produced the first margarine, an immediate success, though much improved since in color, texture, and taste. He was given a prize by Napoleon III.

OCTOBER

1

OCTOBER

RULES FOR DINING

Brillat-Savarin gave as the four indispensables for a dinner:

- Food that was at least passable
- Good wine
- Agreeable company
- Enough time

Among the elements that he felt were desirable, though not essential:

- A maximum of twelve guests
- The room cool (60–68 degrees F), amply lit, and the table linen fresh
- The evening lasting until at least eleven, but not beyond midnight

2

OCTOBER

STILTON

The place of Pushkin in Russian literature was once explained in a lecture in England at Cambridge by a noted scholar, Dimitri Mirsky, with unforgettable brevity. As Shakespeare was to England, as Dante was to Italy, as Goethe was to Germany, he said, so, to Russia, was Pushkin. Any questions?

Something similar might be said about cheeses, ending with, so, to England, is Stilton.

It was in the early 1700s from a coach house, the Bell Inn, on the Great North Road, running from London up the eastern part of England, that the fame of a local cheese began to spread. Though it was not made there, it took the name of the nearest village, Stilton. Naturally blue-veined, creamy yet firm enough to cut and crumble slightly, it is magnificent with red wine or port and with fruit. It is the only English cheese that is legally defined. It must be made from milk coming from English cows in a specific area in the district of Melton Mowbray, a region where iron deposits lie beneath the meadows and may be a factor in Stilton's natural blueing. Stiltons are cylindrical in shape, about ten inches high and eight or nine inches in diameter, weighing about fifteen pounds.

Once done in farmhouses, production has become entirely commercial, with variation in quality, usually the result of the length of aging, which is six months at the minimum and may be as long as eighteen months. The cheese is tested by having a plug of it removed to see if it is ready. Stilton is made from pasteurized milk, though like other cheeses, it was probably better before this practice, and has a self-formed, rough, brown crust that may, if desired, be eaten.

If you buy a whole Stilton, the best way to cut it is in horizontal rounds that can be dug into, the top piece then placed back onto the cheese afterward to keep it moist. When bought in smaller quantities, Stilton should not be allowed to dry out.

3

COFFEEHOUSES

In London, coffeehouses sprang up everywhere with the arrival of the new beverage—coffee—from the Continent in 1652. An advertisement proclaimed: "[It] closes the Orifice of the Stomack, fortifies the heat within, helpeth Digestion, quickeneth the Spirits, maketh the heart lightsome, is good against Eye-sores, Cough, or Colds, Rhumes, Consumptions, Head-ach, Dropsie, Gout, Scurvy, King's Evil and many others."

Gathering places for relaxation and the exchange of information in an age when mail was slow and newspapers in their infancy, London coffeehouses became the centers of social life. For the price of admission—usually a penny—you got not only your first cup, but news of the day carried in by runners distributing gazettes or simply spreading the most recent gossip.

The precursors of a later institution, the English club, they became the place where one was known to be found at certain times of the day or evening. A specialized clientele frequented each place— businessmen in some, politicians or intellectuals in others. For thirty years, John Dryden, whose talk of writing attracted the likes of Pepys and Pope, was to be found at Will's Coffee-House. Conviviality was such that even during the plague the houses were filled, despite the risk of contagion, though clients took the precaution of asking about the health of the others at the table.

Coffeehouses were so popular that in 1675, Charles II issued a proclamation for their suppression, describing them as places of license and libel, but thinking in particular of those frequented by his political rivals. There was such an outcry of protest that the king didn't bother to enforce the edict.

Not only coffee but chocolate drinks and tea were sold, though they were more expensive—in the case of tea, much more expensive. Most customers drank coffee.

Proprietors placed a cup by a sign that read "To Insure Prompt Service," and those able to afford it tossed in a coin. It became "tips."

OCTOBER

EGYPTIAN CUISINE

In Egypt, fish now comes primarily from the Red Sea and Mediterranean instead of the Nile, where it was once so abundant that it was considered the food of the poor. More elaborately prepared, it also appeared on the tables of the rich. It was in Egypt that the technique was developed to force-feed geese, which were then roasted on a spit. Goose meat continues to be a specialty, along with pigeon, cooked in every way imaginable. Lamb and mutton entered the cuisine by way of the Middle East, particularly Turkey. And for drink—past and present—the choice has always been light beer.

On his tour of the Hebrides with James Boswell in 1773, Samuel Johnson observed that a cucumber "should be well-sliced, and dressed with pepper and vinegar, and then thrown out, as good for nothing."

In this instance, the great man was wrong. One of the oldest cultivated vegetables, the cucumber is excellent in salad and makes a fine decoration, a delicious soup, and in England, at tea, a thin and elegant sandwich. Being ninety-six percent water, it has virtually no calories but nevertheless is nourishing, with minerals and vitamins A and C.

A cucumber salad that can be made in twenty minutes, several hours in advance:

CUCUMBER SALAD

1 cucumber, unpeeled and diced	*Red wine vinegar*
1 red onion, diced	*Salt to taste*
1 large tomato, diced	*Pepper to taste*
Extra virgin olive oil	

Combine equal amounts of cucumbers, red onions, and tomatoes. Make a dressing with the vinegar and oil in a proportion of 1:1 or 1:2, adding salt and freshly ground pepper to taste. Serve with some good bread on the side. Serves about five.

6

OCTOBER

GLEANING

Probably the most famous gleaner is Ruth, in the book named for her in the Old Testament. A young widow, she leaves her homeland to care for her mother-in-law, Naomi, also a widow. To make ends meet, Ruth goes to the barley field of a neighbor named Boaz and asks for permission to collect the grain left on the ground after the reapers have finished. With that grain, she feeds herself and Naomi, and eventually Ruth marries Boaz.

Historically, gleaning was a way of helping the poor. A certain portion of the harvest was deliberately left in the field to be gathered by those who needed it. Methods of harvesting are more efficient now, but food is still left in fields and rots if no one collects it, nourishing the soil, perhaps, but not people. Food is wasted in the United States to the tune of something close to 100 billion pounds a year, including what's spoiled in supermarkets or unfinished in restaurants. That comes to about 130 pounds per person. It ends up in landfills, and not even cleaning your plate, as children were once instructed, can diminish that loss very much.

There are volunteer groups around the country who still go into fields to glean on behalf of the poor. In Maine recently, schoolchildren collected fifty tons of potatoes following the harvest. Eastern Long Island is potato country, too. Though some fields have fallen prey to developers, there are still many filled with the low, dark green, bushlike plants. In the fall, heaped trucks take curves a little too fast, causing potatoes to fall off and bounce to the side of the road. We sometimes stop the car, pick up the potatoes, and cook them that night, before the gashes and bruises make them inedible. It is not that, like Ruth, we can't afford them. It's just a way of allowing them to realize their true destiny.

7

OCTOBER

BEET SOUP

Borscht—also known as borshch or bortsch or borsch—is the best-known Russian soup and, along with cabbage soup, the most popular. There are many recipes for borscht: Russian, Ukranian, and Polish, simple and elaborate. Borscht for the czar, as made by Carême, had chicken, veal, duck, sausage, filet of beef, eggs, bacon, carrots, celery, horseradish, and other ingredients. Irma Rombauer's version has only carrots, onions, cabbage, and beets, plus some seasoning.

"Everything I do, I do on the principle of Russian borscht," the poet Yevtushenko said. "You can throw everything into it—beets, carrots, cabbage, onions. . . . What's important is the result, the taste of the borscht."

8

OCTOBER

FIRSTS IN FRANCE

1976. First night together in France. We were in Beaune, the town that is the wine capital of Burgundy. The hotel restaurant had a well-deserved Michelin star. A star in this part of France is usually to be relied on. We had a very good meal; a *fine,* her first, in the bar; and in every way aware of our good fortune, went up to the comfort of our room.

In the morning, trucks were going by. We were hungry enough for breakfast, brought on a tray, and I read the *Paris Trib* in the bath.

The journey had begun.   J.S.

The ecrevisses I ordered, not knowing what they were, arrived looking like a kind of giant shrimp still in their shells. To dismantle them seemed impossible, so, fortified with the Beaune wine, I ate them heads and all. The waiters were inscrutable, the neighboring diners impressed. In the bar afterward, I held the kind of glass I'd seen only in the movies and sipped Cognac with soda, no more intoxicating than the entire night—hotel, man, France.   K.S.

The truffle is the fruiting body of a fungus that grows underground on the roots of trees, usually oaks. In the past and often still, it is considered an aphrodisiac. Some types are found in North America, North Africa, and Spain, but the black truffle found in France, and specifically in Perigord, along with the white truffle of Alba, in Italy, stand apart from all the others. When consumed fresh, they are a great delicacy, either enhancing other foods or by themselves. Truffled turkeys could, before the French Revolution, be found only on the tables of the highest nobility or the best-paid whores.

Truffles are, in a sense, accidental. Why and where they are formed is a mystery. The ancients believed that lightning was a necessary factor in their creation. As with other old notions, there may be an element of truth in this, as it has been observed that certain shocks to the soil in which truffles have previously formed seem to restore them—nearby road building or even the pounding of basketball played on that ground.

It is by their distinct, pungent aroma that truffles are detected underground by dogs or pigs. The latter come by this skill naturally but pose a problem in the separation of the pig from the unearthed truffle.

Truffles begin to grow in the spring and early summer. Even after they reach full size, some time must pass before they are completely mature, so it is in the late fall and early winter that they are at their best. Canned truffles are not to be compared with the fresh ones, and genuine black or white truffles are hard to find in the United States, in addition to being, as everywhere, expensive, several thousand dollars a pound. The white are the more expensive. Chinese truffles, judged inferior, are cheaper.

In the house of one of his mistresses, the actress Mlle George, Dumas wrote that no mercy was shown to the truffle; "it was compelled to yield every sensation it was capable of giving." Sliced into paper-thin leaves by Mlle George's beautiful hands, sprinkled with some pepper and a touch of cayenne, impregnated with some olive oil, they were included in a salad.

10

OCTOBER

BREAKING THE FAST

To eat well in England, you should have breakfast three times a day.
—W. SOMERSET MAUGHAM

Breakfast, breaking the fast since dinner the previous night, is a reflection of the country in which you eat it. A traditional English breakfast, with enough protein to keep you going until teatime, can include ham and eggs, oatmeal, toast, and kippers, which are not for the faint of heart at that time of day. In Japan, breakfast includes rice, miso soup, pickled vegetables, fish, tea, and sometimes a raw egg. For Germans, it is cold cuts, cheese, yogurt, and heavy, dark breads. The French, on the other hand, subsist on a croissant and coffee, and the

Italians, going a step further, have what seems to be a dinner roll in place of the rich, buttery croissant.

11

OCTOBER

HAM

There are two kinds of ham, raw and cooked. Raw really means preserved, treated with salt or brine, and then, in many cases, smoked.

Prosciutto is an example of raw ham, the most famous being *prosciutto di Parma,* for which the pigs are fed on whey left over from the making of cheese. The ham—from the rear leg—is laid on trays of rock or sea salt and turned weekly for at least a month, then dried in the upland air for three to six months or even longer. It is served in paper-thin slices, mild and velvety.

Among other notable raw hams are *jambon d'Ardennes* from Belgium, Westphalia ham, and *jambon de Bayonne,* smoky and dark, from France.

Kentucky ham is renowned, as is Virginia. Smithfield ham is the cream, so to speak, of Virginia hams—lean, smoked over hickory and applewood, and aged for at least a year. It should always be cooked, usually baked after soaking and simmering first.

A little ham goes a long way, and shreds of it are enough to give flavor to lentils, for example, or minestrone or bean soup.

There was a time when trichinosis—a sometimes fatal parasitic disease caused by roundworm in poorly cooked or raw meat, particu larly pork—was widespread. At 140 degrees F the meat becomes safe, though the USDA inspection stamp on meat virtually ensures safety.

12

OCTOBER

CURNONSKY

In 1872, Maurice Edmond Sailland, a food writer who was to become known as Curnonsky, the near-legendary Prince of Gastronomy, was born this day in Angers, France.

He assumed his pen name in 1890 after the publication of an open letter he had written to Emile Zola that he signed with the pseudonym Curnonsky, and that was followed soon afterward by a money order from the paper's editor, along with a request for more articles. For more than two decades he was on the staff of newspapers. In the 1920s, he turned to writing about food and gastronomy.

A large man, popular and bear-like, he was a lover of the good life and in 1927 was chosen as Prince of Gastronomy in a publicized election sponsored by the newspaper *Paris-Soir*. From then on he was addressed as Prince and was prominent at every dinner and banquet of distinction. His image, with a big white napkin tied beneath his chins, was familiar in every restaurant and kitchen, and his name became a household word.

Though he loved public attention, he lived simply and never entertained, describing himself humbly as a poor man of letters. His knowledge of food was great and his passion for it genuine. He could eat huge quantities but not of any dish he considered "just a bit too far from perfection." He was once described as "charming during the hors d'oeuvres, suave during the fish course, in high spirits during the main course, and a little bawdy after the meal."

The author of more than seventy books, many of them with collaborators, and including twenty-four volumes of *La France gastronomique,* in addition to an atlas and an anthology of French gastronomy, he lived to the age of eighty-four and died in an accidental fall from the window of his Paris apartment in 1956.

13

OCTOBER

POTATOES

The ordinary potato, a member of the nightshade family along with the tomato and eggplant, was first brought to Europe in the mid-16th century by the Spanish explorers of South America. It had been cultivated in the Andes of what is now Peru for at least two thousand years. At first potatoes were regarded with suspicion and even thought to be poisonous, but by the time Shakespeare mentioned them in *The Merry Wives of Windsor* between 1597 and 1601, they were in better repute.

Captain Cook took the potato to Australia in 1770, but its popularity oddly skipped over India and the Orient. Since potatoes grew so abundantly, with an acre of land producing up to five or six hundred bushels, and were seeded simply by cutting them into small pieces, each containing one or more eyes, the monarchs of Europe recognized their usefulness. In the late 18th century, Frederick the Great tried to popularize them in Germany by eating potatoes publicly himself, and Louis XVI and his queen, Marie Antoinette, together endorsed them, although Diderot, in his famous *Encyclopédie,* called the potato tasteless no matter how prepared, and Brillat-Savarin said simply, "None for me." In Ireland, however, where they were either first introduced by Sir Walter Raleigh or had washed ashore amid the wreckage of the Spanish Armada in 1565, they had become the mainstay of the diet, destroying, it is said, the art of cooking there.

Potatoes are rich in potassium, iron, and vitamin C. The skin can be eaten but is not nutritious, and most of what is valuable is found in a thin layer beneath it, often pared away if the potato is peeled. Potatoes can be stored for two or three weeks if kept in a cool, dry place and not refrigerated. The cold converts the starch in them to sugar and makes them too sweet, though the process can be reversed by letting potatoes stand for several days at room temperature. Sunlight can turn the skin green, making the area beneath bitter or even toxic.

The floury potatoes—russets and Idahos—bake, mash, and fry well. Red potatoes boil better but don't mash well afterward. None of these freeze well except French fries and mashed or stuffed potatoes. If frozen raw, they become soft. If cooked, as in a stew or soup, they turn mushy and grainy when thawed.

Baked potatoes can be rubbed with a little vegetable oil before being placed directly on the oven rack. They should never be wrapped in foil, which holds in the moisture and essentially steams the potato, resulting in a wrinkled skin and soggy interior.

There are few things that taste better than *rösti,* as the Swiss cook them, or a potato gratin. Just as good are potato pancakes and potato salad. When Waverly Root brought his French wife to the United States for the first time, and they toured eastern cities for a month, he asked her which was the American food she liked best. The Idaho baked potato, she said. According to Root, this potato is unique and doesn't grow in any other place in America. With melted butter and some salt, it almost possesses grandeur.

14

OCTOBER

BERLIN DINING

2002, Berlin. Rainy night, brightly lit restaurant on a corner of the Kurfurstendamm. White tablecloths, a high ceiling, walls filled with pictures, and newspapers in a rack near the bar. In the mirror along the banquettes, every face is visible. The waiter is tall, in white shirt-sleeves and a vest.

We had steak with Kaiserhof sauce—the latter a closely guarded secret—ravioli with wonderfully hot spinach, salad, Bordeaux wine, and bread. We were talking about the city's great expanse, where we'd been that day, places that by contrast made this one seem even warmer and more serene: the bleak square across the street from Humboldt University where Goebbels ordered books heaped and burned in 1933, and later in the afternoon, the chilling remains of Plotzensee Prison, now a memorial, where thousands of political enemies of the Third Reich, in particular Czechs and members of the German Resistance movement, were executed.

The busboy cleared the table. "Did you enjoy your dinner?" he asked. Immensely. The hotel, with its comforts, was just a few long blocks away.

15

OCTOBER

LE PAVILLON

1941. The restaurant that was to become the most exalted in the country for three decades, Le Pavillon, opened this day on 55th Street in New York across from the St. Regis Hotel in a location felt to be unlucky, since two restaurants had previously failed there. The perfectionist owner and maître d', Henri Soulé, had first come to the United States to work at the French Pavilion restaurant at the 1939 World's Fair—a bottle of 1929 Château Margaux was on the wine list at four dollars and fifty cents at the time.

Short, "inclined to stoutness," diplomatic, and unflappable, Soulé was utterly dedicated to his work. He rarely went to the theater or a movie and his hobby, he said, was paying bills. Although the nation found itself at war only seven weeks later and there were many problems, the restaurant was a success from the start.

OCTOBER

MARIE ANTOINETTE

Wheeled through the streets of Paris in an open cart, Marie Antoinette, widow of Louis XVI, who had been executed nine months earlier, went to the guillotine on this day in 1793 after having eaten a little bouillon in her prison cell at the urging of her maid. Though hated by the French for her Austrian background and frivolous ways, she nevertheless had never uttered the words blamed for helping to incite the French Revolution when told the starving masses had no bread: "Let them eat cake."

- *Bouillon* is French for "stock": liquid cooked with some combination of meat, fish, poultry, bones, and seasonings, and then strained.
- Broth is the liquid before being strained.
- *Consommé* is a *bouillon* from which all the smallest remaining particles have been removed by clarifying it.

CRAIG CLAIBORNE

We wanted to invite Craig Claiborne, to whose house in East Hampton we'd been a number of times, both for black-tie New Year's Eve dinners and working lunches, at which he and his longtime collaborator, Pierre Franey, tried out various recipes and ways of cooking—with Franey doing the actual work and Claiborne in half-glasses, standing at the typewriter taking down details.

Claiborne was the celebrated *New York Times* food critic and cookbook writer. He knew the great chefs—some of them cooked at his parties on New Year's Eve—and had eaten at every great restaurant. What and how to feed him?

We decided on lunch instead of dinner, feeling it would be judged less seriously. The matter of the other guests was easily settled: Random House editor Joe Fox; his wife, Anne Isaak; and their houseguests, British publisher Christopher MacLehose and his girlfriend, Susanna Porter, an editor.

We cooked the entire menu in a trial run: Brussels-sprout-and-carrot soup, flounder *à l'Anglaise*—broiled with butter and a simple dusting of bread crumbs—a potato gratin, and a lemon tart for dessert.

At the table we pretended not to notice the reaction to the soup. "Delicious," Craig announced. We felt we were winning. There were requests for seconds on the gratin. Every shred of flounder vanished, as well as the entire lemon tart. Over dessert, Craig, his face cherubic, began to tell a few dirty jokes. Then, among a literary group who ought to know every word in the dictionary, he challenged us to come up with the four words in English that have three sets of double letters, proper names like Mississippi or Tennessee not included.

"Committee," someone finally said after a minute or two.

"That's one."

"Possessiveness," another person said.

"Yes." He was beaming at our difficulty.

At last someone managed to come up with "addressee."

"You're sure there are four?"

"Absolutely."

No one could think of the last one.

It was after three. Craig thanked us effusively. He'd had a marvelous time, he said. It was so nice to be asked to someone's house. People tended to be intimidated and not invite him. What they didn't realize, he said, was that his real pleasure was in the company.

We drifted toward the kitchen door, which, as always seems to happen, was the real entrance, opening into the center of the house. We felt a sense of accomplishment and, it must be said, a certain relief as we walked Craig to his car. It hadn't been comparable to one of his own royal entertainments, but we'd risen to the occasion.

Fox suddenly emerged from the house and came running toward us. "Bookkeeping!" he cried, his face filled with triumph.

We adapted the Brussels sprout soup from Mireille Johnston's *The Cuisine of the Rose,* and in her book it is called *soupe de Nevers,* named for the city:

SOUPE DE NEVERS

36 Brussels sprouts, trimmed
and halved

4 carrots, peeled and sliced
into rounds

3 tablespoons butter

1 tablespoon vegetable oil

8 cups hot chicken broth

Salt (not needed if using
bouillon cubes for the
chicken broth)

Freshly ground black pepper

3 tablespoons minced chives or
parsley

Sauté the vegetables for five minutes in the butter and oil. Place in a large saucepan with the broth and bring to a boil. Cook for fifteen minutes. Add salt and pepper to taste, and garnish with the parsley or chives. Serves eight.

The potato dish, called *gratin dauphinoise Madame Cartet,* is one of many good ones in Patricia Wells's *Bistro Cooking:*

GRATIN DAUPHINOISE MADAME CARTET

1 garlic clove

2 pounds baking potatoes (like russets), peeled and thinly sliced

1 cup freshly grated French or Swiss Gruyère
(or Emmenthaler or the like)

1 cup heavy cream or crème fraîche

Rub a shallow porcelain baking dish with the garlic, cut in half. Preheat the oven to 350 degrees F. Layer half the potatoes. Cover with half the cheese and half the cream. Add salt. Repeat with a second layer. Bake, uncovered, until the gratin is crisp and golden on top (fifty to sixty minutes). Add pepper to the top, if desired. Serves four to six.

18

OCTOBER

LIEBLING

A. J. Liebling, journalist and *New Yorker* writer, was born on this day in 1904. His interest in food was established early, in the days of 1926–27 when he was a student in Paris at the Sorbonne, or at least enrolled there, since he spent most of his time in cafés, inexpensive but worthy restaurants, and on the streets. All of it is vividly brought to life in his memoir, *Between Meals.*

He wrote prodigiously in a style admired for its grace, generosity, and erudition. He was fond of saying that he could write faster than anyone who could write better and better than anyone who could write faster. His favorite subjects were boxing, France, food, and the press, and his favorite people were those who lived precariously or bravely. Among the last things he wrote was a series of articles based on a final, sentimental journey to France, which he had visited many times. He wanted to call it *Recollections of a Gourmet in France,* but his editor at *The New Yorker* objected that no one would ever call Liebling, whose appetite was gargantuan, a gourmet, so the title was changed to *Memoirs of a Feeder in France.*

"The primary requisite for writing well about food," he wrote elsewhere, "is a good appetite. Without this, it is impossible to accumulate, within the allotted span, enough experience of eating to have anything worth setting down."

His more than fifteen books are remarkable for their enduring freshness. He died in 1963, gouty, bald, overweight, a victim of his habits. His last words were uttered in an ambulance, unintelligible, but in French.

19
OCTOBER

JONATHAN SWIFT

Jonathan Swift died on this day in 1745, perhaps the greatest satirist in the English language. His epitaph, which he wrote himself, reflects his view of the world and reads, in part, "The body of Jonathan Swift . . . is buried here, where fierce indignation can no more lacerate his heart."

His father had died before his birth in 1667, and his mother soon abandoned him. Raised by an uncle, he was able to read by the time he was three years old. He became a brilliant writer; his best-known work was *Gulliver's Travels,* later transposed into a children's story. His savage *A Modest Proposal* puts forth a solution to the problem of hunger in Ireland by the sale of the babies of the poor to the rich as food, and is as devastating as on the day it first appeared in 1729.

In *Directions to Servants* he addressed in a similar vein how servants should properly conduct themselves:

"Whoever comes to visit your master or lady when they are abroad," he instructed, "never burden your memory with the person's name, for indeed you have too many other things to remember. Besides, it is a porter's business, and your master's fault he does not keep one; and who can remember names?"

CATHERINE DE' MEDICI

1533. Catherine de' Medici, a fourteen-year-old princess, appeared at the court of France to marry the future Henry II. She arrived with an escort of cooks, along with bags of white haricot beans, broccoli, and artichokes to be planted in her new country. But she brought far more than vegetables—she brought with her the Italian Renaissance.

Women at the time did not dine with the king or great lords, since the act of chewing was thought to spoil their beauty. Instead, they consumed broths in the privacy of their own rooms. But Catherine and her ladies in waiting were accustomed to sharing the table with men and added their presence to the pleasures of the table. Wife of a king and mother of three kings, she was also a glutton. She loved huge banquets at which she could feast on the many dishes of fowl that were then so popular: heron, swan, stork, guinea hen, and even crow. A woman who knew what she liked, she shocked her more respectable subjects by the number of artichokes—considered an aphrodisiac—she consumed.

BABA AU RHUM

On this day in 1677, Stanislas Leszczyński, the nobleman who would twice sit on the throne of Poland and twice be exiled to France, was born in Lwów. He was well liked in France, where he governed Lorraine; beautified its capital, Nancy; and corresponded with intellectuals; and where his daughter, Marie, became the wife of Louis XV and queen of France. He is credited with the idea of improving a small sugar cake by steeping it, still warm, in rum after baking, thus creating baba au rhum. The name, it is said, comes from that of the character he loved best in The Thousand and One Nights, Ali Baba.

21

OCTOBER

APPLE SALES

You cannot sell a blemished apple in the supermarket, but you can sell a tasteless one, provided it is shiny, smooth, even, uniform, and bright.

— ELSPETH HUXLEY

The best-selling apple in the United States is the Delicious, first grown in Iowa in the 1870s, but its taste has deteriorated over the years, and the yellow variety is even worse. The Delicious apple, A. J. Liebling wrote, is "a triumph . . . because it doesn't taste like an apple," and "the Golden Delicious . . . doesn't taste like anything."

CALIFORNIA WINE

Most of the wine consumed in the United States is produced in California. There are fine wineries in the north, around San Francisco, and a huge grape-growing belt in the center of the state. California wines tend to have a high alcoholic content—fifteen percent is not unusual. There is an immense variety, and the choice can be bewildering.

The great California red is Cabernet Sauvignon, along with Merlot and Zinfandel. The best white is Chardonnay. Inexpensive table wine often has a generic name such as Burgundy or Chablis. The better wines usually carry the name of the predominant grape.

The top wines—about thirty or forty producers of red and an equal number of white—are world-class. The price will usually identify this, with names like Mondavi, Caymus, Stags' Leap, and Beringer. There are also a number of expensive proprietary blends that do not give the name of the dominant grape and carry somewhat grand names with no particular meaning: Opus, Dominus, Trilogy, and so forth.

In many cases, bottles will have no vintage year. The long tradition in California has been to make a wine of consistent, reliable quality, often by blending older and newer wine. If there is a vintage, it means that all of the wine must be from that year, and it should be remembered that vintage years in California have no relationship to those in Europe.

People who love wine love life, and in the finest wine areas—Napa and Sonoma, for example—as in comparable places in Europe, there are exceptional restaurants and small places to stay.

I drink when I have occasion, and sometimes when I have no occasion.
—MIGUEL DE CERVANTES

23

OCTOBER

ALICE WATERS ENTERTAINS

Too often when giving a dinner, you are so busy during the evening that you end up feeling you've missed your own party. Alice Waters, of Chez Panisse in Berkeley, understands the temptation of trying to do too much. "At the restaurant, I always cook with a whole group of cooks around me, so even though I trim down the menu for dinner at home, I'm overly ambitious. I always think, the first course will be pasta, and then there will be lamb, and it never works."

She has settled on these rules:

- I have guests come into the kitchen for stand-up hors d'ouvres. I just keep putting things out, almost in the form of tapas.
- The first course is always cold.
- There's only one hot dish that has to be prepared just before the meal. When we go to the table, I bring the hot dish with me. If it is meat or poultry, I always want it to rest for ten minutes between cooking and serving. And since your sense of taste is diminished by really hot food, it is sometimes an advantage for it to cool even longer.
- I love salad, so I often have one afterward that I dress just at the end, served with some cheese.
- I choose fruit or something cold for dessert, like sherbet, but nothing that has to be cooked during the meal.

24

OCTOBER

SOMMELIER

A sommelier, or restaurant wine steward, is often the one who displays the chosen bottle at the table to verify the name and the vintage, opens it, and pours a sample. Frequently, he has created the wine list, choosing wines for variety in type and price range. He's also usually qualified to recommend wines to complement the food.

The name comes from the old French *bête de somme,* or "beast of burden," with a sommelier as its caretaker. The connection with transporting things evolved, until by the early 14th century, it had come to mean the person in charge of the royal baggage during the king's travel. Over the next three hundred years, the sommelier graduated to carrying the wine to royal meals, one of seven officials responsible for the king's table, including the *pannetere,* who served the bread, and the *echansonniere,* who poured both water and wine from silver ewers.

OCTOBER

THREE PLACES FOR LUNCH

There are days, perhaps many, when you long to be somewhere else, and days when you are. It is only a kind of daydreaming, but if you could choose three places in the world where you would like to be for lunch today, where would they be?

First of all, Paris. The Grand Colbert, a brasserie just north of the Palais-Royal on rue Vivienne. Talk, intelligent faces, decent food, a tone of sophistication, and the unmistakable aroma of French cigarettes. You feel you are almost part of it.

Second, a restaurant in a hard-to-reach village, Erice, high above the sea in northwest Sicily. Erice was once the most famous of Mediterranean shrines to the goddess of love, in both a religious and carnal sense, though all that is gone now. From the Via Chiaramonte down a narrow alley, through a private garden, up some steps to a small patio with an awning and a number of tables—this is Ulisse. Level with the treetops, you look out over the tiled roofs of the town.

Tomato and onion salad, *spaghetti al funghi,* half a bottle of wine, a very small check. The sun is pouring down, beating on the awning. As he clears the table, the waiter is singing to himself.

The third would be in New York and, among countless choices, the front room of the Union Square Café on West 16th Street. You are drawn to restaurants above all for their ambience and also for the memories of previous visits. There are other famous restaurants in Manhattan and perhaps, though this is not certain, more glamorous ones, but there are no restaurants that are finer. Food, service, knowledgeable people, publishers, perhaps even someone you know.   J.S.

26

OCTOBER

THREE PLACES FOR LUNCH

After half an hour's ride on a small ferry over choppy November seas from Dinard on the Normandy coast of France, coming to Saint-Malo. Set into the old rampart enclosing the town is À la Duchesse Anne; the apricot and yellow mosaic walls of the dining room are a refuge from the bluster outside. You feel well cared for: the impeccable service and food, deserving of its Michelin star, and the sense of having reached shore.

Twenty-five kilometers west of Florence, near Carmignano, is Da Delfina. The dining room is brown and rustic; the real pleasure is on a broad terrace where lunch is served in the summer and early fall. It overlooks a forested valley, and in the distance stands what is perhaps—or if it is not, it should be—a hunting villa of the Medicis. The impulse is to linger until the October sun is descending toward the treetops.

A few minutes walk from the hotel—the Hilltop—in the university section of Tokyo, down what is almost an alley to a place you would never find if they hadn't told you. I don't remember its name—a soba restaurant, an animated, harmonious room filled mainly with men in business suits. Not another western face to be seen. The buckwheat noodles, freshly made in full view in the kitchen, are served with various sauces in lacquer boxes that are soon piled in front of you. Inexpensive and delicious, and the reason you travel—to enter another world.   K.S.

27

OCTOBER

BALSAMIC VINEGAR

Balsamic vinegar, deep brown in color and aromatic, is a product of Modena, a city also renowned for *zampone,* a sausage that earned the heartfelt praise of Garibaldi.

The genuine vinegar, as made in country houses in the region, can take thirty or forty years or even generations to produce, being moved with exceeding slowness through a series of wooden casks— oak, chestnut, and juniper—absorbing their flavors as well as those of the preceding vinegar. There is evaporation during the hot summers and maturing in the cold, damp winters. The liquid is so prized that in centuries past, small quantities have figured in wills and bequests.

The unique flavor, sweet and tart, is powerful, and only a few drops added to a regular vinegar-and-oil salad dressing, a pasta sauce, or the sauce of cooked meat or chicken will enhance it. Genuine balsamic vinegar is hard to find. The commercial variety is only okay. "Balsamic" means "health-giving." In earlier times the vinegar was used medicinally, and it still can serve as a digestif.

28

OCTOBER

ESCOFFIER

Auguste Escoffier is considered by many to be the greatest chef in the history of cooking. Born on this day in 1846, he may hold the record for the longest active career in the field. He went to work at age thirteen in his uncle's restaurant in Nice. Six years later, he was a chef in his own right in Paris, and by the time he was in his early forties, he was in charge of the kitchen at the world-famous Savoy Hotel in London.

He followed the lead of Prosper Montagne, another great chef at the time, who believed that the quality of restaurant food was suffering at the expense of elaborate presentation. Escoffier became the standard-bearer in favor of simplifying menus, reducing elaborate decoration of food, speeding up service so food would arrive hot at the table, and organizing cooking teams to prepare dishes with more expertise and efficiency.

He created many recipes himself, and according to the fashion of the times, a number were named for celebrated figures in the arts, including Sarah Bernhardt and Verdi. His *tournedos Rossini,* hearts of beef garnished with foie gras and truffles, was in honor of the composer, but the most famous were peach Melba and Melba toast, named for Australian soprano Nellie Melba. He was sometimes even inspired by current events; he created *chaud-froid Jeanette,* a stuffed breast of chicken, served cold, in honor of a ship that had been trapped in polar ice for two years before it was crushed and sank. In its debut appearance, Escoffier's recipe was displayed on top of a ship carved of ice.

In 1898, he left London for Paris to become the first chef of the Ritz Hotel, founded by himself and Cesar Ritz with money from Richard d'Oyly Carte, theater owner and producer of Gilbert and Sullivan's operettas. Known by this time as the king of chefs and chef of kings, Escoffier was awarded the French Legion of Honor in 1920, a year before his retirement after sixty-two years in the kitchen. During his remaining fifteen years he wrote *Ma cuisine* and *Le livre des Menus* and collaborated on *Le guide culinaire,* the three books that essentially codified French cuisine and included thousands of recipes and menus.

29

OCTOBER

FOIE GRAS

Although geese have had food crammed down their throats for centuries, since Roman and even ancient Egyptian times, foie gras, the liver of a force-fed goose or duck, is chiefly associated with France and is one of the glories of French cuisine. The Romans used figs to fatten the geese. The French use corn, and the process—you are better off not knowing the details—involves a funnel and is called *gavage*.

Foie gras makes its main appearance in the winter, and Christmas and New Year's are traditionally the great times to enjoy it. The best quality has a buttery consistency and a marvelous rich, silky taste. It is pale, almost ivory in color, tending a bit toward pink. Despite its astronomic number of calories, good foie gras should not exude any fat. Duck liver tends to be slightly darker, with a more pronounced flavor.

In France, the finest foie gras is served *cru,* or raw. It cannot, however, be legally imported like this into the United States. Lightly and gently cooked, it is called *mi-cuit* or *naturel* or *frais,* and this state is probably preferable for a first experience.

Fresh *mi-cuit* can sometimes be found in the United States, but is more widely distributed in cans or jars. Canning deprives it of little in the way of taste, but careful reading of the label is important. Foie gras *entire* means an entire (or nearly) liver. *En conserve* requires no refrigeration and can be stored for years, even improving with age to a certain point, like good wine or sardines. It should be kept in a cool, dark place and turned occasionally. Cans labeled *bloc* are not as desirable, containing pieces of foie gras—usually only fifty percent of the contents—pressed together. Also to be avoided is foie gras *truffé,* not worth the extra expense, and the flavor of the truffle is minimal.

Foie gras should be served slightly chilled, in thin slices, and is perfect with nothing more elaborate than white country bread. If it is too cold, the flavor is diminished; too warm, and it loses its charm. A cold Sauternes is the ideal accompaniment. In slicing foie gras, use a thin blade dipped in warm water and wiped clean between slices.

30

OCTOBER

IRMA ROMBAUER

Irma Louise Rombauer was born in St. Louis on this day in 1877, the second of two daughters in a solid, German immigrant family. Her father was a doctor. In 1930, to recover from the terrible blow of her husband's suicide, she was urged to distract herself by assembling her ideas on cooking, based to a large extent on seventy-three mimeographed recipes she had gathered for her church group. Over the summer, at a small inn in Charlevoix, Michigan, she began to work on what would become the most famous American cookbook, *Joy of Cooking*. She had three thousand copies printed at her own expense in 1931. Clear, friendly, and precise, it contained five hundred tested recipes and reflected its author's wise, understanding personality.

This was during the Depression. After two years, it had sold just two thousand copies, but a publisher, Bobbs-Merrill, took it on in 1936, and it continued to sell modestly until a revised and enlarged edition with answers to almost every possible question appeared in 1943. It has now sold over fifteen million copies, and its popularity remains unrivaled.

31

OCTOBER

CHESTNUTS

On Manhattan street corners in the fall, the smell of roasting chestnuts is one of the pleasures of the city. A partially gloved hand, fingers blackened by charcoal, fills a small paper bag with seven or eight chestnuts, the curled-back skin crisp and revealing delicious, yellowy insides. Rich in energy and nutrition, chestnuts have been a food of both the rich and poor since earliest antiquity. Xenophon describes the children of noble Persian families being fed chestnuts to fatten them, and they were an important food for the populace in the harsh years following the destruction of the Roman Empire. They were a staple in France until the arrival of the potato. Chestnut meal was the ingredient of the original polenta, and chestnuts were boiled into soup and ground into flour.

There are wild chestnuts, not as tasty, with two or three nuts per shell, and the cultivated, European chestnuts whose shells contain only one. Nothing is easier than to gather them, which was also important for their popularity—when ripe, they fall to the ground.

Chestnut trees are long-lived. One, said to be two thousand years old, planted by the Romans, stood at the foot of Mount Etna until destroyed by an eruption in 1850. There were once great chestnut forests in America that spread from Maine to Florida and west to Arkansas with majestic trees that could reach a height of one hundred feet. All were attacked by a blight at the end of the 19th century; by 1940, they were completely gone.

As a food of the poor, chestnuts have mainly vanished. Instead, there is *crème de marrons,* used to fill crepes and cakes, and chestnut stuffing for roast turkey. Finest are the *marron glaces,* chestnuts poached in syrup until they are infused with sugary vanilla flavor and then glazed, translucent—a slight, uneven color is normal. The process, which the French may have invented in the time of Louis XIV, or the Italians before that, involves sixteen separate steps. Nowadays, frozen chestnuts are shipped from Italy to France, where they can no longer be obtained in sufficient quantity.

When buying chestnuts, choose those that are heavy, hard, and shiny brown. To roast them at home, first cut an X on the top of the shell to allow it to open and expand. On a baking pan covered with a thin layer of salt to prevent the bottoms from burning, roast them in the oven at 400–425 degrees F for twenty minutes or so.

NOVEMBER

CRAYFISH • RESTAURANT GUIDES
SANDWICH • RISOTTO • SIEGE OF PARIS
ROYAL PROGRESS • CHINESE FOOD
SALICE SALENTINO • BÉCHAMEL SAUCE
TAMALES • OYSTERS • ANTONY AND CLEOPATRA
OLIVE OIL • INUIT/ESKIMO
CABBAGE • JASON EPSTEIN ON COOKING
FONDUE • CRANBERRIES • PASTA SHAPES
GRIMOD • THE BEST COOK
CROISSANTTURKEY • ROASTING A TURKEY
CARVING A TURKEY • THANKSGIVING
WISHBONE • CANDY • GROS PLANT
CHURCHILL

NOVEMBER

CRAYFISH

Popular in Europe as early as the Middle Ages, crayfish, or *ecrevisses,* were scooped from the Seine by local citizens as late as the 16th century. By the 19th century, they had become fashionable, in short supply, and expensive. A dish of crayfish was also widely recognized as a preamble to seduction when a man ordered them for a woman in a restaurant.

NOVEMBER

RESTAURANT GUIDES

There are restaurant guides and restaurant guides, and then there is the Zagat, now spread coast to coast in the United States and with foreign editions. The idea behind the Zagat is simple and democratic: let the public decide, informed or ill-informed and regardless of taste or standards. The result is unreliability. The listings are breezy, imprecise, and often conflicting. Frequently the restaurant turns out to be the opposite, in one respect or another, of what is described. If there are high marks for food and low for decor, you might find the reverse. In cases of unchallengeable greatness, the

Zagat will be correct; otherwise it is useful mainly for telephone numbers, type of cuisine, and hours of opening.

The best guide to restaurants is an informed individual, someone whose standards are high, who has a palate, an eye, impartial judgment, and who has been around.

An expert in 1925, J. A. P. Cousin, had a snobbish but succinct scale of classification for the restaurants of Paris:

- Perfection
- The Last Word
- Very High Class
- Smart
- Reliable
- Savory and Plentiful
- Good Little Place
- Good Atmosphere

To these might be added the categories of:

- Innovative
- Welcoming
- Undiscovered
- Inexpensive
- Outrageous

Very little else, other than type of cuisine, is necessary.

3

NOVEMBER

SANDWICH

On this day in 1718, John Montagu, the fourth Earl of Sandwich, was born. He grew up in Cambridgeshire at Hinchingbrooke House, which had been the family home and was the birthplace of Oliver Cromwell. Montagu attended Cambridge but left before earning a degree. Nevertheless, he rose to become first lord of the admiralty and was at the helm (1771–82) when the colonies were lost during the American Revolution. He helped finance Captain Cook's expedition, and when Cook discovered the Sandwich Islands in 1778, he named them for the earl, in place of the name used by the natives and later restored: Hawaii.

Accomplished but dissolute, Montagu spent long days and nights both at his desk and at gambling tables, and it was allegedly at one of the latter that, unwilling to interrupt himself for a meal, he ordered some meat brought to him between two slices of bread. The practice caught on.

4

NOVEMBER

RISOTTO

Risotto is an Italian rice dish, cooked by slowly absorbing liquid and producing exceptional flavor. So many things can be added to the cooking rice—wild mushrooms, seafood, asparagus, meat—that risotto is almost a cuisine by itself. In *The Food of Italy*, Waverly Root lists thirty-seven different recipes. Burton Anderson, in *Treasures of the Italian Table*, has an impressive, detailed account of the rice and of risotto preparation by an Italian chef.

Arborio—an Italian rice that is widely available—is the first choice for risotto. It adheres to itself without becoming gummy and will absorb generous amounts of broth and, hence, flavor. Risotto takes from twenty to thirty-five minutes to make, being stirred and with liquid added a little at a time. It is pleasant to make in an atmosphere of complete informality, as when everyone is sitting at a big kitchen table.

There are two broad types: *Milanese,* which is heavier and a bit drier, and *Veneto,* which is looser and moister. The styles use the same technique but are finished off differently.

Nothing is like real risotto. You will almost never find the authentic thing in restaurants since it is so labor-consuming and, like a soufflé, takes so long to prepare. In restaurants, they usually stop cooking risotto at the three-quarter point and hold it there, resuming when it is ordered but with a lessening in perfection.

The finest risotto we ever had, apart from certain notable efforts of our own, was in a small hotel on Lake Garda in Italy. It was *risotto alla Parmigiana,* the simplest and most pure, nothing in it but rice, butter, shallots, broth, and fresh Parmesan cheese, *all'ondo,* soft and flowing, the way the Venetians like it. It was late in the season, and the hotel was nearly empty. The chef probably had nothing better to do.

Afterward we asked the owner if we could have a larger bulb for the bedside lamp in our room, which shed a very feeble light. He finally agreed, yes, all right. He went to the safe in his office, opened it, and gave us one of his big ones, perhaps forty watts.

RISOTTO ALLA PARMIGIANA

2 cups Arborio or converted	Butter
(not instant) rice	1 cup freshly grated
½ cup finely chopped onion	Parmesan cheese
4 tablespoons olive oil	(optional) mushrooms, fresh
1 ½ cups dry white wine	peas, pieces of fresh aspara-
3 ½ cups (or less) hot	gus or proscuitto or what-
chicken broth, made with	ever you like, already
bouillon cubes	steamed, boiled, or sautéed
Salt to taste	

Rinse and drain the rice. Sauté the onions over medium heat until translucent (three or four minutes) in the olive oil in a large saucepan with a heavy bottom.

Turn up the heat to medium-high or high. Add the rice. Stir and cook for four or five minutes, scraping the rice off the bottom of the pan. Don't let the rice brown. Add the wine. Stir continually, or nearly, until the wine is completely absorbed—about three minutes.

Add the broth slowly, only about a half cup at a time, stirring over relatively high heat. Some salt can be added during the cooking. All the broth should be incorporated in about twelve to fourteen minutes. At the end, the rice should be moist and creamy, not gummy.

Stir in the butter. Remove from heat. (An Italian friend and superb cook says the secret is to remove the rice from the heat before it has completely finished cooking.) Stir in the cooked vegetable or other addition. Add the cheese and serve immediately. Serves five or six.

Opinion says risotto cannot be kept as a leftover, but we make fried risotto flat cakes with it.

5

NOVEMBER

SIEGE OF PARIS

Just as a good story is the theme of its location, so a good meal is the success of its ingredients. What is available and fresh should be the starting point. Certain circumstances can be demanding. In 1870, during the Siege of Paris that climaxed the Franco-Prussian War, the starving populace was forced to eat domestic pets, cats and dogs, as well as rats, and even the occupants of the Vincennes zoo. On the ninety-ninth day of the siege, which happened to be Christmas Eve, there appeared on the menu of Voisin, a distinguished restaurant: elephant consommé and roast camel, along with bear and kangaroo.

6

ROYAL PROGRESS

In medieval times, the households of the English rulers were organized on such a lavish scale that Richard II's kitchen employed over two thousand cooks to feed the ten thousand daily visitors. Even two hundred years later, during Elizabeth I's reign, there were 160 on the kitchen staff and ten times that number of diners at court.

Elizabeth and her successor, James I, made a practice of occasionally touring their kingdom, accompanied by hundreds of courtiers and a caravan of household goods that included carpets, musical instruments, and portions of the royal libraries. They stayed at the great houses of wealthy subjects, who were often strained to the limit to make certain their sovereigns were comfortable and entertained until they moved on.

In Lancashire, Sir Richard Shuttleworth had built an imposing house called Gawthorpe Hall. Completed in 1605, it burned in 1617, soon after Shuttleworth learned that King James was to visit. It was rumored, probably falsely, that Shuttleworth set it afire himself rather than face the even greater cost of a stay by the king. The house was eventually restored, and Charlotte Brontë later spent time there with her friends, the Shuttleworth heirs.

C H I N E S E   F O O D

Through the centuries, food and cooking, inseparable from philosophy and religion, have been subjects of immense importance to the
Chinese. Emperors, scholars, and writers have addressed these matters, as well as Confucius, the greatest Chinese philosopher, for
whom even the way the table was set and the meal served were of
utmost concern, though he also said, "Live humbly."

The Chinese diet is relatively low in calories, perhaps reflecting its
origins in scarcity, with little fat and of that, only a small proportion of
it animal fat. It includes almost no milk or dairy products. Rice is
commonplace, though not an essential element, especially in the
north, where little rice is produced. Essential to any Chinese meal,
however, are three ingredients: fresh ginger, soy sauce, and scallions.

The usual place setting is a bowl, a plate, chopsticks, and a spoon,
and nearly every dish is prepared for these few implements. The
place of honor at the table is given to the oldest guest, and in general,
those who are soon to become ancestors are treated by family, as well
as by the state, with the greatest consideration.

A famous Seven Necessities that no Chinese, even the poorest,
could do without were listed more than a thousand years ago as
firewood, rice, oil, vinegar, salt, soy sauce, and tea.

8

NOVEMBER

SALICE SALENTINO

The owner of a New York shop that sold cookbooks once gave me the name of a favorite Italian wine. It was an inexpensive one that came from southernmost Italy, from Apulia, the long, narrow province that runs along the Adriatic coast. He wrote it down: Salice Salentino, the single *c* pronounced, as usual in Italian, as *ch*.

It proved to be a wonderful recommendation. Salento is the peninsula in Apulia that is the very heel of the Italian boot. The entire province is filled with vineyards, and the production of wine is the second greatest of all regions of Italy—Sicily being the first—though most of it is used anonymously in blending, and only a small percentage ends up in its own bottles. Salice Salentino is one of these, robust but somehow velvety, and normally easy to find in wine shops, where it stands modestly in the crowd. J.S.

9

NOVEMBER

BÉCHAMEL SAUCE

Béchamel, the delicious white sauce for creamed vegetables, soufflés, and croquettes, first appeared in France during the reign of Louis XIV (1643–1715), though it may have been created earlier and elsewhere. It was named for Louis de Bechameil, a handsome, corrupt financier who served as the king's majordomo. He had all the luck, complained an old duke who said he had been serving chicken in a cream sauce since before Bechameil was born, and no one had named any kind of sauce for him.

Béchamel is simple to make and takes only about five minutes. There are a number of variations using more or less butter and flour, depending on the desired thickness, but the foundation for all of them is the same:

BÉCHAMEL SAUCE

2 tablespoons butter

3 tablespoons flour

2 cups milk heated to a boil in a small saucepan

In a saucepan, melt the butter over low heat. Add the flour slowly, stirring until they are smoothly blended without browning. Remove from heat. Add the milk and stir vigorously with a wire whisk. Set over medium heat, stirring until the sauce comes to a boil; then cook for another minute, stirring constantly. Makes two cups.

10

NOVEMBER

TAMALES

The great Aztec lords sat down to tamales, according to Bernardino de Sahagún, who accompanied Cortés in 1519, and tamales were offered as annual gifts to the gods, although this was somewhat less often than it sounds, since the Aztecs had an eighteen-month year.

Not only Aztecs but Mayans and Incas also ate them, often while at war with one another, since tamales could be made in advance and were easily transported for the armies. They were made of essentially the same ingredients used today—corn flour called *masa,* meat or fish, beans, rice, vegetables, fruit, and nuts, though there might also be gopher, frog, and even insects. Then as now, the fillings were wrapped in corn husks or banana leaves and usually steamed.

In Mexico today, tamales are sold by street vendors everywhere—with cheese and chilis replacing the more exotic ingredients—and are also made at home, often for gatherings of family and friends.

11

NOVEMBER

OYSTERS

The unknown and courageous soul who first ate a raw oyster was followed by such fanciers as Nero; Seneca; Casanova, who ate fifty a day; Henry IV, the "Evergreen Lover," who ate as many as three hundred at a sitting; Louis XIV, who consumed nearly as many and had a royal preserve of them; Abraham Lincoln; and innumerable others.

In antiquity, oysters existed in a continuous band four thousand miles long from Scandinavia down past Britain and France, around into the Mediterranean, circling Italy, all the way to Greece. That rich vein survives only in fragments today, and everywhere the abundance of oysters has diminished.

It used to be a rule that raw oysters should be eaten only in months whose names included the letter *r*, that is, September through April. Before the age of refrigeration, they could not be safely transported in hot weather. Now, however, they are safe year-round, though in May through August, oysters spawn and tend to be creamy rather than firm in texture.

Oysters are best when of moderate size and from colder waters. They are best eaten raw with only a squeeze of lemon or the *vinaigre* and shallot mixture served in France. Cold white wine makes them sacred.

12

NOVEMBER

ANTONY AND CLEOPATRA

According to Plutarch, Cleopatra first appeared to Marc Antony sailing up the Cydnus River "in a barge with gilded stern and outspread sails of purple, while oars of silver beat time to the music of flutes and fifes and harps. She herself lay all along under a canopy of cloth of gold, dressed as Venus in a picture, and beautiful young boys, like painted Cupids, stood on each side to fan her."

Shakespeare, who knew a good thing when he saw it, immortalized the scene in Act II of his play:

The barge she sat in, like a burnish'd throne,
Burned on the water, the poop was beaten gold,

Purple the sails, and so perfumed, that
The winds were love-sick with them, the oars were silver,
Which to the tune of flutes kept stroke. . . .
And so forth. It continues:
Upon her landing, Antony sent to her,
Invited her to supper, she replied
It should be better he became her guest. . . .

From that night on, Antony and Cleopatra did everything possible to impress each other with the extravagance and opulence of the meals they ordered to be prepared. He had once made the gift of a house to a cook who had prepared a particularly successful dinner, but now, besotted, he was said to have given a city to one who pleased Cleopatra.

Joining her in Alexandria, Antony established his own court where he could entertain her. One evening, a visitor noticed that eight wild boars were being roasted and commented that many guests must be expected. No, the cook told him, only twelve, but since it was impossible to know exactly when Antony would be ready to dine, and since the roast must be cooked exactly to the minute, eight boars were needed, at different stages of completion, so that one would be perfect when the time came.

13

OLIVE OIL

The olive tree is as old as recorded history. Slow to mature and amazingly long-lived—from three hundred to six hundred years—today's ancient, gnarled specimens with wood like iron may have produced their first fruit not long after Columbus set sail for the New World.

The first olive trees in Greece are said to have been planted in Mycenae, the city that the mythic hero Agamemnon ruled, ruins of which are still in existence. You can stand in what is thought to be the bedchamber where Agamemnon, returned at last from the Trojan War, was murdered by his unfaithful wife and her lover. All around and beneath is the incredible, mountainous countryside with groves stretching off in the distance as far as one can see. To walk through the Lion Gate and up the rocky path to the remains of the palace is to walk the nave of the immemorial.

Olives are green at first and black when left on the tree to ripen. The oil from their pressing comes in great quantities from Spain, France, Greece, California, and Italy, as well as from other places. One of its desirable qualities is that it contains no cholesterol. In the ancient world, it was also used as a medicine and even as a cleanser, there being no soap.

Italian olive oil, among the best, is carefully classified by law, the finest being first-pressed extra virgin: the whole olives are crushed without damaging the pit, and no chemicals of any kind are allowed. Extra virgin means lower acidity and hence, better flavor. Lesser-quality oils are virgin and pure olive oil, the latter usually having had chemicals added to reduce acidity.

For salad and all uncooked uses you should buy only extra virgin. For cooking, a lower grade may be used, although olive oil is not, like other cooking oils, a mere lubricant; it adds its own distinctive flavor.

Oddly enough, Italian law does not require that all the oil be from the region indicated on the label, so it may read Tuscany, but the oil may partly or entirely come from elsewhere, even North Africa. There are so many brands, including some good domestic ones, that it is really necessary to know which are reputable and then to choose the one with the best taste.

14

NOVEMBER

INUIT/ESKIMO

In the Arctic climate, foods high in fat and protein are essential, and meat—whether seal, caribou, fish, polar bear, or walrus—is shared by everyone in the community after the hunt. Despite the influx of processed food, there is still a strong tradition centered around communal meals. The Inuit belief is that food makes friends out of strangers and even doubles in volume when it is shared.

The Inuit of the Canadian northwest have a yearly festival on this day that epitomizes their philosophy. On the day before, the children go from door to door collecting food for the feast. The next day, as they share their meal, the men and women ask for each other's valued possessions, which are freely given, since it's considered bad manners to refuse. Then, when many items have been placed in the hands of their new owners, they all dance together.

15

NOVEMBER

CABBAGE

Cabbage is not mentioned in the Bible, though it was eaten by both Romans and Greeks. The Emperor Tiberius once required the Senate to vote on whether there was any dish in the world superior to corned beef and cabbage.

> Diogenes, to a young courtier: If you lived on cabbage, you
> would not be obliged to flatter the powerful.
> Young courtier: If you flattered the powerful, you would not
> be obliged to live on cabbage.

In Russia, cabbage soup, or *shchi,* is made from cabbage, carrots, meat, onions, celery, and garlic, with a sour flavoring from apples, sour cream, or sauerkraut juice. A favorite for at least a thousand years, it can be found in Russian poems and prose, on the table of both rich and poor, and in the fond memory of every exile.

16

NOVEMBER

JASON EPSTEIN ON COOKING

Like all great cooks, Jason Epstein decides what to cook by seeing what's available and what looks good in the market. In New York City, he lives near Chinatown where vegetables, fruit, fish, and meat are sold by small vendors and are excellent. The mark of a good restaurant is that it remains true to the ingredients and that the ingredients are fresh. This is also his method.

The important thing in preparing a dinner is timing, he says— making sure things are done at the right time. He doesn't write a schedule or make a diagram, but works it out in his head. Another thing worth knowing is how to brown things—fish or chicken, for example—without having them stick to the pan. "You can't brown things in Teflon," he says. The secret is to have the pan very hot before adding the oil and then to wait until it shimmers before adding the food.

Of the countless restaurants in France he has visited, he mentions with particular affection the Relais de la Poste in a small town called Magesq about fifty kilometers from Biarritz. Afterward, we looked it up in the Michelin: 1,218 inhabitants, and the Relais de la Poste, with thirteen rooms, is in red, meaning "especially agreeable." Its restaurant boasts two stars. The specialties include breast of pigeon with wild mushrooms and game in season.

Jason has been there a number of times, the first when traveling with Gore Vidal, "when we were still speaking," he says. "The place never changes. The waiters are always the same. The daughter who brings fresh orange juice to your room in the morning is still twelve years old."

17

❧———————————☙

F O N D U E

A poet's hope: to be
Like some valley cheese,
Local, but prized everywhere.
— W. H. A U D E N

Gruyères (the town is spelled with an *s*, but its notable cheese without one) is about seventy miles northeast of Geneva as you head into the heart of Switzerland. It produces one of the two cheeses—the other being Emmenthaler—that are the basis for fondue, which comes from the French verb *fondre*, "to melt." You can tell an authentic Gruyère cheese by the word "Switzerland" or a crossbow stamped on the rind. Fondue likely originated in remote mountain villages during winters when food was scarce and people softened their old, hardened cheeses over a fire, scooping from the pot with pieces of bread.

There are fondues in which meat is cooked in hot oil or fruit is dipped in melted chocolate, but the classic fondue is made of grated cheese, dusted with flour, combined with white wine, and melted in a pot rubbed with garlic. The pot is brought to the table and kept warm over a flame for a dish that is literally shared.

18

NOVEMBER

CRANBERRIES

Cranberries are one of the three native North American fruits—the other two are blueberries and Concord grapes. They were introduced to the Pilgrims by the Indians, who ate them crushed and mixed with honey or maple sugar. They were also a preservative, combined with dried meat in a mixture called pemmican that helped prolong the life of the meat. In addition, crushed cranberries were used for dyes and as poultices for injuries.

The high acid content that makes them an effective preservative also helps control bacteria, and may help prevent urinary tract infections in women. Their acidity also makes them more long-lasting than other fruits, and even freezing barely alters their nutritional content. And they are loaded with vitamin C. American sailors used to eat them to prevent scurvy, just as their British counterparts ate limes.

The English name "cranberry" comes from their flowers, which bend down into a form rather like the head of a crane. They grow on vines that yield fruit for 150 years if undamaged, and the vines thrive in "bogs," not of water, but of the remains of glacial deposits, with the addition of sand and peat. They're harvested from September through December and are therefore fresh during Thanksgiving and Christmas. The berries have a pocket of air inside that makes them float, so they can be knocked off the vines, the fields flooded, and the berries then raked in.

19

PASTA SHAPES

On Italian menus pasta can be found served in soup, *pasta in brodo;* as a dish with a sauce, *pasta asciutta;* and baked, *pasta al forno.*

There are more names for pasta shapes than stars in the sky, or nearly. They are all in Italian, of course, and many are beautiful. Among them are:

Anelli, "rings," or *anellini,* "little rings."

And *occhi di passeri,* "sparrows' eyes."

Also *risino,* "tiny rice."

And *semi di melone,* "melon seeds."

And *stele* and *stellini,* "stars" and "little stars."

Then, not for soup, there are:

Cappelli di prete, "priests' hats."

And *farfalle,* "butterflies," and *farfalloni,* "large butterflies," and *farfallette,* "little ones."

Also *maruzze,* "seashells," in many sizes, including *maruzzine,* "small seashells."

Rigati means "grooved" and is an additional form of many shapes, *ziti rigati, rigatoni, canelle rigati,* and so forth.

Certain of the countless shapes go well with certain sauces. Sometimes if the dinner is special we make a little menu so that what is going to be served can be anticipated, and it's always a pleasure to write the name of an exotic pasta on it. "Tripolini," they ask, "what is that?" Little bows named in honor of the conquest of Tripoli, of course.

20

NOVEMBER

GRIMOD

In Paris, in 1758, Alexandre Balthazar Grimod de La Reynière was born, misshapen, with rudimentary hands, one like a claw and the other like a goose's foot. Hastily baptized, since it was feared he would not live, he later would claim, among other stories, that his fingers had been bitten off by a sow when he was three weeks old.

A lawyer and also a drama critic, he was unnoticed until he gave a legendary dinner in 1783 at a time when the *ancien régime* was already trembling and the *ancienne cuisine* was also about to disappear. The printed invitations were of enormous size and resembled death notices. When the guests entered the dining room, hung in black and lit by hundreds of candles, a coffin was in the middle of the table. There were nine courses between which Grimod discoursed on his supposedly low-born ancestors. The result was notoriety and a reputation as a madman.

On a later occasion, he dressed a huge pig in his wealthy father's clothes and sat him in the place of honor at a dinner. His parents returned unexpectedly and, outraged, had him confined in a monastery for nearly three years, for his own good, as they said. His great interest in food and dining began at the abbot's table.

He later opened a grocery store in Lyon, but his gastronomic fame rests on *L'almanach des gourmands,* the first guide to the restaurants and food shops of Paris, including sophisticated and witty essays on the preparation and serving of food. The book, which became a series from 1804–12, was immensely successful. Grimod was the first real food critic and can be said to have invented food journalism. He also organized a jury of twelve to judge foods—pastries, meats, anything that was submitted to it—and to issue a verdict and certificate of official recognition.

Having inherited a fortune upon his mother's death, he married the actress who had long been his mistress, Adélaide-Thérese Feuchère, and retired to a château in the country to live among close friends. He died in the middle of a great midnight feast on Christmas Eve, 1837.

One of the recipes he left behind gives the names of various actresses of the time to describe certain ingredients, a woodcock "tender as Mlle Volnais," for example, and a pullet "as white as Mlle Belmont."

21

NOVEMBER

THE BEST COOK

November 21 is the birthday of Lorry Hubbard, the best amateur cook we know. She sets a standard one can't match, but it's enough to be invited to dinner.

Her father cooked pot roasts and soups and had an herb garden. He once raised a goose in the basement and roasted it for Christmas. Her mother had no interest in cooking but said she'd buy the ingredients if Lorry would make Sunday dinners, so Lorry found recipes in the library and in a special Thursday section of the *Chicago Tribune*.

"I simply don't have the time to cook," many people say. Lorry runs a business that produces educational material on art for schools. She has five grown children, two stepchildren, and grandchildren. She keeps a garden and raises golden retrievers for show and breeding. She oversees three houses, including one in France, and her husband, her partner in business, has been in a wheelchair since before they married more than twenty years ago. For relaxation and pleasure, she cooks.

Her idea of a simple menu for a summer dinner party is: hors d'oeuvres of pâté (or fresh foie gras that she makes herself if enough people are coming); salmon carpaccio with a Bibb lettuce salad; duck breast with Cognac sauce; risotto with mushrooms and peas; and for dessert, peaches with a fresh raspberry sauce. If she happens to wake up at five in the morning, she sometimes cooks—an apple strudel from memory, say—because her husband, Tom, likes a little something sweet for breakfast. She occasionally cheats, as she calls it, and uses store-bought puff pastry.

Her houses are filled with cookbooks, of course. Her favorite is Julia Child's *Mastering the Art of French Cooking*. She likes the old version of *Joy of Cooking* more than the revised one, because the new one is "healthier." Her favorite ingredient is sea salt, the exact amount of which to use she knows automatically. After decades of experience, she can look at any recipe and know in advance whether it will be good or not, but she's not bound by what's on the page and improvises freely.

One thing she doesn't worry about is the afterward. "I know women who cook thinking about how much mess they're making, but I never think about that," she says. She and her husband are amazed at how often people go out to restaurants and do it only occasionally themselves. Why would they?

A couple of her many favorite recipes:

FRENCH CHICKEN

1 3–4 pound chicken, rinsed
and patted dry

1 teaspoon dried thyme or
herbs de Provence or

1 tablespoon fresh thyme
(leaves only)

1 teaspoon dried rosemary,
crumbed, or

1 tablespoon fresh
rosemary, chopped
Salt and pepper to taste

3 tablespoons vegetable oil

3–4 slices thick smoked bacon,
cut in ¼-inch pieces

1 large onion, chopped coarsely

2 stalks celery, chopped coarsely

2 large carrots, chopped coarsely,
or 12 small baby carrots

2 cloves garlic, minced

8–12 small, new red potatoes
Handful of small, thin green
beans

½ pound sliced button
mushrooms, sliced

1 cup canned tomatoes, drained

1 cup dry white wine

½ to 1 cup chicken stock;
(start with ½ cup and
add as needed)

¼ cup Wondra flour

Fresh minced parsley

Preheat the oven to 400 degrees F. Sprinkle the inside of
the chicken with half the herbs. Season the chicken with
salt and pepper. Heat the oil in a Dutch oven or metal
casserole (such as Le Creuset) over medium heat until hot.
Brown the chicken on all sides and transfer to a plate.

Add the bacon to the pot and cook until crisp. Add all
of the vegetables and cook for five minutes, stirring
occasionally, over medium heat. Add the wine, the
chicken, tomatoes, chicken stock, remaining herbs, salt
and pepper, and bring to a boil.

Cover the pot, put it in the oven, and cook for fifty
minutes to one hour.

Transfer the chicken and vegetables to a large serving bowl or platter with high sides, and keep warm.

Skim the fat from the cooking liquid and reduce the liquid to about one to one and a half cups. Whisk in the Wondra flour gradually until the sauce thickens slightly. Let simmer over medium heat for about five minutes, while carving the chicken.

Spoon the sauce over the chicken and vegetables and garnish with the parsley. Serves four to six.

ZUCCHINI, EGGPLANT, TOMATO, PEPPER CASSEROLE

1 large zucchini, peeled or unpeeled, sliced into ¼-inch slices

1 large eggplant, peeled, sliced into ¼-inch slices

3–4 fresh tomatoes, peeled, sliced into ½-inch slices

½ green pepper, sliced lengthwise into ¼-inch slices

½ red pepper, sliced lengthwise into ¼-inch slices

1 medium white onion, thinly sliced

1 tablespoon minced garlic

½ cup fresh whole basil leaves

¼–½ cup olive oil

Salt and pepper to taste

3 tablespoons shaved or grated Parmesan cheese

Preheat the oven to 375 degrees F. Sprinkle salt lightly over the zucchini and eggplant and let them sit in a colander for about twenty minutes. Rinse well and pat dry with a paper towel.

Spray a large, low (one and a half inches high) casserole dish with Pam. Place the zucchini slices down one side of the casserole and the eggplant slices next to them. Place tomato slices with one onion slice in between each one alongside the eggplant slices. Add another row of tomato and onion slices, or place another row on top of the first one. Scatter minced garlic over the vegetables. Place the slices of red and green pepper attractively between the rows. Scatter basil leaves over the entire, casserole, and drip the olive oil over all the vegetables. Lightly salt and pepper.

Place the casserole in the oven, covered with foil, for twenty minutes. Uncover, sprinkle the Parmesan cheese over all the casserole, reduce the heat to 350 degrees F, and cook another twenty minutes or until vegetables are done. Serves four to six.

22

NOVEMBER

CROISSANT

Besieged by the Turks in 1686, Budapest, legend has it, was saved from capture by the warning of bakers who, at work in the early hours, heard the sound of tunneling beneath them. The right to bake a special sweet pastry in the shape of the crescent on the Ottoman flag was their reward. Imitated in Paris, it became the croissant.

The actual history of croissants is almost as inexact. They seem to have appeared, or at least been first mentioned, in an 1853 French food book, and the first published recipe dates back to only 1906. Croissants contain a large amount of butter, at least those labeled *croissant au buerre* in Paris bakeries. Those labeled simply *croissant* contain less, or even margerine. Either way, they are what makes a French breakfast.

TURKEY

In Europe, turkey was eaten as early as the 1540s, a full one hundred years before the Pilgrims tasted it in Plymouth. There was the mistaken notion that it was a delicacy of the East, partly because of the confusion about whether Columbus had indeed reached India by sailing west. In France, the bird was called *coq d'Inde,* the "cock of India," which became *dinde* or *dindon.* The English, thinking it came to them from Turkey, named it for its source.

In fact, it is a native of North America and was eaten enthusiastically by the original inhabitants. Columbus may have crossed paths with turkeys on his fourth voyage in 1502, but it wasn't until Cortés's conquest of Mexico in 1521 that they were transported to Spain and from there to the rest of the Old World, where they quickly became popular. In England, large flocks were driven on foot, their feet tied in sacking or leather boots to withstand a walk that often took a week or more from the countryside to London. They were intended to arrive in time for Christmas and soon replaced the goose on holiday tables.

24

NOVEMBER

ROASTING A TURKEY

Benjamin Franklin always believed that the turkey, instead of the bald eagle, should be the national bird, being "much more respectable and a native of North America." He was talking about the wild turkey, smaller than our domesticated variety and a bird described as "wary to the point of genius." The wild turkey is said to have been the one eaten at the first Plymouth Rock Thanksgiving in 1621. Almost 350 years later, vacuum-packed roast turkey with all the trimmings was the first meal eaten on the moon.

Excellent cooks differ in their methods for roasting a stuffed turkey. One way is to set the oven at 325 degrees F and cook the bird covered with a cheesecloth, basting it occasionally. Another—our preference—is to start the browning by putting it in a 450-degree oven for twenty minutes, then turning the heat down to 325–350 degrees and basting frequently through the cheesecloth. A six- to sixteen-pound stuffed turkey should be cooked twenty to twenty-five minutes per pound. Over sixteen pounds, it is eighteen to twenty minutes per pound.

25

NOVEMBER

CARVING A TURKEY

Carving has been considered an art since at least Roman times, when wooden models were provided in the kitchens to instruct servants, and music was played as they practiced to encourage grace and rhythm with the knife.

By the late 18th century, there were thirty-eight terms for carving, depending on the dish: pigeons were "thighed," pheasants "allayed," deer "broken," and salmon "chined." As in the past, it is still an honor to be designated carver, though now the challenges are turkeys and roasts.

For a turkey:

(1) First, remove the thigh and leg from the body by fixing the leg with a large two-tined carved fork. Cut through the skin, then bend the leg outward to cut through the thigh joint close to the body.

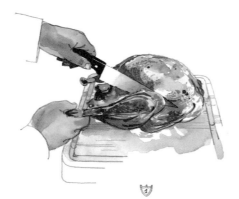

(2) To carve the breast, insert the fork across the middle of the breastbone, which is on top when the bird is on a platter. The breast should be cut in thin slices down from the breastbone, angling slightly toward the wing joint. Carve the entire side nearest you before beginning on the other, which can be kept intact to prevent it from drying out until more meat is needed.

In general, beef seems more tender if cut against the grain of the meat, but with a standing rib roast, it is easier to cut between the ribs, which is with the grain.

26

THANKSGIVING

In 1789, George Washington, during his first year in office, declared November 26 "A Day of Publick Thanksgiving and Prayer," intended to acknowledge "with grateful hearts the many and signal favors of Almighty God." It wasn't the first Thanksgiving celebration, but it was the first official one in the newly formed United States.

The earliest Thanksgiving was in Plymouth, Massachusetts, in 1621, attended by the Pilgrims and Indian chiefs Squanto, Samoset, and Massasoit, along with ninety of their men. For the next 150 years, individual colonies organized their own Thanksgiving remembrances, often tied to specific victories in battle or a good harvest and usually marked not with eating, but with fasting and prayers.

In 1863, President Lincoln proclaimed the fourth Thursday of November a national holiday. President Franklin Delano Roosevelt tried to better that in 1939 by changing the day to the third Thursday of the month in an attempt to extend the Christmas shopping season and boost the economy during the Depression, but there was such an outcry against it that five years later, on this same date in 1941, he signed a bill that changed it back to the fourth Thursday.

WISHBONE

Wishbone lore goes back 2,500 years to Etruscan times, when certain hens were thought to have powers for predicting the future. A circle was drawn on the ground and divided into twenty-four sections, one for each letter of the Etruscan alphabet. The hen was then asked a question, placed in the middle of the circle, and like a feathered Ouija, ate the kernels in an order that signified the answer, such as the name of a husband-to-be or the outcome of a dispute. The hen was then killed and its breastbone dried and used as a lucky talisman.

When the Romans later adapted the custom, two people tugged on the dried bone, each making a wish, the winner being the one who got the longer part of the bone that included the head, hence the term "lucky break."

28

NOVEMBER

CANDY

Candy came from the Arabic word *qand,* which means "sugar"—always its main ingredient. Originally a combination of fruit or nuts with honey, candy came to be made with sugar from cane, imported first from India over five thousand years ago. It has always been valued for the pleasure of its sweetness—in French, the word *bonbon* means "good good."

Like many luxuries, candy belonged exclusively to the wealthy through the Middle Ages, but by the 15th century, the cost of sugar was less exorbitant, and candy became available to almost everyone. One of the most popular forms was marzipan, a paste of sugar, nuts, and egg whites formed into fanciful shapes and still made today. Sugarplums, small balls of candy mentioned in *The Night Before Christmas,* written by Clement Clarke Moore in 1822, have been eaten since Shakespeare's time.

The most popular candy worldwide is chocolate. The non-chocolate variety is divided into "hard" and "soft," depending on when crystallization of the sugar is stopped. "Soft" includes gum-drops, caramels, cotton candy, taffy, and jelly beans, whose centers probably originated in the chewy sweet called Turkish Delight in the Middle East, eaten since Biblical times. Jelly beans established themselves in the United States when they were advertised as something special to send to Union soldiers during the Civil War.

When Mary Poppins said, "A spoonful of sugar helps the medicine go down," perhaps she was aware that until about 1300, candy was sold almost exclusively by doctors to cover the taste of vile medicines.

29

NOVEMBER

GROS PLANT

There's a wine called Gros Plant—Big Plant—named after the vine itself and grown south of Nantes in the Loire Valley, making it a relative of Muscadet. The wine authority Robert Parker says it is so "green"—so acidic—that it takes a masochist to drink it. Others are more forgiving, describing it as an uncomplicated dry white that goes well with seafood. That's how we first met it, in France in the autumn of 1976.

In late November of that year, we were speeding along the highway toward Cherbourg and passage on the last Atlantic crossing of the season on the *Queen Elizabeth II.* Suddenly we caught a glimpse of a large hand-lettered sign: "Gros Plant." An arrow pointed down a dirt road. We turned around and followed the road to a farmhouse with chickens wandering through the yard. In a shed, a man and his ten-year-old son were pasting labels on their wine bottles, the boy applying the glue to the paper, the father positioning it on the glass. We bought a case.

On the dock at Cherbourg, as we waited for the ship, there was a huge stack of wooden cases like ours, except for the words stenciled on the sides: "Blanc de Blancs Taittinger," "Champagne," and the owner's name, "Rockefeller." We felt a limited kinship. At the time, the duty charged on a bottle of wine was ten cents, and there was virtually no limit on the amount of hold baggage.

For a long time it was hard to find Gros Plant in the United States. The quantity produced has never been great—most is drunk locally, and Americans tend to favor an easier, softer wine than this flinty white. You can get it now—it has become more accessible as its neighbor, Muscadet, has grown more popular. It is cheap and, if you like this sort of thing, good.

30
NOVEMBER

CHURCHILL

1874. At Blenheim, the hereditary home of his father and the only nonroyal palace in England, with 320 rooms, a library more than 180 feet long, and vast surrounding lands, in a small room off the Great Hall, which was as far as his young mother was able to go after leaving the ball, Winston Churchill, who was to become England's greatest prime minister and, excepting Shakespeare, perhaps her greatest single individual, was born at one-thirty in the morning.

Throughout his long life, he ate well and drank heartily, and once described a meal as follows: "Well, dinner would have been splendid if the wine had been as cold as the soup, the beef as rare as the service, the brandy as old as the fish, and the maid as willing as the Duchess."

DECEMBER

PIZZA • CHILI CON CARNE
PRESENTATION • ROSTI
BREAD AND HISTORY • LA COUPOLE
FOODS OF INDIA • ASPEN WINTERS
CLARENCE BIRDSEYE • MOVIES • KETCHUP
MADAME BOVARY • FIRST MEAL • FRITTATA
CANDLES • DELMONICO'S • BOSTON TEA PARTY
AMPHOUX • DINING ROOMS • ROQUEFORT
CROSS-COUNTRY DINNER • PANETTONE
CANDY CANES • CHAMPAGNE • CHRISTMAS EVE
CHRISTMAS DINNER • BOXING DAY
LOUIS PASTEUR • BURGUNDY-CHAMBERTIN
MME DE POMPADOUR • COULIBIAC
GREAT MEALS

1

PIZZA

The first pizza ever delivered was ordered by King Umberto I and Queen Margherita of Italy in 1889. Visiting the queen's family near Naples, they heard about a popular handheld meal sold by street vendors and at open-air pizzerias and favored by the poor. They wanted to try it but were unable to mingle with the masses at the local pizzeria. Instead, Rafaele Esposito, the owner of the most famous one, came to them. He brought the ingredients for three different combinations for the royals to try, but it was the one made with tomatoes, mozzarella, and fresh basil—the red, white, and green of the Italian flag—that most pleased the queen. Esposito named it in her honor, and it gave Naples the reputation of having invented pizza.

Its actual origins were far earlier. The Greeks and Etruscans had their versions of rough bread formed with a raised edge to hold bits of other foods on top. In the first century, the Roman statesman Cato wrote about "flat rounds of dough dressed with olive oil, herbs, and honey, baked on stones." The essential tomato wasn't added until fifteen hundred years later, imported from the New World, and those now grown in the volcanic soil near Vesuvius are one of the reasons that Neapolitan pizzas are still considered to set the standard.

Italian immigrants brought pizza to America, and the first pizzeria opened in New York City in 1905. It wasn't until after World War II, however, when soldiers returned from Italy with stories of a wonderful food eaten without utensils, that it took off, and it remains one of the most popular foods worldwide.

DECEMBER

CHILI CON CARNE

"Un coup de rouge," you can say in France, ordering a glass of ordinary red wine. In Texas you can say, "A bowl of red," meaning chili.

Chili con carne—chili with meat—is a redundant term. All chili, except, of course, vegetarian, has meat, and the authentic Texas variety has little else, no tomatoes and, above all, no beans. Chili seems to have originated in Texas, perhaps in the poor Mexican sections in the days—the early 1800s—when Texas was a possession of Mexico. It is mentioned in print as early as 1857. There were the chili queens of San Antonio a little later, whose carts appeared at dusk with large, brightly colored lamps and a great pot of chili together with tables and stools.

Like Coca-Cola, chili conquered the world, or at least North America. There are countless recipes for it, many of them imaginative, but in spreading north and eastward it underwent changes and is commonly found now with both tomatoes and red beans, as well as onions, green peppers, celery, and other things.

The appeal of chili is that anyone, even a child, can make it; the ingredients are easily found; it is delicious by itself or with rice and a variety of toppings; and, like other widely popular dishes, it is as good or better the next day.

A recipe for chili that will please everyone, though it is not of a caliber to win a Texas cook-off:

CHILI CON CARNE

3 tablespoons margarine or
olive oil
2 large onions, chopped fine,
one to be served on the side
2 cloves garlic, minced
1 pound chopped or ground beef,
chuck or round
1 large can tomatoes with basil,
including the liquid
1 green pepper, chopped fine
Sesame oil to taste
Worcestershire sauce to taste

2 tablespoons chili powder
1 tablespoon salt
1 bay leaf
1 teaspoon cumin, powdered
¼ teaspoon cayenne
½ teaspoon celery salt
Basil to taste
1 can kidney beans
Strong cheddar cheese,
to be served on the side
Cooked rice, to be served with
the chili on top

Sauté the onion and garlic in the margarine or oil until golden brown. Add the meat and cook until brown. Add the remaining ingredients and bring to a boil. Reduce the heat and simmer, uncovered, for two to three hours. Add a little water, if necessary. Add the kidney beans fifteen minutes before serving. Serve over rice with the chopped onion and grated cheese as toppings. Serves four.

3

DECEMBER

PRESENTATION

Alice Waters once observed that in her experience, you can tell whether a chef is a man or a woman by looking at your plate: a man builds a tower, a woman makes a nest.

Presentation was once far more complicated. What was known as French service in the early 19th century was highly formalized and meant an enormous number of prepared dishes on the table simultaneously in three succeeding waves: hors d'oeuvres and first courses; then roast and vegetables; and finally, sweets and fruits. The guest could pick and choose, as if from a giant buffet, until that course was cleared and the next appeared, but nothing stayed hot that was supposed to be hot.

In the 1860s, Czar Alexander II's ambassador to France introduced Russian service at his table, which was then quickly taken up all over Paris. Less grandiose, the food was presented one dish at a time to the diners, served from the left, and cleared from the right.

A century later, nouvelle cuisine made its first appearance in France, led by Paul Bocuse, Jean and Pierre Troisgros, Alain Chapel, and Michel Guerard. They took simplification even further, emphasizing freshness of ingredients, less cream and butter, unexpected juxtaposition of flavors and textures, and small portions artistically displayed.

4

ROSTI

In the Alpine villages and towns that over the years have become great ski resorts, there is still the feel of the older, simpler life: the steep, snow-covered meadows where in summer cattle graze; the barns and houses that have stood through centuries of weather, families, fortune and misfortune; houses that are as solid as banks and far more comfortable.

Much of skiing in the Alps is above the tree line, amid only snow and the rugged surrounding peaks. There is the thin, cold air and the feeling of being above every humdrum thing. Further down, the trees begin, and through them you go, riding the soft sound of your skis and at one point seeing ahead a house that is a restaurant or even an inn, set among the trees. Within, it is bursting with noise and warmth, the booths are crowded, the rich smell of cooking in the air. On the *karte* are soups and meats ready to restore one and also, with them, modestly, the delicious potato dish that is characteristic of the mountains, easy to make, impossible to surpass: *rosti*.

ROSTI

2–3 russet or Yukon gold potatoes, smallish,
cooked in their skins the night before
⅓ cup or less diced bacon
1 tablespoon salt
⅓ cup or more olive oil or, better but less healthful, lard

Peel and coarsely grate the potatoes. Mix in the bacon. Heat the oil in an iron skillet large enough to easily accommodate the potatoes. Add the potatoes and bacon, turning them over several times to thoroughly impregnate them with the oil or lard. Cook over medium heat, stirring frequently until the bacon becomes cooked. If the potatoes seem dry, cover the pan. After several minutes, draw the potatoes together into a low, cakelike shape. Raise the heat and cook until a golden crust forms underneath. Turn them out onto a plate, crust up. Serve hot. Serves three or four.

5

DECEMBER

BREAD AND HISTORY

Bread is normally the only food that is kept on the table throughout the meal. The word is almost synonymous with food and, by extension, life.

The English "lord" comes from an Anglo-Saxon word meaning "keeper of the bread" and "lady" from the word for "kneader of the dough." "Bread" is also an equivalent for that other indispensable commodity, money. "Dough" and "bread" are common words used for money in America, and the French use *blé*— "wheat."

In ancient Rome, following some hard times, grain was price-supported, and later it was distributed free—in Julius Caesar's time to 150,000 adult males. Eventually this became free bread rather than grain, and also pork fat and even wine. Grain came to Rome from Egypt, Sicily, and North Africa, carried in ships to the port of Ostia and then in barges up the Tiber to Rome.

Although in ancient Greece there were more than seventy varieties that were baked, by the 17th and 18th centuries in Europe, good bread was expensive, and by the time of the French Revolution, the price of bread was almost ninety percent of an average worker's daily wage.

6

DECEMBER

LA COUPOLE

La Coupole opened in Paris in December, 1927, with twelve hundred bottles of Mumm's champagne. Its twenty-four interior pillars were decorated by local artists. Transformed from a wood and coal store, the restaurant was open from breakfast until after midnight and became the place to be seen. As was said between the two world wars, "Governments are made at Lipp, but they fall at La Coupole."

Not to mention liaisons. Louis Aragon, a founder of surrealism in literature, who had had a long love affair with Nancy Cunard, met Russian novelist Elsa Triolet at the bar soon after La Coupole opened. She was attracted to him immediately and pursued him so directly that at first he thought she was a police spy. They married within the year. He later wrote, "My life can be summed up in one word, 'Elsa.'"

DECEMBER

FOODS OF INDIA

The Indian continent, with over a billion people and 150 languages and dialects, inevitably also has a vast diversity of foods, which vary according to the region. In the north, where the temperatures go from sweltering in summer to very cold in winter, meals are heavier and richer, while in the south, where it is almost always hot, less meat is eaten because it is too heavy for daily consumption. Availability of ingredients makes a difference, too, with coastal regions relying more on fish and arid inland areas consuming more lentils for protein. Rice is eaten all over India, but especially in the south, where it appears virtually at every meal.

In addition, there are religious differences in diet between the Muslim minority, whose Koran prohibits alcohol, and the Hindus, who don't eat beef because the cow is considered sacred. Among the Hindus, there is also a division between the diet of the higher and the lower castes. The higher castes, including the Brahmins, often are vegetarians and tend to choose their foods to enhance both their spirituality and their health, with the focus on vegetables and fruits. The lower—and poorer—classes have traditionally eaten anything except beef.

Most Indian food eaten outside the country reflects northern Indian cuisine, such as *tandoori* dishes from the Punjab, in which meats are marinated in spices and then roasted over a wood fire, along with the regional wheat bread called *naan,* which is an unleavened flat bread, as are all Indian breads, including *papadums,* made of lentil flour into a tortilla-like bread that is roasted over a flame or cooked in oil on a hot griddle until crisp.

In Indian cooking, "curry" simply means a sauce, which can be fiery or mild. Adding coconut milk makes a spicy curry mild. Recipes are handed down over generations, but common ingredients include turmeric, cardamom, chilis, coriander, cloves, ginger, nutmeg, and fenugreek, a cloverlike plant with pungent, aromatic seeds. The spices are dry roasted, then ground on a special flat granite stone with another stone, rather like a mortar and pestle. Curry powder available in Western stores is an approximation of this mixture.

It's not uncommon anywhere in India for food to be served on a simple metal plate called a *thali* or on a banana leaf plate. With a banana leaf, you simply fold it over when finished. Traditionally, food is eaten by hand, but only with the right hand since the left is considered "dirty," with lowlier uses. It's considered offensive to greet anyone or even to pay with the left hand.

The universal beverage is *chai*—the Hindi word for "tea"—boiled with milk, water, and spices such as cardamom, ginger, cinnamon, and cloves, and served with plenty of sugar. It is often poured into a glass from a great height to cool it more quickly.

8

DECEMBER

ASPEN WINTERS

1993. One of a score of winters spent in Aspen and among countless dinners, this one from the annals:

"So the season is beginning. Very little snow so far. A bunch of movie stars—Bruce Willis, Don Johnson, others—are opening a restaurant and pleasure palace called Planet Hollywood a few steps toward the mountain from the Ute City Banque. The rent they are paying is $25,000 a month—just a benchmark. Lorenzo and Joyce [Semple, very close friends] came to dinner. He uncharacteristically drank a couple of bottles of wine and wouldn't go home. The wine was Ruffino Chianti Classico 1989. He had denounced it before tasting it, saying that 1990 was known to be the good year, but then the glassfuls began to disappear. We watched a movie afterward, a French movie called Blue, made by a Pole. Stunning images, limited content—very Aspen."

DECEMBER

CLARENCE BIRDSEYE

On this day in 1886, in Brooklyn, Clarence Birdseye was born. Dropping out of college at Amherst for lack of tuition money, he went to Labrador on a fur-trading expedition and saw there that fish, frozen in the bitter cold after being caught, lost nothing in texture or taste when later cooked. In 1916, together with his wife and young child, Birdseye returned to Labrador. They brought with them several barrels of fresh vegetables and, dipping them in seawater, successfully froze them in the icy arctic wind.

The first mechanical freezing plant in the world had been built about fifty years earlier in Sydney, Australia, and insulated ships had been carrying frozen meat across the oceans, but it was Birdseye who would pioneer the sale of frozen food to retail customers. He formed a frozen seafood company in New York City that failed, but in 1926 started another in Massachusetts. It was called General Seafoods but then, more broadly, General Foods.

By 1929, he was able to sell the company for the then huge sum of twenty-two million dollars, and by 1937, fifty-seven different frozen vegetables, fruits, and meats were being shipped and sold in individualized waxed cartons under the Birdseye brand, which became syn-onymous with frozen food.

Fresh and frozen food have virtually the same nutritional value. Frozen peas, in fact, have more, since they are usually frozen immedi-ately after being picked, while unfrozen peas make their slower way from the farm to the wholesaler to stores, losing vitamins en route.

Almost any food can be frozen, although not eggs when they are in their shells. The more quickly the freezing is done, the better—the ice crystals that form within the food are smaller and affect the struc-ture less. Smaller quantities thus give better results than larger when freezing at home. A year is usually the maximum recommended time for storing frozen food, although many—milk, bacon, hamburger, soups, fish, stews—are better if not kept this long.

10

DECEMBER

MOVIES

Food isn't featured as often in movies as sex, but screen meals leading up to or following it are often more memorable. One unforgettable scene centers on Albert Finney and Joyce Redman gluttonously devouring a chicken and soon each other in *Tom Jones*. Another is the far more decorous Grace Kelly in *To Catch a Thief,* with white gloves and carrying her chicken in a picnic basket. "Breast or leg?" she asks sweetly.

Movies with food as a theme have been made around the globe: *The Baker's Wife* from France, *Babette's Feast* from Denmark, *Tampopo* from Japan, *Like Water for Chocolate* from Mexico, *Monsoon Wedding* from India, *La grande bouffe* from France/Italy, *Life Is Sweet* from Great Britain, and *Eat Drink Man Woman* from Taiwan. American contributions to the field run the gamut from *Diner* and *Big Night,* in which there's a lot of action, to *My Dinner with Andre* and *The Big Chill,* in which talk at the table is the main thing going on, or nearly. And who is able to leave *The Godfather* without the desire to go get some pasta— perhaps because of the length.

11

DECEMBER

KETCHUP

Ketchup evolved over time from far more exotic ingredients than it now contains. Also called catsup, ketchup probably originated in China in the 1600s and was known in the Canton dialect as *ketsiap,* a sauce made of vinegar, spices, and the innards of fish. When it immigrated to Malaysia, it became *ketchap* and traveled with English sailors back to Europe, where mushrooms replaced fish innards in the ingredients. It wasn't until the late 18th century that tomatoes became part of the mix. It was marketed in the United States in 1876, described by a manufacturer as a "blessed relief for Mother and the other women in the household."

12

DECEMBER

MADAME BOVARY

Gustave Flaubert, whose first published work was the masterpiece *Madame Bovary*, was born in Rouen, son of a surgeon, on this day in 1821.

In *Bovary*, there is the great ball of the Marquis of Vaubyessard that Emma Bovary and her colorless doctor-husband attend—the ball she never forgot and which overwhelmed her life with its luxury and great style.

It begins with a dinner at which the many men are at one table and the ladies at another with the host and hostess and one ancient figure, the Marquis' father-in-law, eating as if alone with a napkin tied around his neck and gravy dripping from his mouth. He was a nobleman, too, and  was said to have once been a lover of the queen, Marie Antoinette.

There are bouquets of flowers, crystal, large plates, and fine linen. Fruit in open baskets, lobster, quail, truffles, champagne, pineapple. Then later, after much dancing, a supper of soups, cold meats *en gelée,* and wines.

The next evening, having returned home, Emma and her husband eat onion soup and a piece of veal. The memory of the ball is fresh; it pierces her heart, and the gown she had worn and the satin slippers, the wax of the dancing floor still on their soles, are carefully, devoutly, put away forever.

The longing for the world of sensuality and wealth she had glimpsed never went away. It determined the rest of her life and her death.

13

DECEMBER

FIRST MEAL

The chef is certainly not the same one who prepared the first meal we ate there together more than thirty years ago. But Tante Louise is still there and thriving, a restaurant modeled after a French country inn, an anomaly on the corner of a commercialized strip in east Denver. Since that visit, it has become much more upscale and won many awards for its menu and extensive wine cellar.

I have no idea what we ate that first night. I wasn't really thinking about the food. We'd had a drink and later seen a movie, which I also can't remember. The man across the table from me was everything. I was young and still too inexperienced to be a decent conversationalist. We talked about Europe, which he knew intimately—Rome, Paris, London, Barcelona—a world I had seen bits of on a student tour and longed to know.

It was the first of thousands—at home, abroad, in elegant restaurants and unforgettable dives. A lifetime of meals. He's always said that conversation—and so much of it takes place at the table—is the essence of a shared life. I learned to talk.   K.S.

14
DECEMBER

FRITTATA

Pasta is good the next day, either crisped brown in olive oil or as part of an omelet, although, as Marcella Hazan notes, leftover pasta is a rare commodity. It is even worthwhile, she says, to cook spaghetti specifically to use later in a frittata, a kind of Italian omelet cooked over low heat and on both sides, a flat cake of egg with various fillings mixed in that allows the cook to be creative.

FRITTATA

1 egg per person, or egg substitute plus 1 egg for authenticity
Grated Parmegiano-Reggiano cheese to taste
Salt and pepper
Herbs to taste
Olive oil
Filling: previously cooked pasta, vegetables, seafood, ham, or almost
any leftover (if using spaghetti as a filling, it should be tossed and
coated with butter immediately after draining to keep it from
sticking together)

Beat the eggs in a bowl, add the other ingredients, and combine. Pour the mixture into a preheated frying pan with the olive oil. Cook at very low heat, lifting gently around the edge to allow any uncooked egg to seep underneath. When firm and golden on the bottom, flip the frittata and cook on the other side to the same golden brownness. You can, if you prefer, cook the top by putting the pan under the broiler, though not long enough to brown it. Slice into wedges and serve immediately, or serve later at room temperature.

15
DECEMBER

CANDLES

The simplest meal seems more special when there are lighted candles on the table. The more the better, though that can add up. In Aspen, there was a woman who was planning an elaborate dinner party and went to Wax and Wicks, the local candle shop. She wanted dozens of candles, but the ones the owner began showing her were too expensive, she said. He showed her some others. No, those still cost too much. Were there any that were less expensive? He brought out the most basic of his stock. She still wasn't satisfied. Didn't he have anything cheaper? "I'm sorry, madam," he said coldly, "we do not rent candles."

16
DECEMBER

DELMONICO'S

On this day in 1835, a huge fire destroyed much of lower Manhattan, including a restaurant that, when it was later rebuilt nearby, would become the restaurant of the century, not only in New York but in the entire country. Established by two Swiss brothers and named for them, Delmonico's was acclaimed and widely imitated but nowhere rivaled. It was organized on the principle of European restaurants that offered a variety of dishes rather than the American commonplace fixed meal, and the menu at one time listed 340 entrées.

Delmonico's had outstanding food and service amid sumptuous surroundings. There were silver chandeliers, orchestras, and rooms decorated in satin. The restaurant had French chefs and its own farm to provide fresh produce. The cellars were filled with the finest wine. Price was never a consideration, and the fact that it was expensive was part of the appeal. At its height, late in the 19th century, there were four locations and the clientele was drawn from the best of society, business, celebrity, and the arts. Charles Dickens ate there on his visit to America, and the name of a prodigious feeder of the time, Diamond Jim Brady, is intimately linked to Delmonico's.

Quarrels between heirs eventually spelled the end of the restaurant, and the advent of Prohibition in 1920 sealed its fate. By that time, Delmonico's had been synonymous with excellence for so long that the courts decreed it was part of the general language and the name could be used by anyone.

BOSTON TEA PARTY

On this day in 1773, the most famous tea party of all was held in Boston Harbor by colonists dressed as Indians who, angered by Parliament's decision to cut out American middlemen in the tea trade, threw three shiploads—342 chests—of British tea overboard. One of the "Indians" was Paul Revere, whose historic ride two years later was said to have inspired a recipe for wild rabbit in one of the first United States cookbooks.

17
DECEMBER

AMPHOUX

Mme Amphoux, a Frenchwoman, had a renowned distillery in Martinique in the 1800s and produced liqueurs made from cocoa, coffee, and vanilla. The liqueurs were named after her, and though there is not yet an elegant restaurant called Amphoux, it always seems there could be.

18
DECEMBER

DINING ROOMS

On this day in 1902, President Theodore Roosevelt's cabinet members, seated in the State Dining Room, raised their glasses in a toast to the White House. Remodeling had just been completed, with the living quarters enlarged to accommodate Roosevelt's wife and six children and the public rooms reorganized and renovated.

When Thomas Jefferson was president, he used the State Dining Room as his office and let his pet mockingbird fly around at will. Later, Andrew Jackson, a man used to the rough life of a soldier, nevertheless found it necessary to have the White House stables moved away from the dining room windows, so the smell of manure wouldn't overwhelm the food. Now Roosevelt hung the walls with his hunting trophies and no longer had to have the floor reinforced each time he hosted a dinner.

Dining rooms had only come into fashion during the previous century—first in the country houses of the English aristocracy and then during Queen Victoria's reign—as part of the homes of the middle class. Before that, eating was done in the kitchen, near the fire, on a table pulled away from the wall for meals.

19

DECEMBER

ROQUEFORT

Of the three great blues—Roquefort, Stilton, and Gorgonzola— Roquefort is the only one made from sheep's milk and is also the one with the longest history, going back at least to the first century A.D., when Pliny the Elder praised it. It has always been made in the same location, in the caves of Combalou in southwest France, not far from the sea. Its origin was probably accidental, perhaps when a piece of bread and some dry cheese left together in the caves allowed bread mold to infuse the cheese and transform it.

Roquefort was Charlemagne's favorite cheese, and Casanova extolled it in combination with Chambertin wine as a great restorative. Rabelais, who practiced medicine in the region, claimed he always had Roquefort within reach.

The bread mold, *penicillium roqueforti,* is today still supplied from bread injected with a pure culture of it, and the cheese is perfected during months spent in the caves.

These caves—and no other location has been able to duplicate their exact qualities—have fissures that allow cool, moist air to circulate while the temperature remains a constant 44–48 degrees F year-round. Like certain valuable vineyards, the caves are controlled by a group of commercial societies, more than a dozen of them.

Genuine Roquefort has been protected since 1411 by a charter given to the nearby village of Roquefort-sur-Soulzon. Each cheese weighs about six pounds and is marked by a distinctive stamp of a red sheep. It can be bought in smaller wedges but is better when cut fresh from the whole cheese.

The inimitable Curnonsky, Prince of Gastronomes, recommended that a meal-ending Roquefort be accompanied by a bottle of Clos de Vougeot or Haut Brion. Foolish to disagree.

20

DECEMBER

CROSS-COUNTRY DINNER

Five days before Christmas in 1993, we gave a big dinner party in our old house in Aspen. To begin, there was cross-country skiing at dusk out past the high school. Halfway along the trail, we had a table with small baked potatoes, sour cream, and caviar. Vivaldi was playing on a portable CD player. There was ice, vodka, and candles.

Everyone came back to the house freshened by the cold. There were fifteen of us. A wood fire was blazing. The buffet was gravlax, celery remoulade, cold cucumber soup, and tapenade. Further down the table was a *tien de legumes* from Patricia Wells's *Bistro Cooking* and shepherd's pie. Dessert was *gâteau au chocolat,* pear and almond tart, and coffee. The wine was a simple Cotes du Rhône. It was an unforgettable snowy night.

The cold cucumber soup is a favorite in summer and winter:

CUCUMBER SOUP

4 *tablespoons butter*	1 *teaspoon salt (but not if*
½ *cup chopped onion or 2 leeks,*	*using bouillon)*
sliced and cubed	½ *teaspoon freshly ground*
4 *cups diced, unpeeled cucumber*	*pepper*
2 *cups watercress leaves*	½ *teaspoon dry mustard*
1 *cup finely diced raw potato*	2 *cups heavy cream*
4 *cups chicken broth or chicken*	*Chopped chives, cucumber,*
bouillon	*and radishes for garnish*
4 *sprigs parsley*	

Melt the butter in a saucepan and cook onions or leeks until translucent. Add the remaining ingredients, except the cream and the vegetables for garnish, and bring to a boil. Simmer for fifteen minutes or until the potatoes are tender. Purée the mixture in a blender or food processor. Season as necessary. Chill. (At this point, it can be frozen.) Before serving, stir in the cream and add the garnish. Serves eight.

PANETTONE

Panettone, the light, delicious cake emblematic of Christmas throughout Italy, originated in and is a specialty of Milan. The admirable authority on Italian food, Waverly Root, considered it the world's best accompaniment for breakfast coffee. Made in a high, domed shape that is sometimes thought to honor the domes of Lombard churches, it contains butter, milk, sugar, eggs, raisins, and bits of candied fruit.

It is traditional in Italian households for the head of the family to cut three large slices and for family members to eat a bit of each slice as a guarantee of good fortune. The Duke of Milan himself used to perform the ceremony annually.

The name "panettone" is probably derived from *pane,* meaning "bread," and *tone,* the suffix for "big," although there are competing versions. Panettone should be warmed just slightly before serving to diffuse the buttery flavor, and it is also excellent toasted.

You may be lucky enough to be near a good bakery where panettones are made; otherwise, the big food companies produce respectable versions in quantity. If you happen to be in Milan around Christmastime, there is the Pasticceria Cova, where panettone allegedly began, or the Pasticceria Amrosiana, one of the best in the city.

22

DECEMBER

CANDY CANES

It is said that candy canes were created in 1670 by the choirmaster at the Cologne Cathedral in Germany, who gave them to the children in the choir to pacify them during the long Christmas services. He modeled them after the shape of the crooks carried by the shepherds who, according to the story in Luke, were the first to hear the good tidings of Jesus' birth. It was well over two hundred years later before peppermint was added to the sugar canes, and they took on their distinctive look.

The red-and-white striped pole that signifies a barber's shop didn't mimic candy canes but came much earlier. Until the mid-18th century in England, the Barbers'-Surgeons' Guild performed blood-letting and operations, and their symbolic pole represented bloody rags blowing dry in the wind. When the Surgeons Guild split off in 1745, it abandoned the pole to the barbers, who continued to use keen blades for their own purposes.

23

CHAMPAGNE

Champagne was the drink of Russian nobility and the English race-track, and with the rise of the middle class, the drink of nearly everybody. Stimulating *ab initio,* and stupefying afterward, in its early days it was much sweeter than now and was a dessert wine. It was a favorite of Mme Pompadour, mistress of Louis XV, who felt "full of beauty" after drinking it.

Originating in the area around Reims, where a still white wine had been produced for more than a thousand years, it achieved its sparkling quality when in the 17th century, a monk, Dom Perignon, supposedly allowed wine to ferment in a corked bottle.

Champagne has always been costly to produce and hence expensive. The process involves a first fermentation that comes to a stop in the cold winters northeast of Paris. The wine is bottled and some sugar added, and in the spring, although it has been stored underground at a constant low temperature, a magical event occurs—a second fermentation begins in sympathy with the sap rising in the trees outside. This second, sealed fermentation is the defining one. Sediment is later painstakingly removed, a bit more sugar added, and the characteristic swollen cork and wire muzzle applied.

Made, for the most part, from pinot noir, the grape of the great Burgundies, champagne is pale in color because the grape skins are quickly removed from the liquid during the pressing. Blanc de Blanc, however, is a champagne made from chardonnay or white pinot grapes.

Like all white wines, champagne should be drunk fairly young—except when it is high quality—preferably from a tulip-shaped glass, rather than the wide, flat type that allows the bubbles to quickly dissipate. The bottle should be chilled but not icy. Champagne, like wine, has vintages, some good, some not.

The driest champagne is labeled Brut, then comes Extra Dry, Sec, and Demi-Sec. The larger bottles have, together with burgundies, marvelous biblical names. After the Magnum, which contains two bottles, they are:

Jeroboam—Four bottles

Rehoboam—Six bottles

Methusalem—Eight bottles

Salmanazar—Twelve bottles

Balthazar—Sixteen bottles

Nebuchadnezzar—Twenty bottles

Balthazar was one of the three Magi. Nebuchadenezzar, a great king of Babylon, conquered Judea and destroyed Jerusalem five hundred years before Christ.

24

DECEMBER

CHRISTMAS EVE

For years it was past midnight before the various toys were finally assembled and the gifts laid out under the tree with its strings of lights. Morning came very early, as might be expected. There was the long ritual of the opening of presents amid strewn paper and boxes, who had given what to whom sometimes becoming lost in the confusion.

Peter Matthiessen's wife, Maria, with her German heritage, did it differently. Christmas was celebrated on Christmas Eve with real candles on the big tree. First there was a fine dinner, then the opening of presents. You went to sleep on the full happiness of it.

We adopted her way and also began to always read something aloud on Christmas Eve, sometimes with just the family, sometimes with friends. Most often it was "A Child's Christmas in Wales," Dylan Thomas's glorious remembrance of this holiday, very different from but in a way rivaling Dickens, with its thrilling language and warm heart.

> For dinner we had turkey and blazing pudding,
> and after dinner the Uncles sat in front of the fire,
> loosened all buttons, put their large moist hands over
> their watch chains, groaned a little and slept . . .

We passed the book around, everyone reading a part. We opened presents—most, not all of them—and if it was cold and clear, went out to look at the stars. And so to bed.

25

CHRISTMAS DINNER

The Christmas dinner that Scrooge foresees being served at the Cratchits' in Charles Dickens's *A Christmas Carol* stands as perhaps the most famous meal in English literature.

Mrs. Cratchit made the gravy . . . hissing hot; Master Peter mashed the potatoes with incredible vigor; Miss Belinda sweetened up the apple sauce; Martha dusted the hot plates; Bob took Tiny Tim beside him in a tiny corner at the table; the two young Cratchits sat chairs for everybody, not forgetting themselves, and mounting guard upon their posts, crammed spoons into their mouths, lest they should shriek for goose before their turn came to be helped. At last the dishes were set on, and grace was said. It was succeeded by a breathless pause, as Mrs. Cratchit, looking slowly all along the carving-knife, prepared to plunge it in the breast; but when she did, and when the long expected gush of stuffing issued forth, one murmur of delight arose all round the board, and even Tiny Tim, excited by the two young Cratchits, beat on the table with the handle of his knife and feebly cried Hurrah!

BOXING DAY

Boxing Day, celebrated in England, Canada, Australia, and New Zealand, has grown out of the Feast of Saint Stephen, the first Christian martyr, who was stoned to death. On Christmas Day, presents are exchanged between family members, friends, and associates, but on Boxing Day, gift-giving is meant to flow all in one direction: from the richer to the poorer or from employers to staff. The name probably came from the opening of the church alms boxes to distribute the money to the needy.

A favorite Christmas carol recalls the pious ruler of what is now the Czech Republic, who was assassinated by his brother in 929 A.D. but became the patron saint of Bohemia, Good King Wenceslas. He looked out one cold night to see a poor man, one of his subjects, gathering winter fuel. It was on the Feast of Saint Stephen. To a page he said,

Bring me flesh and bring me wine,
Bring me pine logs hither:
Thou and I will see him dine
When we bear them thither.

While Christmas Day is traditionally spent at home with immediate family, Boxing Day means visits to grandparents who serve ham or even roast lamb instead of the turkey or roast beef of the day before.

LOUIS PASTEUR

Wine can be considered with good reason as the most healthful
and the most hygienic of all beverages.

—LOUIS PASTEUR

In 1822, Louis Pasteur was born this day in Dôle, in the French Jura.
Before he turned his attention to making milk safe to drink, Pasteur,
at the request of Napoleon III, studied the reasons that wine and
beer turned sour, an economic disaster for French producers in the
1850s. Pasteur identified the cause as bacteria and discovered that if
the starting sugar solutions could be heated to 55 degrees C (131
degrees F), the bacteria—and the problem—were eliminated. The
process, eventually called pasteurization, formed the foundation of
microbiology.

Soon after, he also saved the French silk industry by distinguishing healthy from diseased silkworms and in later work developed the
theory of germs as the cause of illness, along with methods of inocu-
lating against rabies, tuberculosis, cholera, and anthrax. He died in
1895 at the age of seventy-two, a national hero. His funeral was held
at Notre Dame, and he was buried in a crypt in the Institute Pasteur,
which he founded and ran and which continues to be a world-class
center for the study of infectious diseases.

28

BURGUNDY-CHAMBERTIN

1832. The Canal de Bourgogne opened after more than two hundred years of planning and about sixty of actual construction. For the first time, the wines of Burgundy could be reliably shipped to Paris and beyond.

Some of the greatest red wines in the world are made from pinot noir grapes, grown in the chalky soil of the Côtes de Nuits, a small region just south of Dijon at the northern end of the Cotes d'Or. One of those is Chambertin, named for Bertin, an owner during medieval times who grew vines on his field (*champ*) and modeled his methods on those of the monks who were his neighbors.

Over hundreds of years, a wine was created on these seventy acres that Napoleon called his favorite. The story is that he issued a standing order: whenever French troops passed this vineyard, they were to present arms. Dumas wrote of the wine, "Nothing inspires such a rosy view of the future." And Talleyrand, a connoisseur of food and drink, took a more modern approach, saying of Chambertin, "When one is served such a wine, one takes the glass respectfully, looks at it, inhales it, then, having put it down, discusses it."

MME DE POMPADOUR

An infant, christened Jeanne Antoinette Poisson, was born this day in 1721 to middle-class parents in Paris. In time she was to become the mistress of Louis XV, who made her Marquise de Pompadour, and for more than twenty years her influence over the king and the government was unrivaled.

She had been taught early that sex and food were the two means of holding a man, and she made good use of both. Intelligent and stylish, she entertained the king at intimate dinners and surrounded herself with writers and artists of the first rank—Voltaire, Helvetius, Boucher. It was said of her that she had been taught everything except morals, which would have stood in her way. When she became, as was described, "no longer fit for love," she arranged for younger women to perform this duty and so remained essential to the king and his close confidant. She died at forty-two.

"Born sincere, she loved the king for himself," Voltaire wrote. "She had justice in her spirit and in her heart; all this is not to be met with every day."

The opinion was not universal. Diderot said, "Mme de Pompadour is dead. So what remains of this woman who cost us so much in men and money, left us without honor and without energy, and who overthrew the whole political system of Europe?"

30

COULIBIAC

2000. *Coulibiac* is the world's greatest dish, Craig Claiborne wrote, nothing to even compare to it. A marvelous kind of pâté-pie made of salmon, mushrooms, onions, rice, hard-boiled eggs, and the dried spinal marrow of a sturgeon—*vésiga* or *vyaziga,* said to add a distinctive quality of taste and texture, though not essential—it arrives baked in a golden crust.

Coulibiac, coulibiaca, or *koulibiaca* originated in the 19th century and had been served to the Czar by the great French chef Edouard Nignon, who during his long career was also head chef to the Austrian emperor and President Woodrow Wilson. The preparation was complicated, but Claiborne was absolutely unequivocal—neither goose nor turkey nor game nor anything else could compare: "Blessed be the holiday table graced with *coulibiac.*"

We decided to make it from his recipe for New Year's Eve.

The next night, we were three couples in evening clothes. We drank champagne, talked, and ate some hors d'oeuvres. There was no appetizer. Claiborne had said he was not convinced there was anything except caviar that could precede *coulibiac.*

We'd worked on the dish for two days. It came to the table in a lightly browned crust that was inscribed with the year just ahead, 2001, embossed on it in dough, and the final half cup of melted butter poured in through a hole that had been made for the steam.

It was an impressive sight. The *coulibiac* was large enough for a dozen people, as it turned out, and fragrant. A delicious aroma filled the room as inch-thick slices were cut. We had omitted the *vésiga* or *vyaziga,* mainly because we couldn't find any. It was not noticed. The *coulibiac* was extremely rich, and even after second helpings, there was enough left for two more meals.

There's a passage in the second volume of Gogol's masterpiece, *Dead Souls,* where Chichikov, the questionable hero, meets a landowner named Petukh while fishing. Petukh is a grand gourmand whose entire life is focused on eating, and after a huge dinner at his house, Chichikov hears his host giving instructions to a servant about the next day's delights.

" 'Make a four-cornered fish pie,' Petukh says. . . . 'In one corner put the cheeks and dried spine of a sturgeon, in another some buckwheat, little mushrooms, onions, some soft roe and, yes, some brains and something else as well, you know, something nice. . . . And see that the crust is well-browned on one side and a little less done on the other. . . .' Petukh smacked his lips as he spoke. . . ."

We needed no help in recognizing what he was describing.

31

GREAT MEALS

Sometimes you forget. A few years back, from the menu that we made:

NEW YEAR'S EVE—1986
SCOTTISH SMOKED SALMON
PÂTÉ DE CAMPAGNE (VEAL AND PORK)
PÂTÉ MAISON (CHICKEN LIVER)
RISOTTO CON FUNGHI
HEARTS OF ARTICHOKE, SPINACH, ENDIVE, AND ROMAINE SALAD
CAMPARI AND ORANGE ICES
SWEETS AND LIQUEURS
WINE: DUHART MILON ROTHSCHILD 1976

The dinner took a day and a half to prepare, but it was for New Year's Eve, and two really good, though amateur, cooks were going to attend, so it was more than worth it. We started eating late and toasted in the new year. There was snow on the ground, and the night was brilliant and dark. Duhart Milon Rothschild is a fourth growth, but it drank like a first. An evening beyond price.

Menu

December 31, 2000

Foie gras
Coulibiac de saumon
Green Salad
Poires bordelaises
chocolats

—

Coulibiac de saumon, in
the opinion of the late
Craig Claiborne, "the
world's greatest dish
(we will see),
as served to
Tsar Nicolas by
Edouard Nignon,
one of the titans of
French cuisine"

Peggy O'Shea and Michael Thomas
Tula Telfair and Spencer Davidson

INDEX

🍃 RECIPES 🍃

❧ A Note on the Authors ❧

James Salter is the author of nine previous books, including the novel *A Sport and a Pastime*; the collection *Dusk and Other Stories*, which won the 1989 PEN/Faulkner Award; and *Burning the Days: Recollection*. Kay Salter is a journalist and playwright who has written for *The New York Times* and *Food and Wine*, among other publications. *Yr. Obedient Servant*, her play about Samuel Johnson, was produced in London under her maiden name, Kay Eldredge. The Salters live in Colorado and on Long Island.

❧ A Note on the Illustrator ❧

Born in Blois, France, in 1962, graphic artist, illustrator, and set and product designer Fabrice Moireau has been sketching his surroundings since earliest childhood. Moireau's illustrations have appeared in such books as Louis Vuitton's *Carnet de voyage* (Paris), Henri Delbard's *Les fruits de ma vie*, and *Carluccio's Complete Italian Food* by Antonio and Priscilla Carluccio. He lives in Olivet, France, with his wife and children.

A Note on the Type

The text of this book was set in Requiem, a typeface designed by Jonathan Hoefler (born 1970) and released in the late 1990s by the Hoefler Type Foundry. It was derived from a set of inscriptional capitals appearing in Ludovico Vicentino degli Arrighi's 1523 writing manual, *Il modo de temperare le penne*. A master scribe, Arrighi is remembered as an exemplar of the chancery italic, a style revived in Requiem Italic.

This book has been produced in association with Callaway Arts & Entertainment:
Nicholas Callaway, Amy Cloud, Cathy Ferrara, Nelson Gomez,
Krupa Jhaveri, Toshiya Masuda, and Joya Rajadhyaksha.
With special thanks to Antoinette White.